The War on Our Freedoms

The WAR on OUR FREEDOMS

Civil Liberties in an Age of Terrorism

EDITED BY

R ICHARD C. L EONE AND
G REG A NRIG, J R.

A Century Foundation Book

P UBLIC A FFAIRS
New York

No part of this book may be reproduced in any manner whatsoever
without written permission except in the case of brief quotations embodied
in critical articles and reviews. For information, address PublicAffairs,
250 West 57th Street, Suite 1321, New York, NY 10107. PublicAffairs books
are available at special discounts for bulk purchases in the U.S. by
corporations, institutions, and other organizations. For more information,
please contact the Special Markets Department at the Perseus Books Group,
11 Cambridge Center, Cambridge, MA 02142, or call (617) 252-5298.

"The Go-for-Broke Presidency" by E. J. Dionne, Jr., draws on work published
in the *Washington Post* in 2002 and 2003, © 2003 The Washington Post
Writers Group. Reprinted with permission.

"'The Least Worst Place'" by Joseph Lelyveld is an updated version of
"In Guantánamo," originally published in the November 7, 2002, issue of
The New York Review of Books. Reprinted with permission.

Library of Congress Cataloging-in-Publication Data
The war on our freedoms: civil liberties in an age of terrorism/edited by
Richard C. Leone and Greg Anrig. — 1st ed.
p. cm.
"A Century Foundation Book."
ISBN 1-58648-210-6
1. Civil rights—United States. 2. September 11 Terrorist Attacks, 2001.
3. War on Terrorism, 2001 – . 4. Terrorism—United States—Prevention.
5. United States—Politics and government— 2001– .
I. Leone, Richard C., 1940– II. Anrig, Jr., Greg, 1960–
JC599.U5W313 2003
323'.0973—DC21
2003046681

Book design by Jane Raese
Text set in 11.5-point Adobe Caslon

FIRST EDITION

1 3 5 7 9 10 8 6 4 2

CONTENTS

vii

CONTENTS

FOREWORD

Immediately after September 11, Americans were more than willing to accept encroachments on established liberties in order to prevent another successful terrorist attack. But more than a year later, after the administration of President George W. Bush has implemented numerous policies that clearly infringe upon basic civil liberties, it is far from clear that the nation is much safer.

Throughout this period, there has been a disturbing absence of information and debate about the genuine and imagined trade-offs between liberty and security. The public needs to know far more so that the choices we make will not be driven either by our fear of the terrorists or by the fiats of our government. In the end, citizens should decide what trade-offs are worth making when it comes to security and liberty. We need to win the war on our freedoms on terms that incorporate long-standing American values.

In addition, most of what we know about the effectiveness of institutions—businesses, nonprofits, and government—is that good performance, over the long haul, depends on transparency and accountability. To those running such institutions, it is easy to embrace the apparent short-term advantages that flow from not having to address outside criticisms. These positive features, however, are almost always overtaken in time by the inevitable weaknesses that flow from bureaucratic inertia and the pursuit of self-interest. Whether one is talking of Enron's management, the American Catholic Church, or the Nixon White House, it is certainly arguable that the worst problems those institutions encountered would have been reduced had there been broad and early public access to emerging problems.

It's not an abuse of power to seize the moment and use the reservoir of support generated by the terrorist attacks to advance a program that may require painful sacrifice in order to substantially reduce the danger to the United States. But such an approach is very different from relying on the special political conditions generated by 9/11 to advance a sharply partisan agenda. Nor should the greatest sacrifice that the American people be called upon to make be some of their liberties. More taxes, more hassles, more caution, even more military and quasi-military actions—all could be part of a reasonable response to 9/11. Our core purpose, however, should remain clear: We must resolve that it is an essential part of winning the war on our freedoms to insist that we keep intact the civil liberties and other freedoms that we have gained in 225 years. That must be freedom's answer to the terrorists.

The distinguished group of authors in this volume set forth what is essentially a wake-up call to the American people. Taken together, the essays document a sea change in issues involving trade-offs between freedom and security. Some changes have ripple effects that cut across a range of freedoms, so several chapters explore the same policies from different standpoints. Collectively, these pieces argue that the trustworthy government we need in a time of crisis can be sustained only by real understanding, open debate, and informed consensus—no matter how cumbersome that process may seem to those in power.

Our hope is that this volume will advance a more thoughtful process of public deliberation.

Richard C. Leone
Greg Anrig, Jr.
April 2003

The War on Our Freedoms

The Quiet Republic:
The Missing Debate About
Civil Liberties After 9/11

RICHARD C. LEONE

There are some circumstances in which holding
your breath is a perfectly appropriate response, but to do
so indefinitely requires that you be unconscious.

THE GOVERNMENT of the United States reacted to the terrible events of September 11, 2001, with sweeping policy departures both at home and abroad. To date, there has been remarkably little debate about many of the changes in national policy, especially those that have significantly compromised the civil liberties of U.S. citizens. Yet history teaches us that bypassing public deliberation almost inevitably leads to outcomes that the nation ends up regretting. Looking back, there is a long list of reactions to other threats in which the absence of open debate coincided with many of the nation's low points. During the twentieth century, the Palmer Raids after World War I, the internment of Japanese Americans during World War II, the Bay of Pigs fiasco, Iran-Contra, the secret war in Honduras, and any number of other ventures went badly astray. Public deliberation entails controversy that can be painful and time-consuming, but it often prevents bad ideas from taking hold while broadening support for policies that are implemented.

After 9/11, the administration of George W. Bush was un-understandably eager to demonstrate to the country that it would respond quickly and decisively to prevent a recurrence of the horrific terrorist attacks. And hardly anyone—not Democrats in Congress, not the media, not even major civil liberties advocates—wanted to be perceived as attempting to obstruct that effort. But in looking back on all that has happened so far during the tumultuous post-9/11 period, it is alarming how little public deliberation has occurred. For example:

- The limited debate about an independent investigative commission to examine and learn from possible intelligence failures leading up to 9/11, was not created until more than a year after the attacks. In contrast, a similar commission was formed within three weeks after Pearl Harbor to find out what happened.
- The initial acquiescence to a limited budget—$3 million— for the commission to conduct its inquiry, in contrast to the $60–80 million being contemplated—and criticized as low—for the inquiry into the cause of the space shuttle *Columbia* crash.
- The lack of argument and dissent over the enactment, just six weeks after 9/11, of the USA Patriot Act incorporating sweeping changes in the ways that the government can monitor and investigate all citizens.

- The lack of curiosity on the part of the politicians, the public, and media outlets about the secret detentions of Muslims.
- The partisanship during the debate over creating the new Department of Homeland Security, with much of the focus on reducing worker protections and not enough on the unusual limits on public access to information about the department.
- The amazing absence of attention to the inclusion in the Homeland Security Act of provisions protecting pharmaceutical giant Eli Lilly from certain lawsuits— a provision that no one in the Senate or anywhere else admits to authoring.
- The muted reaction to the administration's rejection on several occasions of measures to provide significant new funding for many areas of domestic security, including much of the money requested by state and local governments.
- The overt efforts of the Bush administration to discourage debate across the board, exemplified by the following statement by Attorney General John Ashcroft: "To those who scare peace-loving people with phantoms of lost liberty; my message is this: Your tactics only aid terrorists— for they erode our national unity and diminish our resolve."
- The negligible opposition for months to the creation of the Orwellian-sounding Total Information Awareness program, headed by John Poindexter—the same John Poindexter who played a central role in Iran-Contra.

Part of the explanation for all this may simply be that politicians, the press, and the nation remain off-balance, unable to resume the normal rough-and-tumble of democracy. We are still digesting the dramatic alteration of a world in which we felt sure before 9/11 that the United States was preeminent, without conventional military rivals, the unchallenged global economic leader, culturally and politically admired and imitated. This generous self-assessment engendered a degree of confidence, which was one factor in the relatively limited public concern in the wake of such earlier terrorist attacks as the World Trade Center bombing in 1993, the African embassy bombings in 1998, and the attack on the USS *Cole* in 2000. The events of 9/11, however, awoke Americans to the awful knowledge that the modern terrorist threat includes the risk of a Pearl Harbor–like attack, the possibility, however remote, of so-called sleeper cells of operatives hiding next door, and the danger of weapons of mass destruction in the hands of suicidal enemies. While the fact of American strength abides, a shocked nation continues to search for answers to three questions: Why did Al-Qaeda attack on 9/11? Who are the terrorists? And what can we do to prevent them from striking again?

The first question is the most difficult, but at least interim answers have become widely accepted. The explanation that the administration and others emphasize—that the terrorist attacks constitute "a war on our freedoms"—reflects some insight but also begs the larger question. While the terrorists' hostility is rooted in profound cultural and political differences, the economic and foreign policies of the United States—particularly in terms of our unique global role and our long-term involvement in the Middle East—probably deserve pride of place in any story about increasing danger in recent years. Nor can we achieve a clear understanding of our situation without considering the internal conditions in those countries that seem to be producing the largest numbers of potential anti-American terrorists. So far, deeper inquiries into what motivates the terrorists have attracted only limited popular attention.

In partial answer to the second question—"Who are the terrorists?"—the nation took a crash course in modern terrorism, learning about Osama bin Laden while almost contemporaneously attacking his bases in Afghanistan. The evidence also mounted that the pool of potential terrorists might be very broad and deep, including Muslim extremist groups other than Al-Qaeda. In early 2002, the president went further in defining the immediate dangers in the world, describing as an "Axis of Evil" three states (Iraq, Iran, and North Korea) that he said could well threaten the United States with weapons of mass destruction. As of this writing, one of those nations, Iraq, is now occupied by U.S. forces.

The answer to the third question—"How can we protect ourselves?"—is still a work in progress. So far it has included reorganizing major portions of the government, launching a new military buildup, taking direct action in Afghanistan, Yemen, Iraq, and elsewhere, imposing countless additional private and public security measures (notably the great changes in commercial aviation), seeking better intelligence, "hardening" possible targets, and introducing significant changes in the rules governing the justice system, immigration, the courts, privacy, secrecy, press access, and civil liberties.

The reality that the terrorists "took advantage of the vulnerability of an open society" focused special attention on the issue of whether we are simply too "open" for our own good. It is in this context that the phrase "war on our freedoms" raises more questions than it answers. How do we assess the true tradeoffs between freedom and security? How should we decide how much of our freedom we are willing—or need—to give up in the interests of increasing domestic safety? Finding the right answers is not easy, especially in the absence of widespread public understanding of the issues and discussion of the choices. But we need to be very careful, all the more so because the struggle in which we are now engaged may last for an indefinite period. It is important to ask, for example, what mix of openness and secrecy is likely to produce the best performance by the government agencies we depend upon to implement security measures. The struggle against terrorism could continue for generations, and we run the risk of finding ourselves on a slippery slope, making decisions in which freedoms that are set aside for the "emergency" become permanently lost to us. In the end, the freedoms we abridge in the interests of security will be largely the result of choices that we, not the terrorists, make.

"The Constitution is not a suicide pact"

The attacks in New York and Washington, followed closely by the mysterious anthrax mailings and the swift war in Afghanistan, inevitably instigated changes in law enforcement, intelligence operations, and security generally. As U.S. Supreme Court Justice Sandra Day O'Connor predicted on September 29, 2001: "We're likely to experience more restrictions on our personal freedom than has ever been the case in our country." The public strongly supported doing whatever was necessary. In fact, one poll showed 55 percent of citizens were worried that the government *would not go far enough* in fighting terrorism in order to protect civil liberties; only 31 percent were worried the government would go too far in fighting terrorism at the expense of civil liberties.

The specific actions taken seem to be the result of an initial assessment of the nation's possible vulnerabilities, coupled with preexisting attitudes on the part of the nation's leadership. After taking office, the Bush administration had quickly and consistently established its commitment to secrecy as well as hard-line law enforcement. There was little risk that the administration would err on the side of protecting civil liberties—indeed, the Patriot Act that the administration authored, and Congress left almost entirely intact, was arguably the most far-reaching and invasive legislation passed since the Espionage Act of 1917 and the Sedition Act of 1918. It allows the government to look at individuals' retail purchases, Internet searches, e-mail, and borrowed library books. It permits the U.S. attorney general to detain immigrants based on "suspicion," requires businesses to report "suspicious transactions," allows the government to conduct secret searches without notification, grants the Federal Bureau of Investigation and other agencies greatly expanded access to all sorts of personal and business data with little judicial oversight, and allows for surveillance of any number of domestic organizations and advocacy groups. Although the act can permit the government to collect vast amounts of information, it does not provide the agencies involved the resources required to analyze it. As New York University law professor Stephen Schulhofer puts it, "A large part of what we lack [already] is not raw data but the ability to separate significant intelligence from 'noise.'"

While the American Civil Liberties Union, the American Library Association, the Electronic Privacy Information Center, and other privacy and civil liberties groups tried to prevent historic changes in civil liberties from becoming law in the heat of the moment, their efforts went virtually unnoticed. Even members of Congress known as traditionally strong voices in favor of civil liberties said little about the legislation. The administration launched an aggressive campaign on behalf of enactment, implying that anyone opposing the Patriot Act could be considered soft on terrorists. The message echoed President Bush's comment after September 11, "You are either with us or with the terrorists."

A year later, when Congress passed the legislation creating the new Department of Homeland Security, it incorporated provisions creating the Directorate for Information Analysis and Infrastructure Protection, which would maintain a database of public and private information on individuals. It also allowed for broad intelligence information sharing between the Homeland Security Department and other agencies; placed significant limits on the information citizens can request under the Freedom of Information Act; and imposed new criminal penalties for government employees who leak information. Again the debate over such changes was one-sided and lacked virtually any attention to possible unintended consequences. After some initial interest, Congress dropped consideration of a provision suggested by Harvard Law School professor Christopher Edley to create an independent Office of Rights and Liberties to oversee the new agency's actions regarding civil liberties.

Throughout this period, the administration pursued additional changes in law enforcement and surveillance—again with little awareness on the part of the public. The Department of Justice, for example, announced that it might now monitor conversations between attorneys and detainees. Attorney General

Ashcroft rewrote FBI guidelines to allow agents to monitor all political, religious, and advocacy groups without any evidence of wrongdoing and to make it easier to monitor Internet activity. He reversed the policy underlying the Freedom of Information Act that required agencies to begin with the presumption that information should be publicly available. The administration has also required male immigrants already legally in the United States from twenty different countries, mostly Arab and South Asian, to register with the Immigration and Naturalization Service, regardless of their status. Those who fail to register are subject to fines, entry in the National Crime Information Center database, and possible deportation. In the process, the administration detained almost 1,200 men, almost all for immigration violations, and refused to release their names or any other information about them. Many of the detainees were held without any charges filed against them for weeks and months on minor immigration violations, others as material witnesses. Some have been deported, others have been released, but several are still incarcerated. While a few news outlets have reported about particular individuals who appear to have been unfairly detained, by and large these policies have not evoked significant public concern.

Two administration initiatives have provoked enough of an outcry to be rescinded or delayed. Operation TIPS, which called upon postal workers, train conductors, and others to monitor and report the activities of other citizens, reached too far and was withdrawn—at least for now. And Congress eventually blocked funding, at least temporarily, for the administration's Total Information Awareness program, which was to be run by former Iran-Contra figure Poindexter. That office was intended to develop an enormous surveillance system and database of private-sector and government information, including all sorts of personal, commercial, and government information such as hotel reservations, credit card transactions, and phone records. The information would be mined in an effort to detect suspicious behavior patterns. Even leading Republicans balked at the program's vaulting ambitions. Senator Charles Grassley (R-Iowa) said that it could have had a "chilling effect on civil liberties." In January 2003, Congress acted to halt the program in sixty days unless the Pentagon submitted a report assessing, among other things, its impact on privacy and civil liberties—or unless President Bush certified that a halt would endanger national security. So far, the administration has responded by offering special oversight panels to be watchdogs for the operation. But the vigorous reaction and debate about this program represents the exception rather than the rule.

Rally 'Round the Flag

The United States might have been founded by people who were deeply committed to the Bill of Rights, but the American public, particularly in times of danger, seem quite willing to set aside many of those rights. A *Washington Post*/ABC poll, for example, reports that six in ten Americans say the government's ability to keep wartime secrets is more important than a free press. Even in peacetime, 28 percent say the government should have the right to control what information is reported. Yet journalists have received generally high marks for their objectivity during this period. Thirteen percent say the media have been too supportive of the Bush administration, 17 percent say they have been too critical, and 61 percent say "about right."

The administration's actions have been possible, above all, because of broad public support for "emergency measures." Post-9/11 public opinion research has reflected a sharp spike in fear, as well as a revival of trust in government—the ultimate guarantor of safety. Darren Davis and Brian Silver of Michigan State University, tracking public attitudes on these issues, stress that "the context created a greater opportunity for fear to be personalized." Robert Putnam of Harvard University reported a post-9/11 increase of 45 percentage points in those who trust the national government. And some polls indicated that as many as 90 percent of Americans supported the war effort in Afghanistan. In fact, initially, there was virtually universal support for just about everything the administration proposed or did. In Congress, the votes for the Patriot Act were 357-66 in the House and 98-1 in the Senate. More than a year later, in November 2002, ninety senators supported the Homeland Security Act.

Polls also suggest that Americans recognize the possibility of a loss of civil liberties but do not think that the government has gone too far. While 62 percent feel that the FBI's policies may intrude, an overwhelming majority (79 percent) think that investigating threats, even if it results in a loss of privacy, is more important right now than respect for privacy (18 percent). A majority of those polled support random searches of cars, bags, and passengers on commercial airplanes, government scrutiny of library records, and surveillance cameras in public spaces. They draw the line when phone conversations are randomly recorded or mail is randomly opened.

Reflecting the lack of open debate about the wide array of initiatives undertaken since 9/11, 58 percent think civil liberties have stayed the same since before the terrorist attacks. In other words, one reason for the lack of public concern is probably that the limited reaction by elected officials and the media has left most citizens unaware of the changes that are under way. Only 15 percent of Americans polled believe the Bush administration has gone too far in restricting civil liberties to fight terrorism. In contrast, 55 percent believe it has done about the right amount, and 26 percent believe it has not gone far enough.

American history reflects a similar readiness to override civil liberties when confronted by danger. When an "emergency" existed, the government generally had a free hand. But after the fact, many actions were regretted and/or rescinded.

Woodrow Wilson, in his 1915 State of the Union address, attacked unspecified foreign agitators among us, insisting that "such creatures of passion, disloyalty, and anarchy must be crushed." Also, shortly after America's entry into World War I, Congress enacted the Espionage Act (strengthened in 1918 by the Sedition Act), defining all German males over the age of fourteen who were living in the United States and still citizens of Germany as "enemy aliens." Wilson supported measures that prevented enemy aliens from owning firearms or aircraft and from residing in designated parts of the country. In addition, such individuals were prohibited from leaving the country without permission. These laws and regulations anticipated the notorious raids on radicals and aliens ordered by A. Mitchell Palmer, the U.S. attorney general under Wilson, and contributed to the creation of the FBI, the first national police agency. In contrast, to President Bush's credit, he has preached tolerance toward Muslims.

After the attack on Pearl Harbor, likewise, drastic measures were taken, with little vocal opposition. Most notably, in a more openly racist time, Japanese internment camps were largely accepted in the name of the safety of the American public. In 1942, in fact, research at the time indicated that only 31 percent of Americans favored allowing interned Japanese to return to their homes after the war. While we have not seen anything like the treatment of Germans during World War I or the Japanese internment during World War II, holding a large number of individuals incommunicado is among the worst violations of civil liberties since 9/11.

The Cold War was the first conflict in the nation's history involving prolonged danger from an enemy abroad and possibly at home. Our concerns then, like those today, were also multidimensional: fear of subversion by Communists within the country, fear of a devastating nuclear exchange with the Soviet Union, and fear of bloody clashes intended to "contain" communist expansionism, such as the wars in Korea and Vietnam. The consequences of the Cold War for civil liberties were widespread, including extensive FBI monitoring of all sorts of groups and individuals. Notably, at the height of the Cold War, business, political, and even press leaders had great difficulty mustering the political courage to take on Senator Joseph McCarthy's highly controversial crusade against Communists. In a reaction that would be inconceivable today, Arthur Hays Sulzberger, publisher of the *New York Times*, insisted that reporters who took the Fifth Amendment before congressional committees investigating communism should be (and were) fired. Harvard scholars Robert J. Blendon and John M. Benson report that, by the close of the Korean War, 68 percent of Americans opposed allowing Communists to make speeches in their community.

Vietnam, more than any other twentieth-century conflict, came to divide the country. And that division provoked extreme measures by the administrations of Democrat Lyndon Johnson and Republican Richard Nixon to deal with war protestors. The FBI, the Central Intelligence Agency, the military, and local police forces all went beyond recent boundaries despite the fact that there was no actual physical threat to the United States. Even the Pentagon Papers, emerging in 1971 fairly late in the antiwar protest cycle, were deemed too hot for most politicians to handle. Daniel Ellsberg, who eventually leaked the papers to the *New York Times,* wrote that he was turned away by antiwar senators J. William Fulbright, George McGovern, and Charles McC. Mathias. Yet Vietnam did provoke a more powerful opposition movement than did any other twentieth-century crisis. These protests began slowly, however, and during the initial period of conflict there was a broad consensus of support for the war. The anti–Vietnam War demonstrations always had a simple and direct point: The United States should end its participation in the conflict, a demand for something well within the control of the government.

There is another key difference, of course, between all these cases and the situation today. During the two world wars and even during the Cold War standoff with the Soviets, civilians seldom felt personally threatened as they went about their daily lives. The current fears may subside, and historians may look back on this crisis and the resulting consensus about how to balance security and freedom as a mere blip, involving emergency policy choices that, like those in the past, were eventually reversed or moderated. But there is a much better chance of that happening if, as soon as possible, we initiate a much more robust exposition and debate about the nation's options.

Minority Views

One reason the sweeping changes in U.S. policy at home and abroad have failed to provoke much debate is the avalanche of events dominating the media and private conversation, including the anthrax attacks, Afghanistan, the shoe bomber, the Washington-area sniper attacks, Iraq, North Korea, and even the *Columbia* disaster. The administration may have total confidence in its overall strategy, but most citizens can't know how to rank-order the dangers or how to judge whether our approach—heavy on the military and law enforcement, light on debate and diplomacy—is the most effective way to proceed. We do know that the president feels that "the best defense is a good offense."

Not surprisingly, then, criticism of those security measures that have an impact on civil liberties has largely been limited to groups that concentrate on such issues, such as the ACLU, the Lawyers Committee for Human Rights, National Security Archive, Constitution Project, Human Rights Watch, Amnesty International, the American Society of Newspaper Editors, the Reporter's Committee for Human Rights, the Center for National Security Studies, and the Association of Radio-Television News Directors.

On an ad hoc basis, liberals and conservatives have come together under the leadership of the liberal Morton Halperin and libertarian Grover Norquist specifically to criticize aspects of the Patriot Act and the use of military tribunals. And, as an example of groups that respond with special fervor to anti–civil liberties actions, the resistance of librarians and their activism in opposing the gathering of information about what books people read is a recent case in point. Other voices in opposition include the virtual organization Move On, which claims to reach 600,000 and has expanded its activities to include sharp criticism of anti–civil liberties measures.

There is little unrest on campus so far or even in law schools, a situation similar to that in 1965, when Vietnam just began to provoke opposition. And foundations, after an outpouring of grants to help victims of the 9/11 disaster, are at an early stage in terms of responses to the new government policy initiatives. The nation's public priorities have changed swiftly, but most institutions, like the country in general, need time to digest, understand, and react to the rapid evolution in security policies.

The Loyal Opposition

The nature of the current threat to the United States inevitably strengthens the hand of the White House at the expense of other political power centers. All citizens want a president who leads in these circumstances; we want to see him as less a politician, more a head of state and commander in chief. Still, despite the natural tendency to pull together during periods of conflict, there is ample evidence that the public remains uneasy and concerned about the future.

Not surprisingly, rank-and-file Democrats are the most critical of Bush and, according to polls, are less supportive of the measures to curtail civil liberties than are Republicans. Nonetheless, as one Democratic pollster put it, "Right now, even hardcore Democrats are more interested in security than rights." And several other Democratic strategists, asked why Democratic leaders are not pushing back harder, cited other reasons: the president's popularity, the continuing pro-administration news coverage, and some confusion about just what the best policies are in this unprecedented situation.

Many Democrats may well feel that, facing an enemy unlike any other, it is sensible to try to think through, almost from scratch, just how this danger should be confronted and what it means for the basic priorities of their party. At the same time, key officials in the Bush administration have been quick to put forward their own long-standing beliefs about greater government secrecy, less fettered law enforcement, military activism, and unilateral aggressiveness in international affairs as exactly the right remedies for the new threat.

Some of the roots of the cautious Democratic response to the Bush initiatives also may lie in the recent history of the party's approach to major policy issues. In the past couple of decades, a major movement—perhaps *the* major movement—in the party was intended to reduce the apparent differences between Democrats and centrist Republicans. The strategy was largely a reaction to presidential defeats during the 1980s, arguing that the Democratic party had moved too far to the left and was too soft on such issues as crime, defense, and welfare. Democratic dominance in the House and Senate, governorships, and state legislatures was dismissed in the face of an inability to assemble an Electoral College majority. The new approach was refined by the highly successful Democratic Leadership Conference and one of its early leaders, Bill Clinton.

In the current circumstances, however, Democrats might learn something from the man who was known as "Mr. Republican." Speaking less than two weeks after Pearl Harbor, Ohio Senator Robert A. Taft said that as a matter of general principle, I believe there can be no doubt that criticism in time of war is essential to the maintenance of any kind of democratic government. . . . Too many people desire to suppress criticism simply because they think it will give some comfort to the enemy. . . . If that comfort makes the enemy feel better for a few moments, they are welcome to it as far as I am concerned, because the maintenance of the right of criticism in the long run will do the country maintaining at a great deal more good than it will do the enemy, and it will prevent mistakes which might otherwise occur.

Moreover, most Republicans in Congress shared Taft's view that continuing attacks on the administration of Franklin D. Roosevelt were appropriate and politically effective; the GOP scored significant gains in the 1942 congressional races.

Perhaps the current low intensity of Democrats debating the administration's policies at home will alter as the presidential race heats up later in 2003. Some candidates have started to talk about these issues. Senator John Edwards of North Carolina argued last October that "it is wrong in the name of war, in the name of the war on terrorism, to let this administration take away our rights, take away our liberties, take away the freedoms we believe in. It is wrong, and we need to be able to stand up and say that to this president, this administration." And Senator John Kerry of Massachusetts said something similar: "A real threat exists for future terrorist attacks in this country, and it's up to all of us to respond appropriately to prevent them—but we can do that even as we protect the God-given rights and civil liberties which make America the land of the free. Our nation must be secure, but need not become so at the expense of our freedoms, our rights and our liberties."

Nobody Said It Would Be Easy

Robert Taft had a powerful point, and it was not primarily about party politics; it was about democracy and government. The politics of "permanent emergency" are hard and perilous. But they are nothing compared to the dangers of a government that is not transparent and accountable. It's the job of the opposition, the press, and the public to insist on full and open discourse about what we are doing and why.

We should be in the midst of a great debate about how to define the right mix of measures to increase our security and make us less likely to become victims while avoiding the calamity of becoming a garrison state. We know that good decisions often arise from sometimes painful public probing, including the post–Pearl Harbor investigation ordered by President Roosevelt, the Edward R. Morrow broadcasts that contributed to the fall of Joe McCarthy, the Church Commission investigation into intelligence failures in the 1970s, the Ervin Commission's revelations about Watergate, the My Lai investigation, and the publication of the Pentagon Papers. Such self-examination pointed toward the kinds of publicly formulated responses that are often needed to correct for mistakes that are made in the absence of public scrutiny or informed deliberation.

Today, there are new issues worthy of debate and criticism. There was a strong case, for example, that might have elicited considerable public support for including so-called sunset provisions on nearly all, rather than just some, of the new homeland security–related legislation. By building in the need to reenact the new measures through sunsets, Congress would have ensured that key provisions would last only as long as the emergency—or at least be automatically reconsidered after enough time elapsed to review their costs and benefits. More-over, the new Department of Homeland Security is scarcely likely to become a well-oiled machine because it has been ex-empted from the sort of corrective scrutiny that is a main source of improvement in existing agencies. There is also nothing un-patriotic about saying that ranking Iraq far above North Korea and even Al-Qaeda as immediate threats to the United States ought to be open to discussion. Nor is it un-American to ask whether the fact of a professional military, rather than one that relies on the draft, makes vigorous debate about military action both less likely and more important.

It is fundamental for a democracy to debate the conse-quences of more secrecy, less accountability, and reduced press access to information. It is simply common sense to seek greater public understanding of the causes and goals of the present cri-sis. Yet attempts to understand the roots of the hostility to America sometimes have been greeted with, as Joan Didion puts it, "wearying enthusiasm for excoriating anyone who sug-gested that it could be useful to bring at least the minimal de-gree of historical reference to bear on the event."

It's been said that in a democracy the first purpose of a de-bate about civil liberties is not to win, but to educate. If, in fact, the terrorist threat persists for decades, we must think carefully about what can happen to liberty in a nation permanently at war. We also need to insist on transparency and accountability for our governmental institutions, because that is the only way to improve their performance. In the area of intelligence, espe-cially, we need a broader and more searching inquiry in to what can be done to improve out ability to foresee attacks and to find our enemies. It would be unfair to blame the administra-tion for the events of 9/11, but it is essential to open up the conversation about what we have learned since then. An elected government cannot demand trust; it must be earned and maintained over time.

The Quiet Republic

America has faced dangers before, but for many, this threat seems uniquely personal. It may not be incidental that large numbers of elites who care about civil liberties live in the two cities, New York and Washington, most often mentioned as potential targets of future terrorist attacks. This new fact of life affects what people think about on their way to work and how people react to their families and friends. It is the elephant on the table that nobody wants to talk about. Thus, even those with little sympathy for President Bush's overall policies want an administration that is confident; we want the reassurance that comes from believing that we are in good hands.

For the public at large, this desire to be taken care of may even undermine the basics of democracy. Two University of Nebraska researchers recently reported that they had found that nearly half of all Americans would prefer that government's most significant decisions were made by "experts or business leaders" rather than by elected officials. One could also hazard a guess that this study suggests that the public is tired of partisanship and yearns for less "political" leadership.

Today, many American families would agree that they are confronted by more risk than in the recent past, reflecting both the sense of physical dangers associated with the terrorist attacks and the evaporation of the economic optimism of the 1990s. In these circumstances, the president might have reacted to 9/11 in quite different political terms, seeking, if not quite a government of national reconciliation, at least major efforts toward bipartisanship. He might have named a prominent Democrat, for example, to a key homeland security job. But this administration obviously believes in its ambitious and divisive domestic and international agendas. So what we have is a one-sided continuation of politics-as-usual—a lack of balance in the political process that seems completely at variance with a decade of elections reflecting a roughly 50-50 split in the nation.

Patriotism and anger can be channeled into support for conflict; increases in fear and trust can be translated into acquiescence for more security even at the expense of freedom. But in the end, neither of these sources provide the abiding strength of a nation armed not only with the latest security hardware but also with a deep belief in its course. The great benefit of vigorous debate is that it will serve to educate citizens about the issues. A consensus based upon understanding and informed judgment must be politically more valuable and more durable than one founded upon deeply felt but inevitably transitory emotions.

CHAPTER 1

A Familiar Story:
Lessons from Past Assaults
on Freedoms

ALAN BRINKLEY

THE HISTORY OF CIVIL LIBERTIES in America, like the history of civil rights, is a story of struggle. Even in peacetime, Americans have engaged in an ever-changing negotiation between the demands of liberty and the demands of order and security. But in times of national emergency, the conflict between these two demands has become intense—and the relative claims of order and security naturally become stronger. As we enter a new period of apparently open-ended crisis, the lessons of these past experiences with war and emergency are clear. We cannot reasonably expect the highly robust view of civil liberties that we have embraced in recent decades to survive unaltered. Every major crisis in our history has led to abridgements of personal liberty, some of them inevitable and justified. But in most such crises, governments have also used the seriousness of their mission to seize powers far in excess of what the emergency requires. At such moments, it has been particularly important that vigilant citizens make the case that the defense of our liberties is not an indulgence but rather an essential part of our democratic life.

Put simply, civil liberties are not a gift from the state that can be withdrawn when they become inconvenient. They are the product of continuous effort, which has extended over two centuries and must continue into a third—in dangerous times as well as in tranquil ones—if personal freedom is to remain a vital part of our national life.

"140 years of silence"

It is part of our national mythology that the Framers of the U.S. Constitution guaranteed civil liberties to all Americans through the Bill of Rights and that we are simply the beneficiaries of their wisdom. But not even the Framers were confident that the Bill of Rights provided sufficient protections of liberties. James Madison opposed the Bill of Rights altogether, arguing that any effort to enumerate rights would serve to limit them—one reason for the largely forgotten (until recently) Tenth Amendment, which states that "powers not delegated to the United States by the Constitution" are "reserved to the States . . . or the people." Proponents of the Bill of Rights feared that the amendments alone would not be sufficient to protect individual liberties—and they were well justified in those fears.

During most of the first century of the history of the United States, the Bill of Rights had relatively little impact on the lives of most American citizens. There were widespread violations of civil liberties that by modern standards would seem exceptionally oppressive, inspiring one scholar, remarking on the early history of the Bill of Rights, to describe it as "140 years of silence." Even ignoring the egregious violations of rights and liberties inflicted on both enslaved and free African Americans, Native Americans, Mexicans, Chinese, and many other groups of immigrants, and the routine limitations of the rights of women, the abridgements of civil liberties were severe and routine. Local governments routinely banned books, censored newspapers, and otherwise policed "heretical" or "blasphemous" speech. Standards of public decorum and behavior were rigidly enforced, and unconventional conduct was often criminalized. The legal rights of the accused in criminal trials had few effective protections, and obedience to the Fourth, Fifth, and Sixth Amendments was often token or nonexistent. Freedom of religion did not always extend to Catholics, Jews, free thinkers, agnostics, or atheists; and such people had no protection against discrimination in education, jobs, and even place of residence. Perhaps more important, popular support for an expansive view of civil liberties was thin and, in some places, nonexistent. As a result, there was little pressure on any level of government to work vigorously to defend them. The only exception was the vigorous use of the Bill of Rights to defend property rights.

The Alien and Sedition Acts of 1798—prompted by the quasi-war with France and designed to strengthen the government's authority to deal arbitrarily with aliens and dissenters—produced widespread popular hostility and led to the defeat of President John Adams in 1800. But this powerful reaction should not obscure the degree to which similar abuses of constitutionally protected freedoms occurred routinely, without legislative support, even in more normal times. Similarly, Abraham Lincoln's controversial suspension of the writ of habeas corpus during the Civil War only increased a vulnerability of citizens to arbitrary arrest and imprisonment that was already widespread.

It would be too much to say that the Bill of Rights was an empty shell during the nineteenth century. Things would surely have been worse without it. But to a significant degree, it remained contentless in the absence of popular, legislative, and judicial support—all of which were intermittent and often grudging for over a hundred years.

The Nation Unravels

Our modern notion of civil liberties was, in fact, not born with the creation of the Bill of Rights. A more important turning point may have been the U.S. involvement in World War I, which created some of the most egregious violations of civil liberties in our history—and, indirectly, some of the first vigorous defenses of them.

When the United States entered the war in April 1917, the administration of Woodrow Wilson was acutely aware of how much of the public remained hostile to the nation's intervention. It responded much like the Adams and Lincoln administrations had in earlier conflicts—with an aggressive campaign of intimidation and coercion designed to silence critics and root out opposition.

At the center of this effort were two pieces of wartime legislation: the Espionage Act of 1917, and the Sedition Act of 1918, which empowered the government to suppress and punish "disloyalty and subversion." The Espionage Act, among other things, permitted Postmaster General Albert Sidney Burleson to ban all "seditious" materials from the mails, a task that Burleson approached with great relish, announcing that "seditious" materials included anything that might "impugn the mo-

tives of the government and thus encourage insubordination";
anything that suggested "that the government is controlled by
Wall Street or munitions manufacturers, or any other special interests"; anything, in other words, that Burleson considered
somehow radical. All publications of the Socialist party were
banned by definition.

The Sedition Act, passed the next year to strengthen the
provisions of the Espionage Act, made it a criminal offense to
use "any disloyal, profane, scurrilous, or abusive language about
the form of government of the United States or the Constitution of the United States, or the flag of the United States, or the
uniform of the Army or Navy," or any language that might
bring those institutions "into contempt, scorn, . . . or disrepute."
This second law was particularly useful to the government as an
instrument for suppressing radicals and labor unionists. The
greatest number of prosecutions under the law were directed
against members of the Socialist party and its radical offshoot,
the Industrial Workers of the World (IWW). Eugene V. Debs,
the Socialists' leader, was convicted and imprisoned for questioning American involvement. Bill Haywood, head of the
IWW, fled to the Soviet Union during the war to avoid imprisonment. Others were imprisoned for casual remarks about the
president or the conduct of the war effort. Hiram Johnson, the
progressive senator from California, caustically described the
provisions of the law: "You shall not criticize anything or any-
body in the government any longer or you shall go to jail."

This state-sponsored repression did not occur in a vacuum. It
both encouraged and reflected a widespread popular intolerance
of dissent that very quickly became coercive and occasionally
violent. In 1917, private volunteers formed the American Pro-
tective League (APL) to assist the government in the task of

maintaining loyalty. The APL received the open endorsement of the U.S. attorney general, who called it a "patriotic organization . . . assisting the heavily overworked federal authorities in keeping an eye on disloyal individuals and making reports on disloyal utterances." It received $275,000 in government funds to finance its activities. Its members wore silver badges, as if they were official law enforcement authorities (although there was no screening process for entry); ordinary citizens were generally unaware of the distinction between them and legitimate authorities. By the end of the war, the organization had 250,000 members—men and women who defined their mission as spying on their neighbors, eavesdropping on suspicious conversations in bars and restaurants, intercepting and opening the mail and telegrams of people suspected of disloyalty, and reporting to the authorities any evidence of disenchantment with the war effort. They made extralegal arrests. They organized "slacker raids" against perceived draft resisters. The APL constituted only the largest of a number of such organizations. There was also the National Security League, the American Defense Society, even one modeled on the Boy Scouts—the Boy Spies of America.

Much of this repression was directed at labor leaders, radicals, and other dissidents. But its greatest impact fell on immigrants. Both Woodrow Wilson and Theodore Roosevelt denounced "hyphenated Americans" in 1916, and neither discouraged assaults on them once they began. Popular passions against dissidents and immigrants soon ran amok. The primary target, although not the only one, was German Americans. The California Board of Education, for example, banned the teaching of German in public schools, calling it "a language that disseminates the ideals of autocracy, brutality, and hatred." Libraries removed German books from shelves. Merchants and others dropped German words from the language. ("Sauer-kraut" became "liberty cabbage"; "hamburger" became "liberty sausage.") German faculty members were fired from universities. German musicians were fired from orchestras. There were widespread rumors of plots by German Americans to put ground glass in bandages sent to the front, and so people with German names were barred from the Red Cross. In Minnesota, a minister was tarred and feathered because he was overheard praying with a dying woman in German. In southern Illinois, a man was lynched in 1918 for no apparent reason except that he happened to be of German descent; the organizers of the lynch mob were acquitted by a jury, which insisted that what they had done had been a patriotic act.

This overwrought nativism—generated, even if inadvertently, by government policy and rhetoric—extended to other ethnic groups as well: to the Irish (because of their hostility to the English), to the Jews (because many were hostile to an American alliance with the anti-Semitic Russian government), and to others simply because their ethnic distinctiveness came to seem a threat to the idea of "One-Hundred Percent Americanism," a phrase widely used at the time to describe national unity. Immigrant ghettoes in major cities were strictly policed and became frequent targets of vigilante groups. Even many settlement-house workers came to feel it their duty to impose a new and more coercive conformity on the immigrants they served. A settlement worker in Chicago said in 1918 that the war had made her realize that "we were a nation only in a very imperfect sense. We were stirred to a new sense of responsibility for a more coherent loyalty, a vital Americanism."

Woodrow Wilson reputedly predicted in early 1917, "Once lead this people into war, and they'll forget there ever was such a thing as tolerance. To fight, you must be brutal and ruthless, and the spirit of ruthless brutality will enter into the very fibre of our national life, infecting Congress, the courts, the policeman on the beat, the man on the street." It proved in large measure to be a self-fulfilling prophecy—and not just for the war. The behavior Wilson predicted, and helped to create, continued well after the Armistice of November 1918. In some ways, it intensified, most notably during what has become known as the Red Scare.

The great Red Scare was in part a response to the Bolshevik Revolution in Russia and the tremendous fear that it created throughout the capitalist world. It was also a product of the great instability of postwar America, something that many middle-class people believed to be orchestrated by revolutionaries. There was widespread labor unrest, racial conflict in cities, economic turbulence, and a small but frightening wave of terrorist acts by radicals. But the Red Scare was above all a result of the deliberate strategies of ambitious politicians, who saw a campaign against Bolshevism in America as a useful spur to their careers.

The U.S. Justice Department, under Attorney General A. Mitchell Palmer (who had presidential hopes for 1920), was the leading actor in inflaming the Red Scare. An attempted bombing of Palmer's house helped legitimize the major campaign against radicals that he was already planning and that he launched in 1920. On New Year's Day, he ordered simultaneous federal raids (orchestrated by the young J. Edgar Hoover) on suspected radical centers all over the country. There were 6,000 arrests, amid enormous publicity. They have become known to history as the Palmer Raids.

This crackdown was supposed to reveal and destroy what Palmer claimed was a national, revolutionary conspiracy. In fact, the raids netted three pistols, no explosives, and only a small smattering of radical literature. Most of the people arrested were not radicals at all, and even the relatively few genuine radicals rounded up could not be shown to have violated any laws. Most were eventually released, although many remained in custody for weeks and even months without facing formal charges. While detained, they were denied access to attorneys or even to their own families. Several hundred foreign radicals and presumed radicals were deported to Russia, where they arrived—many of them speaking no Russian and knowing nothing of the country—in the middle of a civil war. Palmer himself looked back on this sorry episode a year later without repentance. "Like a prairie fire," he said,

> the blaze of revolution was sweeping over every American institution of law and order a year ago. It was eating its way into the homes of the American workman, its sharp tongues of revolutionary heat were licking the altars of the churches, leaping into the belfry of the school bell, crawling into the sacred corners of American homes, seeking to replace marriage vows with libertine laws, burning up the foundations of society.

As during the war, popular vigilante groups took their cue from the government and leaped into the battle. In the state of Washington, a mob dragged a member of the IWW from jail, where he had been placed after arrest on vague charges of "subversion," castrated him, and then hung him. In New York, soldiers and sailors (eager to strike back at people who had opposed the war effort) invaded the offices of a socialist news-paper, smashed the presses, and assaulted the staff. And just as German books had been burned, German teachers had been fired, and German ideas had been suppressed during the war, now books and teachers and ideas presumed to be radical were burned and fired and suppressed.

The Silver Lining

The federal government's assault on civil liberties during and after World War I may have been the most egregious in its history. It stifled dissenters who gave no evidence of being a danger to the nation. It permitted the persecution of German Americans who posed no threat to security. It produced a wide-ranging legal assault on men and women based on nothing but their presumed beliefs. And it routinely suspended such ordinary rights as freedom of speech, freedom of association, and freedom from arbitrary arrest.

But in acting so aggressively to abridge civil liberties, the government in these years inadvertently gave birth to a powerful new movement to protect them. Indeed, it is not too much to say that World War I was the birthplace of our modern notion of civil liberties; that in its aftermath, the Bill of Rights began to have an expansive meaning in American life for the first time. The backlash against the wartime excesses helped create three new forces committed to defending civil liberties in the future: popular support; formidable institutions; and the first serious evidence of judicial backing.

Popular support for civil liberties prior to World War I had been almost entirely theoretical. Most Americans would, if asked, have claimed to support the Bill of Rights. But except for a few dissenters and free thinkers, most took little notice of, and expressed little alarm about, the many ways in which its provisions had been made almost meaningless by the operation of state and local governments. People of wealth and standing assumed, generally correctly, that they faced little danger of repression, censorship, and arbitrary arrest. People without property had no realistic expectation that the civil liberties promised by the Constitution would mean very much to them. As Zechariah Chafee, a great champion of free speech in the 1920s and 1930s, later wrote of this period: "The First Amendment had no hold on people's minds, because no live facts or concrete images were then attached to it. Consequently, like an empty box with beautiful words on it, the Amendment collapsed under the impact of Prussian battalions, and terror of Bolshevik mobs."

The heavy-handed actions of the federal government, however, created popular alarm where other abuses had not, largely because of the greater suspicion with which Americans viewed federal power. The Palmer Raids in particular produced widespread denunciations in the press; destroyed A. Mitchell Palmer's political career; nearly crushed in the bud J. Edgar Hoover's prospects for bureaucratic advancement; and badly damaged the Wilson administration and the Democratic party. Republicans, sensing a political opportunity, took up the cause of civil liberties as a way of attacking the Democrats and helped give the issue popular credibility. In the absence of scientific polls, it is impossible to measure the extent of this shift in public opinion. But not since the Alien and Sedition Acts of 1798 had violations of civil liberties aroused so much evidence of popular and political condemnation.

The war and its aftermath also energized the small and once largely powerless community of civil liberties activists, who suddenly saw an opportunity to establish their cause in the public mind. Among them was Roger Baldwin, a settlement-house worker in St. Louis who, inspired by a speech of Emma Goldman, became deeply committed to resisting state efforts to limit individual freedoms. He became a civil liberties activist during World War I, and he spent the rest of his long and active life building institutional support for protections of this relatively new concept. (He believed, with some justification, that he was responsible for introducing the term "civil liberties" into American public discourse.)

In 1917, Baldwin and a few other critics of government policies created the National Civil Liberties Bureau, whose original purpose was to criticize state repression and build support for protecting personal freedoms. Baldwin's approach to this task was deliberately controversial. He rejected the suggestions of some allies that he target only the most indefensible violations (such as the government's brutal treatment of conscientious objectors). He insisted, rather, that the best way to establish the principle of robust civil liberties would be to defend the most unpopular people and causes. He was especially outspoken on behalf of the radical anarchists of the IWW, arguing that by standing up for the "Wobblies" he was casting light not only on the role of government but also on the role of industrial capital in repressing the rights of individuals.

The National Civil Liberties Bureau attracted relatively little attention during the war itself. But the reaction to the 1919 Palmer Raids suddenly thrust it into prominence. In January 1920, it was reorganized and renamed the American Civil Liberties Union. Baldwin suddenly found himself with a host of prominent supporters, among them Clarence Darrow, Jane Addams, Felix Frankfurter, Helen Keller, Norman Thomas, and John Dewey, and he began to envision a larger role for his organization. It would no longer simply denounce assaults on liberty. It would use its influence to attack them through the legal system.

The third great contribution to the creation of the modern regime of civil liberties was the slow but growing support for the idea within the judiciary. Not until the Supreme Court decisions of the 1950s and 1960s, under Chief Justice Earl Warren, did protecting civil liberties become a major item on the Court's agenda, and even then the lower courts were slow to embrace the cause. But the gradual shift of judicial thinking on the issue became visible within months after the end of the war, less in the actual decisions of the courts than in several notable dissents that created the intellectual foundation for an expanded legal notion of free speech.

The most important figure in this process was Oliver Wendell Holmes, Jr. During and immediately after the war, Holmes, an associate justice of the U.S. Supreme Court, showed little more inclination than any other members of the Court to challenge the government's aggressive use of the Espionage and Sedition Acts to silence opposition. Early in 1919, the Court accepted an appeal on behalf of Charles Schenk, a socialist who had been convicted of violating the Espionage Act for passing out leaflets denouncing the war and encouraging young men to resist the draft. Holmes wrote the majority opinion, which affirmed Schenk's conviction and the constitutionality of the law. "The question in every case," he wrote in a controversial decision, "is whether the words used are used in such circumstances and are of such a nature as to create a clear and present danger that they will bring about the substantive evils that Congress has a right to prevent." Schenk's "words," he insisted, were designed to undermine the draft and were therefore unprotected speech. "When a nation is at war," he added, "many things that might be said in time of peace are such a hindrance to its effort that their utterance will not be endured so long as men fight, and that no Court could regard them as protected by any constitutional right."

Holmes's decision evoked a storm of protest from eminent legal scholars whose opinion the justice evidently respected; and by November 1919, he had clearly revised his views about protected speech. In *Abrams v. United States,* the court reviewed the conviction of Jacob Abrams, a Russian immigrant who had been convicted under the Sedition Act for distributing leaflets criticizing President Wilson's decision to dispatch U.S. troops to Russia in 1918, during the civil war that followed the Bolshevik Revolution. As in the *Schenk* case, there was no evidence that Abrams's actions had in any way impeded the course of the war. But a lower court had claimed that it was enough that his actions *might* have jeopardized U.S. policy to justify a conviction; and the Supreme Court agreed, upholding both the conviction and the law. But this time, Holmes (joined by Justice Louis Brandeis) vigorously and famously dissented, in language that many consider the classic initial argument for a robust view of the First Amendment. Defenders of the Sedition Act, Holmes said, had rested their case on the overwhelming importance of sustaining support for the war and the dangers dissenters posed to that effort. But no one should be so confident that the passions of the moment are irrefutable, Holmes suggested:

When men have realized that time has upset many fighting faiths, they may come to believe even more than they believe the very foundations of their own conduct that the ultimate good desired is better reached by free trade in ideas—that the best test of truth is the power of the thought to get itself accepted in the competition of the market, and that truth is the only ground upon which their wishes safely can be carried out. That, at any rate, is the theory of our Constitution. It is an experiment, as all life is an experiment. Every year, if not every day, we have to wager our salvation upon some prophecy based upon imperfect knowledge. While that experiment is part of our system, I think that we should be eternally vigilant against attempts to check the expression of opinions that we loathe and believe to be fraught with death. . . . I had conceived that the United States, through many years, had shown its repentance for the Sedition Act of 1798.

A year later, Louis Brandeis made another significant contribution to the case for expanding the definition of free speech. In a dissent against the ruling in *Gilbert v. Minnesota*, in which the Supreme Court upheld a Minnesota law under which Joseph Gilbert had been convicted of speaking against the draft, Justice Brandeis wrote:

I have difficulty in believing that the liberty guaranteed by the Constitution . . . does not include liberty to teach, either in the privacy of the home or publicly, the doctrine of pacifism. . . . I cannot believe that the liberty guaranteed by the Fourteenth Amendment [in other words, the Fourteenth Amendment's guarantee of First Amendment and other protections to all citizens] includes only liberty to acquire and to enjoy property.

And in 1927, still dealing with the fallout from wartime repression, Brandeis wrote yet another influential opinion in *Whitney v. California.* He concurred on technical grounds with the 1919 conviction of Anita Whitney for joining a communist party in California and advocating the overthrow of the U.S. government, but he dissented sharply from the Court's expansive view of the state's power to suppress "dangerous" speech:

> Those who won our independence by revolution were not cowards. They did not fear political change. They did not exalt order at the cost of liberty. To courageous, self-reliant men, with confidence in the power of free and fearless reasoning applied through the processes of popular government, no danger flowing from speech can be deemed clear and present [a not very subtle slap at Holmes's *Schenk* decision], unless the incidence of the evil apprehended is so imminent that it may befall before there is opportunity for full discussion. If there be time to expose through discussion the falsehood and fallacies, to avert the evil by the processes of education, the remedy to be applied is more speech, not enforced silence. . . . It is therefore always open to Americans to challenge a law abridging free speech and assembly by showing that there was no emergency justifying it. . . . The fact that speech is likely to result in some violence or in destruction of property is not enough to justify its suppression. There must be the probability of serious injury to the State. Among free men, the deterrents ordinarily to be applied to prevent crime are education and punishment for violations of the law, not abridgment of the rights of free speech and assembly.

In these and other dissents, Holmes, Brandeis, and a slowly expanding group of other judges and justices began laying out much of what became the legal and moral basis for our modern conception of civil liberties.

Fighting the Last War

As the United States prepared to enter World War II, no one in authority was unaware of the enormous price the nation (and the Democratic party) had paid for the legal and popular repression of 1917–1920. Nor were officials unaware of the new bulwarks defending civil liberties—the American Civil Liberties Union and related organizations, as well as the still frail but nevertheless visible body of precedent in the courts. As a result, there was no equivalent to the Alien and Sedition Acts in World War II, no government encouragement of vigilante action against dissenters (who were, in any case, many fewer than in the previous war), no demonization of German Americans or Italian Americans. Although the government censored press reports from the front, there was no effort to interfere with what newspapers printed at home. Loud and often vicious attacks on the president and the Congress went unpunished and largely ignored.

But the new regime of civil liberties was not yet strong enough to protect racial minorities against the repressive passions the war helped unleash. African Americans, Mexicans, and others continued to confront the long-standing barriers to liberty that had been part of American racial practices for centuries. Even those who joined the military were required to serve in segregated units and were often denied the most elementary rights of protest and self-protection. A catastrophic explosion at Port Chicago in Los Angeles in 1944 left 320 Navy workers, two-thirds of them African Americans, dead. When black workers refused to return to work at Port Chicago several weeks later, claiming correctly that little had been done to increase safety at the site, they were court-martialed, given fifteen-year prison terms, and dishonorably discharged.

Most vulnerable of all were the small communities of Japanese Americans on the Pacific Coast. In the aftermath of Pearl Harbor, many Californians, not implausibly, feared enemy attacks on the American mainland. Less plausibly, they feared that the slightly more than 100,000 Japanese Americans in California (two-thirds of them U.S. citizens) might be conspiring with the Japanese government to facilitate such attacks.

As in World War I, far from attempting to dampen these fears, public officials inflamed and legitimized them. Earl Warren, the California attorney general at the time, stated publicly: "To assume that the enemy has not planned fifth column activities for us in a wave of sabotage is simply to live in a fool's paradise." John L. DeWitt, commander of Army forces on the West Coast, proposed the relocation of "enemy aliens" to a site far from the coast and rejected all suggestions that distinctions be made between aliens and citizens, or between the loyal and disloyal. "The Japanese race is an enemy race," he insisted. "Racial affinities are not severed by migration." Even second- and third-generation Japanese Americans could not be trusted because, he said, "the racial strains are undiluted."

DeWitt won the support of Secretary of War Henry Stimson, who then persuaded President Franklin D. Roosevelt (despite the strenuous objections of Attorney General Francis Biddle) to sign an executive order authorizing the removal of all people of Japanese ancestry from the Pacific Coast. This act—not the most far-reaching but surely one of the most extreme and shameful violations of civil liberties in American history—was not an inevitable result of popular sentiment, which could have been mollified by appropriate assurances from people in authority and which, in any case, subsided relatively quickly after Pearl Harbor. It was a result of deliberate decisions by men in the War Department whose single-minded commitment to the pursuit of victory in the war left little room for consideration of such abstract notions as civil liberties and civil rights. It did not matter to them very much whether or not the Japanese were truly disloyal. If they were erring, they believed, it was better to err on the side of security. Relocation was a way of avoiding the difficult task of determining loyalty and also a way of assuaging (rather than trying to change) public opinion. The fact that the victims of this action were of Japanese ancestry, linked to a people whom both the federal government and the popular culture were energetically demonizing through an extraordinarily racist propaganda campaign, made the decision still easier.

The question of the constitutional validity of the internment orders reached the U.S. Supreme Court in May 1943. Only a week before the case arrived, the justices overturned a state court ruling (and one of the Court's own decisions of three years before) that had upheld the expulsion of Jehovah's Witnesses from public schools because they refused on religious grounds to salute the flag. But consistent with its historic reluctance to challenge wartime governments on constitutional issues, it showed no such sensitivity to civil liberties in deciding the case of Fred Korematsu, a San Francisco welder who had resisted relocation two years earlier. In a 6–3 decision announced in 1944, the Court ruled, in effect, that the internment policy was constitutional simply because the military claimed it was necessary. Justice Hugo Black, justly remembered as having been a great civil libertarian through most of his career, brusquely dismissed Korematsu's claim as without merit, even though he conceded there was no evidence of the plaintiff's disloyalty. Justice Frank Murphy, dissenting, stated bluntly: "This exclusion of 'all persons of Japanese ancestry, both alien and non-alien,' from the Pacific Coast area on a plea of military necessity in the absence of martial law ought not to be approved. Such exclusion goes over 'the very brink of constitutional power,' and falls into the ugly abyss of racism." The American Civil Liberties Union, and indeed almost the entire civil liberties community, remained virtually silent throughout.

Just as the Espionage Act, the Sedition Act, and the Palmer Raids created a generation of efforts to avoid the mistakes of the past, the internment of Japanese Americans became a case study for several decades after World War II of security measures run amok. Even at the height of Cold War hysteria, when civil liberties violations were widespread, there was never a serious effort to intern communists and subversives (although the 1950 McCarran Act made provisions—never implemented—for such internment camps). But a civil liberties regime constantly fighting the last war is not always well prepared for the next one; and in the 1950s, the defenses of civil liberties painstakingly built up in the four decades since the Palmer Raids proved a frail protection for the left when confronted with the second great Red Scare. Accustomed to protecting citizens from prosecution for exercising free speech, defenders of civil liberties seemed unable to frame an effective response to newer violations: people being dismissed from jobs, blacklisted in their professions, libeled by public officials on the basis of their presumed beliefs and past associations, and in some cases jailed because of their reluctance to testify against others.

A familiar pattern emerged after the demise of Senator Joseph McCarthy: a widespread, retroactive repudiation of the guilt-by-association tactics of those who hunted down suspected Communists, as well as a heightened sensitivity to protecting academic freedom and challenging arbitrary prosecutions and job dismissals on political grounds. This aggressive effort to create bulwarks against a repetition of the harrowing events of the early 1950s also contributed to the dramatic growth in the protection of political, cultural, and religious dissent in the 1960s and to the expansion of legal protections available to those accused of crimes. Interest in civil liberties was so intense in the 1960s that during the Vietnam War, with some notable exceptions, the usual wartime infringements of civil liberties were surprisingly rare. Reporters in Vietnam were permitted to cover the war without censorship or any serious control by the military. Opponents of the draft openly denounced the system without significant legal jeopardy. A powerful antiwar movement emerged with only minor, and largely incompetent, assaults from the government it was attempting to challenge.

By the end of the Vietnam War, it seemed to many Americans that civil liberties were now firmly established and well defended; that despite the continued need for vigilance, the largest battles had been won. And in the glow of that apparent victory, it became tempting to think of the growth of civil liberties protections in the twentieth century as part of a consistent, linear, progressive story—moving almost inevitably from an inferior past to a superior future. But the real lesson of the growth of civil liberties in the twentieth century is not that progress is inevitable. Instead, the lesson is that society's definition of civil liberties is fluid and constantly changing; that new situations create new threats, for which prior experiences are often poor preparation; and that public support for protecting basic freedoms is highly contingent and can evaporate quickly.

Backlash

Well before September 11, 2001, a large segment of right-wing opinion had become firmly committed to the idea that the 1960s had produced an irresponsible and excessive regime of civil liberties; that radicals and dissenters and foreigners did not deserve the protections they had belatedly received; that the press had become a dangerous and even subversive force that must somehow be curbed; and that it should be the task of conservative politics to roll back these rights and increase the ability of the state to protect itself from its challengers.

One powerful orthodoxy of conservative (and military) opinion—despite an almost complete absence of supporting evidence—was that an unrestrained and critical press had undermined the ability of Americans to fight effectively in Vietnam. And so, beginning in the early 1980s, when the press was entirely excluded from the U.S. invasion of Grenada, reporters faced significant new barriers to covering wars. In World War II, photographers and reporters were among the first Americans on the beaches of Normandy. The great war photographer Robert Capa was, in fact, ahead of the troops—taking dramatic pictures of thousands of young men landing and, in many cases, dying in the waves behind him. In Grenada, Panama, Kuwait, and Kosovo, the U.S. government—claiming to be concerned about the safety of reporters, despite the insistence of the press that they themselves were not deterred by possible danger—almost never let the media anywhere near the fighting. The public had to rely on official military accounts of what had happened, many of which later turned out to be incomplete or false.

At the same time, aggressive efforts to fight crime produced a series of attacks on the legal protections of accused criminals that the Warren Court had painstakingly constructed. Police and prosecutors pushed hard and sometimes successfully to expand their ability to conduct random searches. Despite many protests, law enforcement relied heavily on racial profiling. The erosion of legal services gradually made a mockery in some places of the right of the accused (and, most alarmingly, of those facing the death penalty) to be represented effectively by counsel. By the end of the twentieth century, in other words, civil liberties—though far better protected than they had been a half century and more before—were already under assault. There were powerful forces arguing that civil liberties had expanded too far and too fast, that they had become a threat to social order. The attacks of September 11 became, among other things, a vehicle for advancing an assault on civil liberties that was already under way for other reasons.

The United States faces grave dangers in the aftermath of the attacks of September 2001, and the aggressive efforts of the government to seize new powers and to curb traditional liberties cannot be dismissed as cynical or frivolous. Some alteration in our understanding of rights is appropriate and necessary in dangerous times, as even the most ardent civil libertarians tend to admit. But the history of civil liberties in times of emergency suggests that governments seldom react to crises carefully or judiciously. They acquiesce to the most alarmist proponents of repression. They pursue preexisting agendas in the name of national security. They target unpopular or vulnerable groups in the population less because there is clear evidence of danger than because there is little political cost. During World War I, the victims of government repression were labor leaders, anarchists, and socialists—none of whom posed any threat to the war effort but all of whom were widely disliked. In World War II, the victims were Japanese Americans, who were stripped of all the rights of citizenship not because there was evidence of disloyalty but because of racist fears. In the current emergency, the victims are mostly Arab Americans and foreign nationals, who have been subject to mass arrests and considerable harassment on the basis of virtually no evidence of danger or disloyalty.

Citizens naturally react to great crises viscerally and often vent their fears in the form of demands for unconscionable actions. It is government's role to see beyond the understandably passionate feelings of the public and frame a reasoned response to the dangers we face: not to defend all civil liberties reflexively, certainly, but to give them considerable weight in choosing how to balance the competing demands of freedom and order. And it is up to those organizations and individuals who care about civil liberties, and who are committed to continuing the more than two centuries of struggle to legitimize and strengthen their place in American life, to insist that our leaders do just that.

CHAPTER 2

Security and Liberty:
Preserving the Values of Freedom

ANTHONY LEWIS

*Security is like liberty in that many are the crimes
committed in its name.*

—Justice Robert H. Jackson,
dissenting in *Knauff v. Shaughnessy* (1950)

ELLEN RAPHAEL, born in Germany, went to England
in 1939 as a refugee. She served in the Royal Air Force
for three years during World War II, then got a job as a
civilian employee of the United States Army occupation forces
in Germany. There she met and married another civilian
employee, Kurt W. Knauff, a German-born naturalized U.S.
citizen who had served in the U.S. Army during the war. In
1948 she sailed for the United States to become a citizen under
the War Brides Act, which allowed swift naturalization for
women newly married to soldiers or former soldiers. But at El-
lis Island she was denied admission and detained. The U.S. attorney general excluded her on the ground that she was a

security risk, without telling her the reasons for that finding or giving her a hearing. She sued, challenging the secret process— and lost in the Supreme Court by a 4-3 vote.

The majority opinion, by Justice Sherman Minton, emphasized the power of the president, delegated here to the attorney general. "Upon the basis of confidential information," the opinion said, the attorney general had concluded "that the public interest required that Mrs. Knauff be denied the privilege of entry into the United States. He denied a hearing on the matter because, in his judgment, the disclosure of the information on which he based that opinion would itself endanger the public security."

Justice Jackson, himself a former attorney general, rejected that logic. "The menace to the security of this country," he said,

> be it great as it may, from this girl's admission, is as nothing compared to the menace to free institutions inherent in procedures of this pattern. In the name of security the police state justifies its arbitrary oppressions on evidence that is secret. . . . The plea that evidence must be secret is abhorrent to free men, because it provides a cloak for the malevolent, the misinformed, the meddlesome and the corrupt to play the role of informer undetected and uncorrected.

The dangers that Justice Jackson saw half a century ago have returned in more menacing form since September 11, 2001. In his war on terrorism, President George W. Bush has asserted the power to designate any American citizen an "enemy combatant" and to detain that person indefinitely without charge or trial, barring the detainee from speaking to a lawyer and denying him the right to contest the factual basis of his detention in court.

Secrecy marks other steps taken since September 11 by the president and Attorney General John Ashcroft. In the months after the terrorist attacks, more than 1,000 aliens were taken into custody and detained for long periods; their names were kept secret, on the grounds that disclosing them would give terrorists clues to the effectiveness of U.S. intelligence. At the behest of Attorney General Ashcroft, the chief immigration judge ordered that all deportation hearings involving allegations of terrorist connections be held in secret. The government imposed blanket secrecy on the detention camp at Guantánamo Bay, Cuba, where alleged fighters for Al-Qaeda and the Taliban were imprisoned.

Secrecy puts civil liberties at risk for a reason stated by Justice Potter Stewart when the Supreme Court decided the Pentagon Papers case (*N.Y. Times Co. v. United States*) in 1971. The usual legislative and judicial checks on executive power scarcely operate on national security matters, he wrote. Thus,

> the only effective restraint upon executive policy and power in the areas of national defense and international affairs may lie in an enlightened citizenry—in an informed and critical public opinion which alone can protect the values of democratic government. For this reason, it is perhaps here that a press that is alert, aware, and free, most vitally serves the basic purpose of the First Amendment. For without an informed and free press there cannot be an enlightened citizenry.

To Justice Stewart's adjectives for the kind of press needed to check executive power—"alert," "aware," "free," "informed"—one more must be added: "courageous." The American press found its courage in the Vietnam War. Through most of the twentieth century it had had a cozy relationship with the holders of executive power; columnists and Washington bureau chiefs were intimate with secretaries of state. In Vietnam, journalists broke from that close relationship to speak truth to power—to challenge official talk about the light at the end of the tunnel with the facts on the ground. The decision of the *New York Times,* the ultimate establishment newspaper, to publish the Pentagon Papers, the secret history of the war, symbolized the end of coziness. Then came the *Washington Post*'s dogged pursuit of Watergate.

But the war on terrorism is like World War II, not Vietnam: a good war, with a genuinely evil enemy. American journalists naturally sympathize. They know that there may be more terrorist attacks, inclining the public to want security at any cost. They may be concerned about looking unpatriotic if they criticize the government's methods—especially when officials denounce criticism as siding with terrorists. Three months after September 11 Attorney General Ashcroft said: "To those who scare peace-loving people with phantoms of lost liberty, my message is this: Your tactics only aid terrorists, for they erode our national unity and diminish our resolve. They give ammunition to America's enemies."

As ALAN BRINKLEY DESCRIBES in Chapter 1, this is not the first time in American history that civil liberties have suffered during war or national alarm; it has happened again and again. Each time the country later regretted what had happened.

To recall past episodes of repression is to realize that there is something different about incursions on liberty today. The war on terrorism is being waged against a hidden enemy who is not going to surrender in a ceremony aboard the USS *Missouri*. There is indeed no way to foresee how or when this war will end. The fear of terrorism may well go on for the rest of our lives. We may not have breathing space to understand and regret punitive excesses. If we are to preserve constitutional values—the values of freedom—understanding and resistance must come now.

In another way, too, the war on terrorism is more threatening to civil liberty than past crises. It provides more potential justifications for secrecy. The classic formula for silencing the press in war emergencies was laid down by Chief Justice Charles Evans Hughes in 1931 in the case of *Near v. Minnesota*. The government, he said, may prevent the publication of such things as "the sailing dates of troop transports." The troopship rule, as it came to be known, played a central part in the Pentagon Papers decision. The Supreme Court had to decide, as Justice William J. Brennan, Jr., put it, whether in the material the *New York Times* had, there was anything "kindred to imperiling the safety of a transport already at sea." But terrorism may strike in myriad ways: by the commandeering of civilian airliners, the smuggling of small containers of nerve gas or biological weapons, and so on. Anything may be a troopship, and the government demands unencumbered power to deal with it.

The claim of executive power is the heart of the matter. There has been no more sweeping claim, in living memory, than the Bush administration's assertion of power to hold any American in detention forever, without a trial and without access to counsel, simply by declaring him to be an enemy combatant. That claim is presented, legally, in two cases now going through the courts: the cases of Jose Padilla and Yaser Esam Hamdi.

Padilla

Jose Padilla was born in Brooklyn in 1971, became a gang member, and was held for murder as a juvenile, age fourteen. Criminal records show a half-dozen other arrests and several jail sentences. After release from a Florida prison in 1992 he apparently married a Muslim woman, and he took the name Abdullah al-Muhajir. A declaration filed in court by the government, prepared by a Defense Department official, Michael E. Mobbs, said that Padilla traveled to Egypt, Saudi Arabia, and Afghanistan. Unnamed confidential sources quoted in the declaration said Padilla approached "senior Osama Bin Laden lieutenant Abu Zubaydah" in Afghanistan and proposed stealing radioactive material in the United States in order to build a bomb that would spread radiation when it exploded. The government alleged that he did research on that project at an Al-Qaeda safe house in Pakistan.

One of the confidential sources said he did not believe Padilla was a member of Al-Qaeda. But the Mobbs declaration said he had "extended contacts with senior Al Qaeda members," "received training from Al Qaeda operatives in furtherance of terrorist activities and was sent to the United States to conduct reconnaissance and/or conduct other attacks on their behalf."

On May 8, 2002, Padilla flew into Chicago from abroad. He was taken into custody at O'Hare Airport by federal agents. The Justice Department went before a U.S. district court in New York and obtained a warrant for his arrest and detention as a material witness for a grand jury sitting there to investigate the September 11 attacks. Padilla was then moved to a jail in New York. On May 15, he was brought before Judge Michael B. Mukasey, who appointed Donna R. Newman as his lawyer.

Newman, after conferring with Padilla in jail, moved to vacate the material-witness warrant. The judge set June 11 for a hearing on the motion.

But on June 9, the government told the judge that it was withdrawing its subpoena for Padilla to testify before the grand jury. It disclosed to Judge Mukasey that President Bush had designated Padilla an enemy combatant and directed Secretary of Defense Donald Rumsfeld to take custody of him. Padilla was flown to a Navy brig in South Carolina and kept in solitary confinement, forbidden to see his lawyer, his family, or any other outside person.

The next day, June 10, Attorney General Ashcroft, who happened to be in Moscow, made a statement that was broadcast on television to the United States. "We have captured a known terrorist," Ashcroft said. "While in Afghanistan and Pakistan, al-Muhajir trained with the enemy. . . . In apprehending [him] as he sought entry into the United States, we have disrupted an unfolding terrorist plot to attack the United States by exploding a radioactive 'dirty bomb.'"

On June 11, the date originally set for a hearing on the material-witness warrant, Newman, Padilla's lawyer, told Judge Mukasey that she was not allowed to visit Padilla in South Carolina or speak with him; government lawyers said she could write him a letter, but he might not receive it.

Newman filed a petition for habeas corpus, the ancient writ that requires any authority holding a prisoner to show justification for the imprisonment. She asked for an order allowing her to consult with Padilla. Government lawyers, in response, raised technical objections, arguing, for example, that the case belonged in South Carolina, not New York. On the merits, they argued that Judge Mukasey should defer to the judgment of

President Bush and the Defense Department because courts were not competent to weigh wartime necessities.

What was done in the case of Jose Padilla made a radical change in our assumptions about the limits on government power. At the start, Attorney General Ashcroft's statement in Moscow effectively convicted Padilla of grave crimes—without a trial or even an indictment. "We have acted," Ashcroft said, under "clear Supreme Court precedent, which [establishes] that the military may detain a United States citizen who has joined the enemy and has entered our country to carry out hostile acts." That was evidently a reference to the 1942 case of *Ex parte Quirin,* in which the Court upheld the military trial of a group of German saboteurs—one of them an American citizen—who were landed on Long Island by a submarine in World War II. But to call that decision a clear precedent could politely be called an exaggeration. The Nazi saboteurs, unlike Padilla, were given a trial. They had full access to lawyers, and very able lawyers they were. (One of them, Kenneth C. Royall, was later secretary of the Army.)

If Padilla in fact did what Attorney General Ashcroft said, why was he not indicted and tried for those offenses? Plainly, it is much more convenient for the government simply to hold him without going through the effort, and very likely the awkwardness, of producing the evidence and convincing a jury of his guilt. *The Economist* magazine speculated that prosecutors at first hoped he would cooperate and provide information, but he would not. Detaining him without trial obviated having to disclose sources of intelligence that the government might want to keep hidden. It avoided the publicity of a trial. And it allowed the government to keep trying to persuade Padilla to talk.

The hope of getting Padilla to talk was, in fact, cited by government lawyers to Judge Mukasey as grounds for barring his access to counsel. With considerable candor, their briefs said any consultation with a lawyer would interfere with the continuing process of questioning Padilla. Of course, there is an irony in that. One of the very reasons the U.S. Constitution guarantees all criminal defendants the right to counsel, and the Supreme Court in the case of *Gideon v. Wainwright* in 1963 held that poor defendants must be given counsel by the state, is that defendants on their own may be overborne by police and prosecutors.

But this was not a criminal case, the government argued. It was an effort to meet the ongoing threat of terrorism. And letting Padilla talk with his lawyer would "jeopardize the two core purposes of detaining enemy combatants—gathering intelligence about the enemy, and preventing the detainee from aiding in any further attacks against America." The first of those two aims, government briefs said, required continued, unimpeded questioning. The second ruled out access to a lawyer because Al-Qaeda operatives are trained to use intermediaries such as lawyers to pass messages to fellow terrorists even if the "intermediaries may be unaware that they are being so used." The government coupled these particular arguments on the issue of Padilla's access to counsel with a general warning that judges should not interfere with a president's conduct of a war: that judges must pay that power great deference.

Judge Mukasey decided the case on December 4, 2002, in a 102-page opinion that will likely be a landmark in the conflict between liberty and security. He deferred to the president's war power in broad terms, but he declined to withdraw entirely from the judicial duty of scrutinizing official action that impinges on individual liberty.

First, Judge Mukasey held that the president has the authority to order American citizens held, without trial, as "unlawful combatants." He accepted the government's argument that *Ex parte Quirin* (the Nazi saboteurs case) went at least that far, by its application to one American among the group of saboteurs. "It matters not," he said, "that Padilla is a United States citizen captured on United States soil." But he went on to say, "It would be a mistake to create the impression that there is a lush and vibrant jurisprudence governing these matters. There isn't." *Ex parte Quirin* said nothing about how to make the threshold determination that someone is an unlawful combatant, because it stipulated that the saboteurs were.

Second, on the crucial question of Padilla's right to see a lawyer, Judge Mukasey gave Padilla a limited victory. He rejected the government's contention that a lawyer could unwittingly transmit advice from Padilla to terrorists as "gossamer speculation." But Padilla could consult with Donna Newman for only a limited purpose, he held: to prepare for submission to the court any facts challenging the Mobbs declaration and the president's finding that he was an unlawful enemy combatant. (In March 2003, Judge Mukasey reaffirmed that Padilla be allowed to meet with a lawyer in the face of continuing resistance from the Justice Department. "Lest any confusion remain," the judge wrote, "this is not a suggestion or a request that Padilla be permitted to consult with counsel, and it is certainly not an invitation to conduct a further 'dialogue' about whether he will be permitted to do so. It is a ruling—a determination—that he will be permitted to do so.")

Third, Judge Mukasey said the court would scrutinize the finding that Padilla was an enemy combatant—but would hold the government to a very low standard of proof. He said the court would consider only whether there was "some evidence to support" the president's "conclusion that Padilla was, like the German saboteurs in [*Ex parte Quirin*], engaged in a mission against the United States on behalf of an enemy with whom the United States is at war." Merely "some evidence," not "a preponderance of the evidence," is the standard in civil cases in this country, much less than "proof beyond a reasonable doubt," the test in criminal cases.

A *Washington Post* editorial characterized the decision as "a pointed reminder that even during wartime, the president's power to lock up an American citizen must be justified to the courts, and that hearing from the accused is essential to the court's task." The judge understood, the *Post* said, "that without access to a lawyer and at least some ability to contest the government's claims in court, nobody's rights are safe."

How safe will we be if Judge Mukasey's formula becomes the final legal rule? The fact remains that an American citizen was seized at a Chicago airport and detained in solitary confinement, without a trial, for what could be, for all we know, the rest of his life. And that was done on the say-so of government officials alone, with no check except the rather slim possibility of the citizen showing that the government had not even "some evidence" of his wrongdoings—in other words, that it had no evidence. *The Economist*, which has kept a sharp eye on the state of American liberties since September 11, wrote shortly after Judge Mukasey's decision: "It is hard to imagine that America would look kindly on a foreign government that demanded the right to hold some of its own citizens in prison, incommunicado, denying them access to legal assistance as long as it thought necessary, without ever charging them with a crime."

A few hours after Attorney General Ashcroft's June 10 statement on Padilla, President Bush made an eloquent statement on the importance of the rule of law. In the war on terrorism, he said, the "rule of law" and "limits on the power of the state" were "nonnegotiable demands of human dignity." At this writing, Jose Padilla remains in isolated detention while the government is seeking an expedited appeal of Judge Mukasey's decision.

Hamdi

"This case appears to be the first in American jurisprudence where an American citizen has been held incommunicado and subjected to an indefinite detention in the continental United States without charges, without any findings by a military tribunal, and without access to a lawyer."

With those blunt words, U.S. District Judge Robert G. Doumar of Norfolk, Virginia, began an opinion and order in the case of Yaser Esam Hamdi. Judge Doumar was skeptical of the basis for the government's assertion that Hamdi was an "unlawful enemy combatant." He wanted to look over at least some of the evidence himself. The U.S. Court of Appeals for the Fourth Circuit intervened, admonishing Judge Doumar to show proper deference to decisions of the military and repeatedly setting aside his orders. But the appellate court's chief judge, J. Harvie Wilkinson III, also said he was reluctant to embrace "a sweeping proposition—namely that, with no meaningful judicial review, any American citizen alleged to be an enemy combatant could be detained indefinitely without charges or counsel on the government's say-so."

Hamdi's case was, as Judge Doumar said, the first in which the Bush administration sought to imprison a suspect without trial instead of prosecuting him. It presented the issue of presidential power less starkly to the public than Padilla's case because Hamdi had more of the indicia of an ordinary prisoner of war. He was actually captured on the battlefield in Afghanistan, or so the government alleged. That made his situation seem less menacing to an ordinary American's rights than that of a citizen seized on arrival at O'Hare Airport, but the legal issues were not all that different.

Hamdi was "affiliated" with a Taliban unit in the Afghan war, according to the government—a rather strange description that caught Judge Doumar's eye. The unit surrendered to the Afghan Northern Alliance in November 2001, and in due course he was turned over to the U.S. military. In February 2002, he was flown to the prison camp at Guantánamo Bay. But he claimed American citizenship; his father, a Saudi engineer, was working for Exxon on a petrochemical project in Baton Rouge, Louisiana, where the boy was born. The U.S. Army checked the claim and apparently found it correct. In April, he was moved to a Navy brig in Norfolk. On the assumption that he would be charged with a criminal offense, he was assigned a lawyer, Frank W. Dunham, Jr., a federal public defender. There was no prosecution, but Frank Dunham became a dogged advocate of Hamdi's rights.

"He surrendered with an enemy unit, armed with a military-style assault rifle, on a foreign battlefield," government counsel argued in one of its numerous briefs. So whether or not he was a citizen, he was "subject to capture and detention by the military during the conflict." That was a powerful argument, for, after all, prisoners of war do not usually have the opportunity to contest their status in court. The difficulty—one of the difficulties, at any rate—arose from the brief's phrase "during the conflict." This conflict is not likely to come to a defined end. There is no one on the other side with whom to negotiate, no one who would agree to a surrender or armistice or peace. So the government view could mean a life sentence for Yaser Hamdi, without any kind of meaningful legal process.

But the more acute issue posed by the government argument was whether its description of Hamdi was accurate. And how could that question be answered without giving Hamdi a chance to challenge the government's version through counsel? That was the point on which Judge Doumar focused in his extended consideration of the case.

The government relied on a declaration by Michael Mobbs, whom it described as special adviser to the undersecretary of defense for policy, the same man who filed a declaration in the *Padilla* case. It was a two-page paper that in nine paragraphs made the case—all that the government wanted to make—that Hamdi was an unlawful enemy combatant. Judge Doumar was not satisfied. He said the declaration raised "more questions than it answers." For one thing, it said Hamdi was "affiliated with a Taliban military unit" but did not explain what "affiliated" meant. It did not say whether that unit was ever in any battle in which Hamdi participated. The declaration said he was classified as an enemy combatant by "military forces" in Afghanistan. Which military forces, U.S. or Northern Alliance? The declaration did not say. The declaration cited an interview with Hamdi as confirming that he surrendered and gave up his weapon, but the judge said the Mobbs declaration merely paraphrased the interview. What did Hamdi actually say? Judge Doumar asked to see the text of any interviews. He noted that, according to Hamdi's counsel, Dunham, some of those texts were given to counsel for John Walker Lindh, the American who actually was prosecuted for fighting with the Taliban.

To all this, the government's answer was that to reexamine decisions of the military, some made on the battlefield, would be a heavy burden and "could significantly hamper the nation's defense." If there was to be any judicial review in such cases, government counsel said, a secondhand statement like the Mobbs declaration should satisfy it. More would be too intrusive.

The case went back to the U.S. Court of Appeals for the Fourth Circuit, and on January 8, 2003, it gave the government a sweeping victory. The opinion, by Chief Judge Wilkinson, said courts owed deference to the executive on issues of war and national security. It said flatly that Hamdi was "not entitled to challenge the facts presented in the Mobbs declaration." It was enough, the court said, that Hamdi had been captured "in a zone of active combat operations abroad." (The court said its reasoning was not intended to cover a case like Padilla's of someone arrested in the United States.) But the fact that Hamdi was on a foreign battlefield, suspicious though it surely is, cannot be legally conclusive as the Fourth Circuit said. Persons other than combatants are found on battlefields—journalists, for example—and in the chaos of Afghanistan, many might be.

Hamdi's case, like Padilla's, came down to a question of power: the power of the executive branch and the power of the courts. The Framers of the Constitution and the Bill of Rights would surely have been outraged at the notion that a president's appointees could take a citizen into custody and keep him there forever, in silent isolation, on their unilateral assertion that he was an enemy. Yet the Framers could not have imagined the danger of a terrorist enemy that had already killed thousands of American civilians and might acquire weapons of mass destruction.

In this conflict over a broad claim of presidential war power, one thing must be kept in mind: Past assertions by U.S. governments that national security would be at risk if courts applied the Constitution have repeatedly turned out to be wrong. Government lawyers virtually predicted that the Vietnam War would be lost if the *New York Times* published the Pentagon Papers. On the fourth day of publication, by the *Times* and then the *Washington Post*, counsel for the *Times*, Alexander M. Bickel, observed dryly to the judge, "The Republic still stands." There was no impact whatsoever on the war. So one should be skeptical of the claim that, if the government were forced to give the courts firsthand evidence to support its designation of someone as an enemy combatant, it "could significantly hamper the nation's defense."

Any assertion may look convincing if it has not been tested by the time-honored means of the law: cross-examination, checking of the evidence. Anyone who has seen a courtroom drama knows that the most convincing story can explode under the hammer of the legal process. Indeed, one case brought by the Bush administration after September 11 makes the point in a dramatic way.

An Egyptian student, Abdallah Higazy, spent the night of September 10–11, 2001, at the Millenium Hilton Hotel, overlooking the World Trade Center in New York. After the terrorist attack, a security guard in the hotel said he had found an aviation radio in the room Higazy had occupied. Higazy denied that it was his. He was given a lie-detector test and was told he had failed it. He then confessed to owning the radio. After weeks of detention in solitary confinement, he was indicted on a charge of lying when he said the radio was not his. But within a few days of the announcement of his prosecution, a pilot came forward and said it was his radio—he had left it in another room at the hotel. The security guard admitted that he had made up his tale of Higazy owning the radio. And Higazy was released. So a prosecution that looked ironclad turned out to be based on falsehood. (Why did Higazy make his false confession? He said his FBI interrogators told him they would harm his family if he did not talk. The FBI denied that.)

"A cardinal protection of liberty in this country," the *Washington Post* said in one of a remarkable series of editorials on the *Hamdi* case,

> is the requirement that the government justify deprivations of freedom. Yet the emerging hallmark of the enemy combatant cases is the unwillingness of the government to do precisely that. In Hamdi's case, the Justice Department initially argued that its designation was unreviewable by any court. Even now . . . the government contends that the courts should not look beyond the sketchiest of evidentiary statements it has offered in justifying its view of Hamdi. . . . It is critical that Judges remember how the doctrine they are creating could be used against people other than the ones whose cases they are currently seeing. The government's case against Hamdi may be solid. But if it is allowed to detain him without some procedure that requires a persuasive showing, it will create a rule that allows Americans to be exempted from the protections of the Bill of Rights on the strength of a two-page statement the government condescends to present in court.

THE BUSH ADMINISTRATION robustly denies that its measures against terrorism have unnecessarily or wrongly harmed civil liberties. To get the administration's viewpoint, I spoke with the assistant attorney general for legal policy, Viet Dinh. He has played a large role in designing the antiterrorist policy. And for reasons of both skill in legal articulation and personal history, he is a remarkable spokesman for the policy.

Viet Dinh came to this country from Vietnam in 1978, three years after American helicopters lifted off from the embassy roof in Saigon and the Communists took over. He was ten years old. Other members of his family came at different times, some escaping Vietnam on hazardous boats. His father was in a reeducation camp for years.

Viet Dinh's life in the United States has been the immigrant story in dramatic form. A dozen years after he arrived as a refugee he was an editor of the *Harvard Law Review*. He was a law clerk on the U.S. Court of Appeals for the District of Columbia Circuit, then for Justice Sandra Day O'Connor on the Supreme Court. He was thirty-three years old when he became an assistant attorney general.

In a speech in June 2002, Dinh defined "liberty" by quoting Edmund Burke, the hero of enlightened conservatives. "The only liberty I mean," Burke said, "is a liberty connected with order; that not only exists along with order and virtue, but which cannot exist without them at all." In other words, Dinh said, "ordered liberty. Order and liberty, under this conception, are symbiotic; each is necessary to the stability and legitimacy essential for a government under law."

In our conversation, Dinh emphasized the distinctive character of the war against terrorism as compared with traditional wars. "The underlying fact," he said, "is that this so-called war operates not on the usual battlefield, geographically located. Here the war knows no bounds. The terrorists have made it the world."

That has legal consequences, Dinh said, involving the two high functions of the president: as chief law enforcement officer and military commander in chief.

> In traditional wars past the division between the two functions was clear. This time you have a confluence, by Al-Qaeda's choosing, where both hats come into play. An enemy activity may be both a violation of the laws of war and of domestic law. The president may choose to deal with it as law enforcement officer or commander in chief. The decision is his, and the commander in chief has a significant function even in the United States, because Al-Qaeda has made the U.S. a target.

How does that justify the denial of counsel to detainees like Padilla and Hamdi? "There's no question," Dinh said, "but that if the armed forces capture someone on the battlefield, you wouldn't have the panoply of the legal process." The key question is whether the president's role as commander in chief requires deference. If it does, as the government believes and argues, then an enemy detainee has no more right to counsel than he would have, say, a right to jury trial.

But what about the factual question of whether he is *in fact* an enemy combatant? How can that be left to the uncontrolled discretion of the executive? "Frank Dunham [the public defender acting on behalf of Yaser Hamdi] is doing a wonderful job," Dinh said. "He has a right to challenge the designation as enemy combatant. But the law gives him a very limited license to challenge the president's judgment and the intelligence underlying it." That is not much of a right, is it? "No, because he's a battlefield detainee, an enemy combatant. The intelligence may indeed be faulty. . . . But when the president acts as commander in chief, he's entitled to a lot of deference. The stakes are so large in war." The department was confident of its legal position before the administration took its various legal actions, Dinh said. "It's not to say our judgment is infallible. We constantly reevaluate what we do."

At the end of the conversation, I said I had a tough question to ask. Dinh laughed—and laughed and laughed. He knew what I was going to ask: He and his family left Vietnam to escape from a totalitarian society where there was no way to challenge the rulers. In the United States, from the beginning, everything has been subject to check. Yet you are introducing a system where there is no effective check. How does that strike you, as a human being who left that other system?

"It's a question I've asked myself, obviously, many a time," Viet Dinh said.

The thing that I love so much about America . . . and appreciate so much every day is that government works—both in the sense that it is effective for stability and that it provides safeguards against encroachments.

I think it is critical that one recognize that the first function—even if you are an ardent anarchist you have to recognize—that the function of government is the security of its polity and the safety of its people. For without them there can be no structure so that liberty can survive. We see our work not as balancing security and liberty. Rather we see it as securing liberty by assuring the conditions for true liberty. I do not see, therefore, that there is a contradiction between the measures that we have taken and the Constitution or my personal history.

I do not think that we have sacrificed the mechanisms of accountability and appropriate review. We have simply recognized the constitutional authority and deference that the government has, and needs to have, in order to do its job. . . . What we're trying to do here is protect authority so the liberty of law-abiding people can flourish. We will not take advantage of the moment to sacrifice the core values of liberty. . . .

Unlike economists, we don't have the luxury of assuming away the problem.

No one could argue the case for the administration's measures better than Viet Dinh. But is he really correct when he says that he and his colleagues are not, like economists, assuming away the problem? Most lawyers, and most Americans, would have thought that the right of anyone detained by the state to consult a lawyer was one of "the core values of liberty."

The Courts

The distinctive American contribution to the philosophy of government has been the role of judges as protectors of freedom. Over the past half-century, the Supreme Court has greatly expanded that role, defining and enforcing constitutional rights in new ways. And other countries have for the first time given their courts the function of enforcing written constitutions, copying the American pattern. Germany, France, South Africa, India, and now even Britain have vested that power in judges.

But the story is different in wartime. Then judges, wary of imposing their views in areas where they do not feel competent and where lives may be at stake, tend to defer to military and civilian war leaders. Chief Justice William H. Rehnquist summed up the practice in a 2000 speech. "While we would not want to subscribe to the full sweep of the Latin maxim *inter arms silent leges*—'in time of war the laws are silent'—perhaps we can accept the proposition that though the laws are not silent in wartime, they speak with a muted voice."

A striking example of that reality was the Supreme Court's 1943 decision in *Korematsu v. United States,* which upheld President Franklin Roosevelt's order removing 100,000 people of Japanese descent from the West Coast and confining them in desert camps. The majority opinion was written by the Court's most ardent advocate of civil liberties, Hugo L. Black. Its rationale was deference to the executive's military judgment—even though that turned out later to have been based on scare stories about Japanese-American subversion.

Will the Supreme Court adopt such a deferential attitude when it judges the constitutionality of the Bush administration's antiterrorism measures? The answer to that question will likely determine the fate of the president's claim of power to detain Americans indefinitely without trial and without counsel after designating them enemy combatants. It will similarly affect challenges to the secret detention of aliens and secret deportation hearings. And it may define the limits on new ways of invading privacy of communication in order to ferret out possible terrorist plans.

The outcome may turn on another question: Is this a war?

President Bush responded to September 11 at once by announcing a "war on terrorism." Congress quickly authorized him to take sweeping measures. But it is very different from other wars, against known enemies with defined territories and military aims. Judges will be aware of those differences. They will surely know that this "war" could go on for decades, so deference to the president's war power could effectively change the balance of the Constitution and make the executive branch the dominant institution in the tripartite system created by the Framers.

There is, or at least there should be, a further constraint on the Supreme Court's willingness to give presidential orders judicial sanction. It is that a constitutional ruling of the Court would give more permanent meaning and legitimacy to temporary measures.

Justice Jackson made that point, eloquently, when he dissented from the majority in *Korematsu,* the decision upholding the removal of Japanese Americans from their homes. "A military order," he said,

> however unconstitutional, is not apt to last longer than the military emergency. . . . But once a judicial opinion rationalizes such an order to show that it conforms to the Constitution, or rather rationalizes the Constitution to show that the Constitution sanctions such an order, the Court for all time has validated the principle of racial discrimination in . . . transplanting American citizens. The principle then lies about like a loaded weapon ready for the hand of any authority that can forward a plausible claim of an urgent need!

That passage in Justice Jackson's dissent was quoted by the president of the Supreme Court of Israel, Aharon Barak, in a

2002 article in the *Harvard Law Review*. He was making the point that a judge deciding a question of human rights during a time of terrorism must not deceive himself by believing that "at the end of the conflict, I can turn back the clock."

Israel has struggled with terrorism for years. Its supreme court has not been entirely consistent in resolving the conflicting claims of security and liberty. But in recent years the court has increasingly defended human rights against challenged Israeli government practices. Notably, it forbade torture of detainees that officials said was needed to discover terrorist plans.

"Terrorism does not justify the neglect of accepted legal norms," Barak wrote in the law review article. "This is how we distinguish ourselves from the terrorists themselves. They act against the law, by violating and trampling it, while in its war against terrorism, a democratic state acts within the framework of the law and according to law. . . . It is, therefore, not merely a war of the state against enemies; it is also a war of the Law against its enemies."

One of the particular issues in the *Hamdi* case and others before the American courts—whether judges should closely examine the facts underlying security claims—was also touched on by Justice Barak. "Security considerations are not magic words," he said. "The court must insist on learning the specific considerations that prompted the government's actions. The court must also be persuaded that these considerations actually motivated the government's actions and were not merely pretextual. Finally, the court must be convinced that the security measures adopted were the available measures least damaging to human rights."

Justice William J. Brennan, Jr., of the U.S. Supreme Court chose Israel—specifically the law school of the Hebrew University in Jerusalem—as the site of an important speech on civil liberties in times of security crises. Again and again, he said, "sudden national fervor" had led "people to exaggerate the security risks posed by allowing individuals to exercise their civil liberties and to become willing 'temporarily' to sacrifice liberties as part of the war effort." Looking at American history, he warned about the exaggeration of security concerns: "The perceived threats to national security [that] have motivated the sacrifice of civil liberties during times of crisis are often overblown and factually unfounded," he said.

The rumors of French Intrigue during the late 1790's, the claims that civilian courts were unable to adjudicate the allegedly treasonous actions of Northerners during the Civil War, the hysterical belief that criticism of conscription and the war effort might lead droves of soldiers to desert the Army or resist the draft during World War I, the wild assertions of sabotage and espionage by Japanese Americans during World War II and the paranoid fear that the American Communist Party stood ready to overthrow the government were all so baseless that they would be comical were it not for the serious hardship that they caused during the times of crisis.

Will American judges look at the issues of terrorism and freedom in the spirit of Justices Barak and Brennan? Judges are not immune from the sense of vulnerability, of fear, instilled in Americans by the attacks of September 11. A majority of the current Supreme Court may be instinctively inclined to defer to presidential power in wartime—to "speak with a muted voice," as Chief Justice Rehnquist put it. Yet this is an exceptionally bold Court, not shying away from making up new constitutional law of federalism—or from deciding a presidential election. An imperial Court, it has been called. Will it enforce constitutional limits on a newly imperial presidency?

ELLEN KNAUFF'S STORY did not end when the Supreme Court rejected her appeal. The attorney general of the day, J. Howard McGrath, moved by press and public attention to her case, ordered that she be given the immigration hearing that she had theretofore been denied. At the hearing, in March 1950, three witnesses said that while working for the army in Frankfurt she had spied for a Czechoslovak mission there. She denied the charges and said she had never seen those witnesses before. On November 2, 1951, Attorney General McGrath ordered her admitted to the United States.

In 1957, Ellen Knauff was remarried to William B. Hartley and took his name. She and her husband wrote many books and articles, a number of them for children. Both of them died in 1980, when Ellen Hartley was sixty-five.

"PERHAPS IT IS A UNIVERSAL TRUTH that the loss of liberty at home is to be charged to provisions against danger, real or pretended, from abroad."

This was Madison again, in a letter written to Vice President Thomas Jefferson on May 13, 1798. How foresighted he was. What he perceived proved true again and again in the next two centuries. But perhaps we should take some satisfaction from that record. For the fact is that, with all the dark episodes in those years, all the harm to individuals, the United States at the millennium was an astonishingly free country.

The question is whether Americans' commitment to freedom will prove as resilient in an endless conflict with terrorism. The signs so far are mixed. The Bush administration seems determined to press its every measure to the limit, dismissing civil libertarian concerns. Congress has not emerged as a guardian of liberty. But the print press is finally beginning to take hold of such issues as the detention of Americans as enemy combatants on the president's say-so. Nearly two dozen cities have passed ordinances urging respect for civil liberties. Some have long been identified with libertarian causes—Boulder, Colorado, for example, and Berkeley, California. But they may reflect a larger stirring of concern.

Much is at stake. America's extraordinary prosperity and strength have been produced by an open society, where every policy was subject to debate. American power in the world has been as much the power of its ideals—of freedom—as of its weapons. If terrorism leads us to close down the society, then the terrorists will have won.

"Freedom and fear are at war," President Bush said in an address to Congress on September 20, 2001. In a sense different from what he meant, they are.

CHAPTER 3

No Checks, No Balances: Discarding Bedrock Constitutional Principles

STEPHEN J. SCHULHOFER

A s EXPECTED, September 11 has prompted an expansion of law enforcement powers at almost every level. The domain of individual rights has contracted. And who would have it otherwise? For those of us who live and work in Manhattan, September 11 was not just a single horrific day but an extended nightmare. For weeks, kiosks, store windows, and parks displayed flyers by the thousands, pleading for information about loved ones still missing. National guard units seemed to be everywhere. Day after day, the air, gray and acrid, carried the smell of burning flesh.

No, the "war" metaphor is not just convenient political spin. And despite shameless hyping of so-called sleeper cells and color-coded threat levels, no responsible person can dismiss the

---

Portions of this essay appeared in different form in the March 2003 issue of *American Prospect*.

danger of devastating future attacks. Actions to strengthen law enforcement are not simply the product of panic or paranoia.

But the particulars are troubling—and worse. Predictably, there has been overreaction and political grandstanding. More surprising is the neglect. Inexcusably, the administration of George W. Bush has swept aside urgent security needs while it continues to win public acclaim for toughness by targeting and scapegoating civil liberties.

An accounting of the state of our liberties should begin with the positives. To his credit, President Bush has preached tolerance and respect for our Muslim neighbors. Unlike previous wartime governments, this administration has not sought to prosecute dissenters for political speech, has not attempted anything comparable to the internment of Japanese Americans during World War II, and (technically, at least) has not tried to suspend the writ of habeas corpus.

But to measure performance by these standards is to set the bar terribly low; these were sorry historical embarrassments. And 9/11 has already produced several comparable missteps. The administration's efforts to stymie habeas corpus rival the civil liberties low points of prior wars, as does its determination (wholly without precedent) to hold American citizens indefinitely on disputed charges without affording them a trial in any forum whatsoever. Likewise without precedent are the oddly imbalanced means chosen to fight this war. Never before in American history has an administration claimed emergency powers while stinting on urgent national security expenditures and making tax cuts its top wartime priority. Conventional wisdom about "striking a balance" between liberty and security obscures the fact that responses to 9/11 are deeply flawed from *both* perspectives.

Specifically, the domestic security policies of this administration encroach on three principles that are fundamental to the preservation of freedom: accountability, checks and balances, and narrow tailoring of government's power to intrude into the lives of citizens. In each case, the administration has overlooked or dismissed alternative approaches that would strengthen the nation's security at least as effectively without weakening fundamental freedoms. The encroachments on bedrock principles, altogether unnecessary even in this perilous time, are especially evident in four realms of policy: domestic surveillance, new guidelines governing the Federal Bureau of Investigation, the detention of foreign nationals, and the erosion of habeas corpus.

Domestic Surveillance

Expanded surveillance powers have reduced privacy rights that most of us took for granted before September 11. Yet even without knowing the details, many Americans see no need to worry about the civil liberties impact of the new laws. They feel that law-abiding citizens should have nothing to hide, and they welcome rather than fear this enhancement of government surveillance powers. Others (a relatively small minority) argue that sacrificing any of our pre-9/11 privacy rights will simply make us less free without making us more secure and will amount to destroying our freedom in order to defend it. Neither of these positions captures the complex reality of the expanded surveillance powers.

Some of the provisions included in the October 2001 USA Patriot Act simply correct oversights in prior law or adapt technically worded statutes to new technologies and practices. For example, the authority included in the act for judges to permit surveillance of mobile phones in foreign intelligence investigations (a power long permitted in domestic law enforcement) and to issue search warrants with nationwide effect reflect legitimate law enforcement needs that raise no new privacy concerns.

But other new powers are more problematic. The Patriot Act undermines checks and balances by giving investigators new authority to track Internet usage and to obtain previously confidential financial records without having to demonstrate probable cause or obtain a judicial warrant. The Treasury Department expanded its authority to require banks, brokers, and other businesses to report cash transactions and "suspicious activities," which include any transaction that differs from ones the customer typically conducts. Though the Justice Department created a furor with its proposal for Operation TIPS to encourage voluntary snooping by private citizens, the Treasury Department's regulations *require* private citizens and businesses to become eyes and ears for the government—again without any oversight by the judicial branch. Compounding this problem, the new FBI and Treasury Department powers are not narrowly tailored to investigations potentially related to terrorism; the government can invoke most of these new powers even when it seeks only to investigate routine criminal offenses.

The Patriot Act also made especially important changes in the complex Foreign Intelligence Surveillance Act (FISA). The expanded FISA provisions now allow FBI agents to obtain business and educational records, without any need to certify that the targeted customer or student is considered a foreign agent or a suspect in any way. Before 9/11, FISA gave investigators access to the records of a narrow category of travel-industry businesses, provided that the person targeted was a foreign agent. The Patriot Act now permits FBI access to all the records of any business and any nonbusiness entity, apparently including noncommercial entities such as a synagogue or mosque. And the new authority (like that for financial and educational records) drops the requirement that the records pertain to a suspected foreign agent. Formerly confidential records concerning any American citizen are now available for FBI inspection on a clandestine basis whenever an investigator thinks they may be relevant to a terrorism investigation, whether or not the person concerned is a foreign agent or a suspected criminal offender. Again, this is the antithesis of government restraint: Judicial oversight is allowed no role as a check on the executive branch, and the powers granted extend far beyond the international terrorism suspects that are the legitimate targets of concern.

The Patriot Act also eliminated a technical but highly significant limitation on FISA's reach. Prior to 9/11, FISA was not considered a law enforcement tool; its function was exclusively preventative. FISA surveillance powers were available only when the primary purpose of an investigation was to obtain foreign intelligence, including counterespionage and counterterrorism information. In that unique setting, FISA authorized surveillance under flexible conditions that are considered unacceptable when the government's objective is to gather evidence for criminal prosecution. In a criminal investigation, the Fourth Amendment prohibits searches except when investigators have "probable cause" to believe that a search will reveal evidence of criminal activity. A neutral judicial officer, concurring in that assessment, must authorize the search in a court order that "particularly describ[es] the place to be searched, and the persons or things to be seized." In electronic surveillance and wiretaps, this particularity requirement in effect mandates narrow tailoring of the time, place, and duration of the surveillance—all subject to close judicial oversight.

This constitutional regime is a concrete expression of our commitment to effective checks and balances. The Framers of the U.S. Constitution knew that without some outside control well-intentioned investigators in the executive branch would too quickly find "probable cause" and too easily abuse their power to search. The Fourth Amendment therefore requires that the judgment about probable cause ordinarily be made by a neutral judicial officer, who will narrowly define the permissible scope of a search before it occurs.

This centuries-old requirement of independent judicial approval obviously casts no doubt on the wisdom and decency of our current president and attorney general. As most attorneys general have themselves understood, checks and balances—and the warrant requirement in particular—reflect the consistent verdict of history that grave abuses are all too likely if investigators—even conscientious, well-trained investigators—are permitted to search without judicial approval.

Foreign intelligence surveillance, because of its predominantly preventive purpose, traditionally has been allowed more leeway. The differences from the regime applicable to criminal investigations are important to notice:

- FISA surveillance is permitted after showing only a diluted form of suspicion not equivalent to the traditional criminal standard of probable cause.
- FISA authorizes intrusive investigative techniques, such as clandestine physical searches, that are normally impermissible in criminal investigations.

- Surveillance and physical searches can continue over more extensive periods of time, with less judicial supervision.
- The person targeted normally is never notified that he was subjected to surveillance.
- If that person is prosecuted, his attorneys normally cannot review the surveillance documents for purposes of his defense, as they could if surveillance had been conducted under conventional law enforcement standards.

The Patriot Act gives prosecutors, for the first time, the ability to use these broad FISA powers when their primary objective is not preventative but is rather to gather evidence for criminal prosecution. Moreover, FISA does not require that the person targeted be a foreign spy or an international terrorist. Foreign nationals *and* U.S. citizens qualify as "foreign agents" subject to clandestine searches and broad FISA surveillance when they are merely suspected of having ties to foreign organizations or governments, and even when they are merely employed by various *legitimate* foreign organizations. The Patriot Act permits prosecutors to subject these individuals to surveillance that would be unconstitutional if based only on probable cause to believe that the target was a serial killer or rapist.

Concern about the broad reach of these FISA amendments, and their potential to undermine the traditional wall between law enforcement and preventive counterintelligence, led to unique litigation and two historic judicial decisions. FISA has long required the FBI and the Justice Department to establish "minimization" procedures to protect the privacy rights of American citizens by maintaining "rigorous and strict controls" over the use of information about Americans gathered under FISA's exceptional powers. When a foreign intelligence operation uncovers evidence of crime, those procedures authorize agents, with appropriate approval, to discuss their investigation with federal prosecutors and to turn over to them leads they have uncovered. But until 9/11, the regulations barred prosecutors from intentionally or inadvertently "directing or controlling the [foreign intelligence] investigation toward law enforcement objectives." The concern, of course, was that prosecutors lacking grounds for a conventional warrant might otherwise instruct FISA teams to conduct expanded surveillance of American citizens as part of a fishing expedition seeking to build a criminal case.

In a memorandum dated March 6, 2002, Attorney General John Ashcroft initiated a significant change in these minimization procedures. The memorandum instructed FBI and Justice Department officials that FISA powers could now "be used primarily for a law enforcement purpose, so long as a significant foreign intelligence purpose remains." To this end, Ashcroft authorized prosecutors pursuing criminal cases to give advice to foreign intelligence investigators concerning the "initiation . . . or expansion of FISA searches or surveillance," and he deleted the previous caveat that barred prosecutors from "directing or controlling" the scope of FISA surveillance.

The March 6 memorandum drew attention to an obscure body known as the Foreign Intelligence Surveillance Court. Composed of sitting federal judges, the FISA court meets in secret to consider applications for FISA surveillance warrants. From 1979 to 2001, the FISA court approved without modification all but five of more than 14,000 surveillance applications. Its judges have detailed familiarity with foreign intelligence operations and with the workability and shortcomings of the minimization procedures in place before 9/11. And there is little reason to doubt their appreciation for legitimate law enforcement needs. The presiding judge, Royce C. Lamberth, was named to the federal bench by President Ronald Reagan, and five of the six judges who comprised the remainder of the panel in March 2002 were likewise appointed by Republican presidents. All of the FISA judges had been selected for the assignment by Chief Justice William Rehnquist.

Nonetheless, the FISA court unanimously rejected key provisions of the Ashcroft memorandum. In a secret ruling on May 17 (made public in late August), the court specified that "law enforcement officials *shall not* make recommendations to intelligence officials concerning the initiation . . . or expansion of FISA searches or surveillance," and it insisted on rules to ensure that prosecutors "*do not* direct or control the use of the FISA procedures to enhance criminal prosecution." The court noted tartly that any need for prosecutors to direct "the use of highly intrusive FISA surveillances . . . is yet to be explained."

The FISA court did not have the last word, however. The FISA statute gives the Justice Department the right, never before invoked, to appeal an adverse ruling to the Foreign Intelligence Surveillance Court of Review, comprised of three federal judges also selected by Chief Justice Rehnquist. The FISA court of review had never before met, and it heard arguments only from the Justice Department, technically the only party to the case.* The court of review concluded that the Patriot Act amendments did indeed permit prosecutors to use FISA in criminal investigations, without complying with conventional statutory and constitutional limits on law enforcement surveil-

---

*The court did, however, accept amicus curiae briefs supporting the FISA court's decision from the American Civil Liberties Union and other groups.

lance, as long as foreign intelligence gathering was a primary *or subsidiary* purpose of the surveillance. And the court of review ruled that given the importance of the counterterrorism effort, use of these exceptional powers was not unconstitutional. For now, the conclusions of the court of review are final because the only party to the case, the Justice Department, prevailed. There are apparently no means to bring the issue before the Supreme Court, unless and until evidence acquired by expanded FISA surveillance is introduced against a defendant in a criminal prosecution.

This controversy about the wall that traditionally separated intelligence-gathering from law enforcement poses one of the most difficult problems arising out of the 9/11 attacks. September 11 made clear that a rigid division between law enforcement and foreign intelligence operations can be artificial and counterproductive in the context of fighting international terrorist groups like Al-Qaeda. The court of review rightly stressed this point, but then, in a non sequitur, concluded that it was either impossible or too dangerous to attempt any separation of these functions. Yet law enforcement and counterterrorism operations are not always inextricable. And law enforcement can easily slide into prosecutorial fishing expeditions and other dangers to a free society, when it operates free from close judicial scrutiny.

The importance of containing both dangers—the danger of international terrorism and the less obvious, less acute, but still significant danger of prosecutorial abuse—suggests the need to avoid the court of review's all-or-nothing approach. Flexibility for FISA teams to share evidence of crime obtained in foreign intelligence operations was always part of the FISA system and can be enhanced without significant danger to basic Fourth Amendment values. The risk of overreaching arises when the same team uses broad FISA tools to pursue both intelligence and law enforcement goals. In a world of unlimited resources, therefore, we would surely insist that law enforcement and counterterrorism investigators be confined to distinct teams. The difficulty here, as the court of review recognized, is that resources are limited. At the highest levels of the FBI and the Justice Department, senior executives will almost inevitably have responsibility for both functions. And barriers to a blending of roles could (rightly or out of excess caution) inhibit efforts to use criminal investigators in the field for vital counterterrorism measures.

What seems hard to justify, even against this background, is the core of the Ashcroft innovation: the provision granting the department's litigating lawyers the power to *initiate* FISA surveillance, and to *enlarge* its scope, in order to develop evidence for a criminal prosecution. Here, as the initial FISA court decision stressed, flexibility and appropriate coordination are no longer at issue. Rather, the remedy has expanded to encompass rules making FISA's highly intrusive, lightly restricted surveillance powers available for objectives not primarily concerned with preventive intelligence-gathering. The need for some blending of functions does not come close to justifying the Ashcroft innovation that grants prosecutors primacy in initiating and directing the use of broad FISA powers. As the FISA court's initial decision recognized, the need for prosecutors to control the scope of FISA surveillance has never been explained.

The FISA changes, of course, are just one part of the multidimensional expansion of government surveillance powers, an expansion that encompasses the many new FBI and Treasury Department capabilities just mentioned. An overall assessment of these developments must begin by acknowledging that the counterterrorism payoff from the new powers, though not scientifically measurable, can't be dismissed as insignificant. And many Americans probably feel ready to sacrifice all the privacy interests that these new powers affect, if only to obtain even a small nugget of information about Al-Qaeda's plans. Nonetheless, the rollback of privacy rights has three flaws that should trouble us all.

First, worries about terrorism provide no reason to expand law enforcement power across the board. Yet FBI and Treasury agents can use most of their new powers to investigate allegations of prostitution, gambling, insider trading, and any other offense. Prosecutors can now use open-ended FISA surveillance powers to gather evidence for a conventional fraud or income-tax prosecution. Treasury regulations impose reporting obligations that can even be used to police compliance with ordinary government regulations. Far from respecting the imperative to tailor government power narrowly, even in times of peril, we have seen inexcusable opportunism on the part of the law enforcement establishment, which has exploited the momentum of 9/11 to expand government power to intrude on privacy in pursuit of wholly unrelated goals.

Second, accountability measures, though neglected in the rush to pass the Patriot Act, need not impair the usefulness of the new powers and, if well designed, will enhance them. The new provisions not only dilute traditional checks and balances; they neglect many of the internal supervision and control procedures that are staples of effective management in government and the private sector alike. The FBI's Carnivore system for spying on e-mail, for example, desperately needs procedures to preserve audit trails and ensure the accountability of agents who have access to it.

Finally, nuggets or even piles of telling information are useless unless our agencies have the capability to make sense of them. It is now well known that before September 11 the FBI and the Central Intelligence Agency had important clues to the plot in hand, but as one FBI agent put it, "We didn't know what we knew." Since a large part of what we lack is not raw data but the ability to separate significant intelligence from so-called noise, pulling more information into government files will not help and may aggravate the difficulty. Even before 9/11, Treasury officials complained to Congress that the staggering volume of reports they received (more than 1 million every month) was interfering with enforcement. Absent a substantial infusion of resources (which the Bush administration has not yet provided), powerful new surveillance tools can give us only a false sense of comfort.

New FBI guidelines

In May 2002, headlines featured for days the startling news that during the summer of 2001, before the terrorist attacks, agents in Minneapolis and Phoenix had urged investigations of Zacharias Moussaoui and the flight schools, only to be stifled by FBI headquarters—an enormous blunder. In response, on May 30, 2002, Attorney General Ashcroft called a press conference to denounce "bureaucratic restrictions" that were preventing FBI agents from doing their jobs.

The rules he had in mind grew out of extensive FBI abuses

in the 1950s and 1960s. Free to pursue random tips and their own hunches, FBI agents of that era intimidated dissidents, damaged the reputations of many who were not, and produced thousands of thick dossiers on public figures and private citizens. Agents spent years monitoring political groups of all stripes, from the Socialist Workers Party to the Conservative American Christian Action Council. They maintained files on student clubs, civil rights groups, antiwar groups, and other social movements. By 1975, FBI headquarters held more than a half-million domestic intelligence files.

Such sprawling dragnets are as inefficient as they are abusive, and rules to rein them in, adopted in 1976 under President Gerald Ford, were carried forward by every president since. Nonetheless, Attorney General Ashcroft ridiculed these guidelines as absurdly restrictive. He said, incorrectly, that the rules barred FBI agents from surfing the Internet and even from observing activities in public places. He announced that he was solving this problem by allowing FBI agents to operate with much less supervision.

The civil liberties community responded with furious criticism. But far from hurting the attorney general's popularity, the criticism reinforced his intended message: that law enforcement had been tied down by defendants' rights. The failure to pursue the flight school leads was in effect blamed on the American Civil Liberties Union, and the Justice Department presented itself as taking firm corrective action.

What actually occurred was rather different. One part of the rules the attorney general relaxed governs investigations of "general crimes"—gambling, theft, and other offenses *not* related to terrorism. The other rules he relaxed govern investigations of *domestic* terrorist groups. Unnoticed in the brouhaha, the rules that govern international terrorism cases—the ones that apply to Al-Qaeda—were not affected by the changes at all.

Behind the screen of this public relations maneuver, damage was inflicted in several directions. Public frustration with central oversight was understandable under the circumstances, but none of the previous guidelines, even the more restrictive domestic regimes, impeded the kinds of investigative steps the Minneapolis and Phoenix agents had urged. What the field offices needed was better supervision, not less of it. Yet Ashcroft's actions obscured responsibility for FBI missteps, and instead of censure, the FBI was rewarded with greater discretion. As in the case of the Patriot Act, fear of terrorism offered an occasion for the bait-and-switch: The guideline revisions are irrelevant to the concerns about Al-Qaeda that preoccupy the American public, yet they leave us with a large risk to civil liberties and large losses to effective management of the FBI.

Detention of Foreign Nationals

In the months following September 11, federal agents arrested approximately 1,200 foreign nationals. Hundreds were held for months before being cleared and released; others (the precise number is unknown) remain in detention, ostensibly to await deportation. Courts are still sorting out the many issues posed by these actions.

The length of these detentions and the absence of any judicial finding on the need for it are one of the primary concerns. Preventive detention is not unknown in American law, and the extraordinary uncertainties in the days after September 11 presented a virtually unique public safety emergency. Nonetheless, even making ample allowance for the pressure of circumstances, the outer boundaries of executive power in emergency situations were easily reached and exceeded in these roundups.

The most glaring of the problems posed is that the executive branch assumed the power to decide *unilaterally* who would be detained and for how long. Supreme Court decisions make clear that for preventive confinement to satisfy due process, measures like these be strictly confined to limited time periods, with adequate safeguards against the arbitrary exercise of executive power. At a minimum, there must be provision for prompt *independent* review of relevant evidence in an adversary hearing, and the judge must find a substantial government need, reasonably related to the nature and duration of the detention.

The 9/11 detentions of foreign nationals are sharply at odds with these norms. Without statutory authority—and in apparent violation of the extended seven-day period for precharge detention that the Patriot Act allows in terrorism cases—the Immigration and Naturalization Service held some of these suspects for months without affording hearings and without charging any violation of criminal or administrative law. Even after review by semi-independent administrative judges, immigration law violators who would normally be excused or deported were held, and are still being held, for preventive and investigative purposes without any independent review of the grounds for suspicion or the relation of government need to the individual hardship created. Aside from the relocation of Japanese Americans during World War II, the 9/11 detentions appear to be unprecedented in terms of the unilateral, unreviewable executive branch powers on which they rest.

Equally troubling is the extraordinary secrecy surrounding

these sweeps. The government has refused to release the names of any of the detainees, and when they are charged and afforded immigration hearings, all hearings are closed to the press and even to their own families.

The government's justifications for secrecy are revealing. Secrecy, Attorney General Ashcroft stated, is necessary to protect the privacy of detainees. Since many of the detainees desperately wanted their names made public (so that aid organizations and lawyers could contact them), and since the Justice Department could have provided secrecy to detainees who requested it, the privacy claim was painfully disingenuous. In litigation, Justice Department lawyers added the argument that releasing the names of terrorists would give their cohorts clues about the progress of the investigation. This "road map" argument, though harder to dismiss outright, is still embarrassingly thin. Because all detainees have the right to make phone calls, and because gag orders have not been imposed on their family members or on their lawyers, the true terrorists among them can easily find ways to signal their confederates.

The shallow character of these arguments led the U.S. Court of Appeals for the Sixth Circuit to rule unanimously in August 2002 that the government's secrecy policy violates the First Amendment. The court accepted that secrecy might occasionally be warranted, when case-specific reasons for it were accepted by a judge. The crucial point was to provide an independent check on the supposed necessity and ensure that a closed-door policy did not become a cloak for government incompetence or abuse of power.

In October 2002, however, the U.S. Court of Appeals for the Third Circuit, in a 2-1 decision, reached the opposite conclusion, relying on the government's assertion that openness could damage national security. But as Judge Anthony Scirica (a Reagan appointee) noted in his dissent, the issue was not whether deportation hearings should be closed; at issue was only the question of who should make that determination. Closure of all proceedings, regardless of circumstances, was clearly unnecessary, he stressed, because a simple alternative to protect national security was available: Judges could determine national security needs on a case-by-case basis, in a closed proceeding if necessary, just as they do when national security matters arise in a formal criminal trial. In determining the need for secrecy, moreover, judges would of course give great weight to the national security interest and would extend great deference to executive branch expertise.

Secrecy across the board, without any obligation to present case-specific reasons for it to a court, has less to do with the war on terrorism than with the administration's consistent efforts, firmly in place before 9/11, to insulate executive action from public scrutiny. The cumulative effect of these efforts is an unprecedented degree of power—an attempt simultaneously to cut off the right to counsel, judicial review, and even any ability of the press to report what happens to individuals arrested on our own soil. As Judge Damon Keith wrote in the Sixth Circuit decision striking down the blanket secrecy order:

> The Executive Branch seeks to uproot people's lives, outside the public eye, and behind a closed door. Democracies die behind closed doors. The First Amendment, through a free press, protects the people's right to know that their government acts fairly, lawfully, and accurately in deportation proceedings. . . .

The Framers of the First Amendment "did not trust any government to separate the true from the false for us." They protected the people against secret government.

The Erosion of Habeas Corpus

In Chapter 2, Anthony Lewis describes in detail the case of Jose Padilla—a case that also merits scrutiny from the standpoint of judicial review. Padilla, the so-called dirty bomber who allegedly planned to explode a bomb laced with radioactive material, was arrested at O'Hare International Airport in Chicago and held for a month as a material witness. Counsel was appointed for him, and he was due to be brought to court on June 11, 2002. Instead, two nights before the scheduled hearing, President Bush decided that Padilla was an "enemy combatant," a finding that the Justice Department tenaciously argues cannot be reviewed by any federal judge.

That night, without notice to his court-appointed counsel, Padilla was taken from federal detention in Manhattan, put on a military plane for South Carolina, and thrown into a Navy brig. That was on June 9, and Padilla has not been heard from since. The government has refused to let him speak to the press or to his own attorney and has done everything in its power to deny him access to the courts.

Enemy infiltrators have posed acute threats to public safety before, notably during the Civil War. Abraham Lincoln, a straightforward man, responded by suspending the writ of habeas corpus.

That is not the Bush administration's style, however. When Padilla's lawyer, Donna Newman, tried to file a habeas petition on his behalf, the government suggested no need to suspend the writ. Its argument was the "narrow" one that the Padilla petition was invalid because he hadn't signed it. Having deliberately blocked all contact between Padilla and the outside world, the government told the court that a valid habeas petition required his signature, that Newman couldn't sign for him (how do we know that Padilla still wanted her to obtain his release?), and that she—his own lawyer—had no standing to ask the court's help because she had no "significant relationship" with him.

Federal Judge Michael Mukasey ultimately dismissed these arguments as frivolous. He ruled that Newman had to be granted access to her client and that he would review the enemy-combatant designation to be sure it was supported by "some evidence."

Mukasey's decision was announced on December 9, 2002; yet Padilla remains incommunicado. The government responded to Mukasey's order by demanding yet more time and finding several allegedly new reasons why Newman should be denied all contact with her client. In March 2003 Mukasey, finally losing patience, reaffirmed his original ruling and insisted that a visit be permitted. Rather than comply, however, the government obtained yet another stay and appealed Mukasey's ruling to the U.S. Court of Appeals, a move that is certain to leave Padilla isolated for many more weeks, or, more likely, months.

The *New York Times* and the *Washington Post* praised Mukasey for his courage in standing up to the government. But we should take little comfort from his decision. Normally detention without a hearing becomes unconstitutional after forty-eight hours, and regardless of the context (civil, criminal, immigration, or military) detention incommunicado has never been permitted for any appreciable time at all. Yet, as of this writing, Padilla's detention (incommunicado, to boot) has continued without any judicial review for nearly a year.

More important, what is left of the writ of habeas corpus? Paradoxically, Padilla was lucky, because the government initially treated him as a material witness, and a judge appointed counsel to represent him. Next time, federal agents will be free to send the detainee straight to the Navy brig, without stopping first in a federal court. The Navy won't let him communicate with the outside world, and there won't be any Donna Newman to file a habeas petition for him.

The only way to get a case like that before a judge would be for a family member to claim standing. That should work, though this Justice Department seems seriously capable of litigating whether a detainee has a "significant relationship" with his mother. There is also a less technical problem: the secrecy policy. If the person detained has not been in regular contact with his mother, she may not know that he has dropped from sight. And since the Justice Department insists on the importance of maintaining a shroud of categorical secrecy over the identities of those it detains as suspected terrorists, how will a detainee's mother know that he is in military custody?

When they come to assess these maneuvers, future historians may decide that Lincoln was a far less astute strategist than George W. Bush. Lincoln made himself look tyrannical by suspending the Great Writ, and the Supreme Court ultimately held that he had been wrong to do so. If he had had lawyers like John Ashcroft, he could have called himself a champion of civil liberties and at the same time made sure he never had to defend any case in court.

The other worry in Judge Mukasey's decision, for any case that gets to court, is the standard of review: "some evidence."

The charge against Padilla is based on the affidavit of a Pentagon employee, Michael Mobbs. The so-called Mobbs declaration describes intelligence reports from confidential sources —captured Al-Qaeda operatives who were interrogated in detention. According to these sources, Padilla traveled to Pakistan, met with Al-Qaeda operatives, received training, and explored the possibility of setting off a radioactive dirty bomb. One of the government's sources cautioned that Padilla is not a "member" of Al-Qaeda. But informants claimed that Padilla "had significant and extended contacts with senior Al-Qaeda members and operatives" and that he "was sent to the United States to conduct reconnaissance and/or other attacks on their behalf."

Of course, it is currently impossible to cross-examine these informants to test their accusations. And although the declaration states that "certain aspects" of their reports have been corroborated, it says nothing about what those aspects were and whether the details corroborated related to Padilla in any way. As a result, the affidavit provides no basis for crediting the allegations that relate specifically to Padilla. To the contrary, the Mobbs declaration itself acknowledges (in a footnote) several grounds for concern about the informants' reliability. It concedes that "these confidential sources have not been completely candid" and that "some information provided by the sources remains uncorroborated and may be part of an effort to mislead or confuse U.S. officials." It also notes that while under interrogation, one of the sources was being given unspecified drugs "to treat medical conditions."

Information subsequently disclosed (but apparently not presented to the president or the court) reveals an even more troubling detail about drugs that this confidential source was *not* given: The informant against Padilla was interrogated while severely wounded; when he refused to cooperate, pain-killing medication was withheld until he agreed to talk and name names.

Confidential tips given under these circumstances obviously cannot provide proof of guilt beyond a reasonable doubt. They do not even establish probable cause sufficient to support a routine wiretap, because for that purpose the law requires that an affidavit provide a basis for trusting the reliability of an informant's tip. But there is *some* evidence.

If the Supreme Court upholds the "some evidence" standard, it won't matter whether detainees get to file habeas petitions. An unsupported tip from a confidential source is still some evidence, and that will be all it takes to require deference to a president's finding. That finding of enemy-combatant status, in turn, is enough in the administration's view to support detention for the long duration of this conflict, without any trial at all.*

The government's approach is rooted, it says, in its need to continue incommunicado interrogation, for an indefinite period, in order to find out what Padilla knows. If he hasn't talked at this point, after almost a year of interrogation, it is hard to

---

*In principle, the administration should be forced to elect whether to treat Padilla as a lawful or unlawful enemy combatant. A lawful combatant can indeed be detained without trial, as a prisoner of war, for the duration of hostilities. But prisoners of war must be granted numerous rights relating to decent treatment, contact with outsiders, and freedom from interrogation. The Bush administration clearly regards Padilla as an *unlawful* combatant entitled to none of those rights. But even an admitted enemy combatant cannot be considered an *unlawful* combatant, and cannot be stripped of the rights of an ordinary prisoner of war, until he is tried by a military tribunal and found guilty of unlawful acts. In effect the administration seeks to confine Padilla to legal limbo, entitled neither to the privileges of a prisoner of war, nor to trial as an unlawful combatant.

believe another six or twelve months will do the trick or that whatever Padilla knows has not gone stale. But we cannot completely rule out the possibility that after many months (or years) of isolation, a suspect might eventually reveal something useful.

The problem with that argument is the Constitution—not just its fine points but the very idea of a government under law. If the mere possibility of a useful interrogation is enough to support indefinite detention incommunicado, then no rights and no checks and balances are available at all, except when the executive chooses to grant them. If a ruler in any other country claimed unilateral powers of this sort, Americans would be quick to recognize the affront to the most basic of human rights.

Nonetheless, the government claims that two lines of precedent support its approach.

The first is *Ex parte Quirin*, the German saboteurs case. In World War II, eight German naval officers, one of whom claimed to be a U.S. citizen, landed secretly on beaches in the United States, buried their uniforms, and began preparations for sabotaging war production facilities. They were arrested; after conviction by a military tribunal, six were executed. The U.S. Supreme Court held that since they were acknowledged members of the German armed forces, the military had jurisdiction (just as it did over members of our own armed forces) to put them on trial. The Court said that military jurisdiction was permissible because the defendants were "admitted enemy invaders."

In the media and in court, the Bush administration argues that *Quirin* squarely settles its power over Padilla. They are right only if there is no important difference between being an admitted enemy and being an accused enemy. The argument boils down to the claim that since a person who admits guilt can be punished, the law should allow the same result when the president reviews a secret record and finds the crucial facts in the privacy of the Oval Office.

The government's other precedents are the cases holding that military discretion is unquestioned on the battlefield. And in this war on terror, they say, the entire nation is a battlefield. That analogy is not completely false, but if the military can do within the United States whatever it could do in Afghanistan, then again, checks and balances are over for the duration.

The American homeland has been threatened before. The Civil War brought four years of fighting on American soil, and Hawaii was a theater of active military operations throughout World War II. In both situations the military argued the need for displacing civilian courts, and in both situations the Supreme Court rejected that argument explicitly. "Martial law," the Court said in *Ex parte Milligan,* "cannot arise from a threatened invasion. The necessity must be actual and present, . . . such as effectually closes the courts. . . . If martial law is continued after the courts are reinstated, it is a gross usurpation of power."

The presumption against military detention, whenever civilian courts are functioning, is not merely a doctrinal technicality. The central premise of government under law is that executive officials, no matter how well intentioned, cannot be allowed unreviewable power to imprison a citizen. Even in times of dire emergency, the Supreme Court has been consistent and emphatic on this point. However much we respect the good intentions of the current attorney general and secretary of defense, such disregard for traditional checks and balances is a recipe for bad mistakes and serious abuses of power. Unchecked executive power of this sort, when exercised in other countries, is what we immediately recognize as a dangerous step in the direction of tyranny.

Perverse Logic

The Bush administration's counterterrorism strategy is not captured by the cliché about "shifting the balance" from liberty to security because so many of its actions encroach on liberty *without* enhancing security. Even within the executive branch, the rush to be tough, and to appear tough, has triggered disregard for accountability principles that lie close to the core of effective management. And the White House's determination to enlarge unilateral executive power has prompted unprecedented measures to bypass checks and balances that do not impede legitimate national security efforts. At the same time, the administration, brushing aside traditional commitments to narrow tailoring of intelligence-gathering power, has taken far too many steps that are demonstrably irrelevant to the Al-Qaeda threat; 9/11 opportunism in the law enforcement establishment has fueled successful efforts to expand investigative and surveillance powers wholly unrelated to terrorism.

Yet this lack of caution concerning encroachments on freedom coexists with great restraint in pursuing security needs that require the commitment of significant financial resources. The decision to blame civil liberties and to draw attention away from other aspects of an effective counterterrorism strategy is logical for an administration that puts tax cuts ahead of all other priorities. But for a nation facing unprecedented threats, it is a dangerous and indefensible choice.

CHAPTER 4

"The Least Worst Place": Life in Guantánamo

JOSEPH LELYVELD

F THERE'S A CIVIC HUB on the naval base that the United States has occupied since 1898 on two spits of dry scrubland here on Cuba's southeastern heel, it's the section locally known as Downtown on the windward side of the bay. Downtown consists of "Cuba's only McDonald's," as the franchise is often described, and a smallish mall with a supermarket, pizzeria, ATM, and video store that displays a regularly updated selection of T-shirts poking ironic fun at "Gitmo," as the base is known in Navy talk. "The Least Worst Place," proclaims the legend on the latest, repeating a solecism that stumbled off the tongue of Donald Rumsfeld. The defense secretary, trying to echo Winston Churchill on democracy, had been explaining how Guantánamo got chosen as the warehouse for former Taliban fighters and supposed Al-Qaeda terrorists picked up in Afghanistan and other precincts of the global war on terrorism.

Irony attaches to any description of the life on this isolated base but never to the war or to the mission. Nor is it evoked by a familiar symbol on a flagstaff on the approach to Downtown:

the black banner memorializing the POWs and MIAs lost in Vietnam more than three decades ago, especially those who might have been held in perpetual captivity after our own government perfidiously affirmed, according to truly diehard adherents of this faith, that all captives had been returned. Commonplace as it still is on military bases and across America, this black banner provides a small jolt in the least worst place, a reminder that the United States once championed the Geneva Convention on the treatment of prisoners of war. At the Vietnam War's end there were 50,000 prisoners of war, Vietcong guerrillas as well as regular North Vietnamese troops, in South Vietnamese camps visited regularly by the International Committee of the Red Cross (ICRC), which Hanoi (to use a verb recently favored by George W. Bush) stiffed.

At the United States Naval Station at Guantánamo Bay, by contrast, there is not a single certified prisoner of war among the estimated 650 Taliban and Al-Qaeda detainees. The procedures laid down by the Geneva Convention have been overridden by fiat of the president, who determined at the start of the year that they didn't apply in this case; that none of the detainees needed to be treated as prisoners of war under the terms of the convention; and, therefore, that there was no need to determine their status individually before the tribunals it prescribes, which are also prescribed by U.S. military regulations. Otherwise, President Bush on February 7, 2002, decreed that Taliban captives would be treated humanely "in accordance with the Geneva Convention."

He had the grace not to say that it was better than they and their Al-Qaeda brethren deserved, and that we are prepared to hold the lot of them at Guantánamo until the distant day, if it ever comes, when Islamic terrorist networks have been universally uprooted. Yet this, basically, appears to be the administration's position. What cannot be said in so many words becomes increasingly apparent as we enter the second year since the first detainees arrived from Afghanistan in January 2002 at Guantánamo in shackles, earmuffs, and blackened goggles: that a system of preventive detention has been established in Cuba on the American side of the fence. Why Cuba? Two federal district courts, casting aside the due process arguments of humanitarian and civil liberties groups, have already bowed to the U.S. Justice Department's contention that it is foreign territory and therefore beyond the jurisdiction of "any United States court," as the administration's lawyers put it in their formal response to a habeas corpus petition in the U.S. District Court for the District of Columbia.

As a matter of international law, the American position can be described as selective or balanced, tricky or nuanced. It can also be described as careless, in that it probably was not necessary for the United States to act as if it were making up international law as it went along. Some experts in military law—including, there is reason to believe, some still in uniform—think a solid legal argument could have been made for a detention regime not all that different from the one that has been brought into being here. But as a matter of practical statecraft and political judgment, the American position contains its own rationale and calculations. These, however, can be inferred or pieced together only on the basis of occasional asides by various officials.* Just because this administration is allergic to

---

*Asked in a television interview on February 17, 2002, whether the detainees might be held indefinitely, Deputy Secretary of Defense Paul Wolfowitz replied, "I think that's probably a good way to think about it." A few weeks later Assistant

explanations, it doesn't necessarily follow that it is without arguments on its side, or that the arguments it chooses not to make so as to avoid rebuttals in courtrooms or print are devoid of common sense.* Its case, I believe, goes something like this:

Jihadists are different from other warriors, in that their struggles won't obviously be ended by an armistice or surrender proclaimed from on high. The overriding objective of any detention regime in these circumstances has to be the gathering of intelligence about the network and its targets that may serve to prevent future attacks. Prevention is more important than prosecuting individuals for past actions. If you are looking to the future, it's hard to say who among the detainees is important—that is, dangerous—and who's not. If

---

Attorney General John Yoo concurred, asking, "Does it make sense ever to release them if you think they are going to continue to be dangerous even though you can't convict them of a crime?" See Warren Richey's article in the *Christian Science Monitor,* April 9, 2002. Following briefings he got on the way to Guantánamo, Alabama Republican Senator Jeff Sessions said: "If these people are committed terrorists who are going to take release as an opportunity to attack again, then it would be insane to release them." See Bob Drogin's article in the *Los Angeles Times,* January 27, 2002.

*Two weeks before visiting Guantánamo Bay, I approached the Pentagon with a request for a background conversation on such matters as the operational considerations that led to the current detention regime and what had been gained from this approach that might have been sacrificed by closer adherence to the framework of the Geneva Convention. I also said I wanted to discuss the possible evolution of the current regime. I said I was interested in hearing an authoritative explanation of the administration's position and would not insist on attributing what I heard to official sources. A definite response came after I was already in Cuba. It said that "much of the information you requested was at a level of detail that we cannot provide."

future actions are the primary concern, it would be reckless to release persons who have already shown themselves to be adherents of movements that directly or indirectly supported the suicide attackers of September 11.

None of these is a legal argument and, since there has been a dearth of reliable information about actual happenings inside the security fences and interrogation rooms at Guantánamo since the detainees began to arrive, none of them can be evaluated in the light of known results. But the underlying logic I attribute to the administration, in a temporary suspension of journalistic disbelief, leaves hanging the question of whether the toughness of the detention regime is a product of anything other than the legitimate security concerns raised by a combustible mix of hostile inmates.

If the overriding priority is intelligence-gathering, as clearly seems the case, it's no great leap to conclude that it's calculated as well to make the detainees less resistant to the ongoing interrogations by demoralizing them. ("If we put them in the Waldorf Astoria, I don't think we could get them to talk," one officer said during my visit to the base.) Could it also be a form of punishment for persons who have yet to be charged with crimes? The answer seems obvious enough. The interrogations by military intelligence agents, the Federal Bureau of Investigation, and the Central Intelligence Agency, among others, had hardly gotten under way here when President Bush voiced his blanket conclusion that the Guantánamo detainees were "killers." Defense Secretary Rumsfeld said they were "hardcore, well-trained terrorists." Attorney General John Ashcroft said they were "uniquely dangerous."

Later on other officials started to allow for the possibility that these broad-brush conclusions might not, after all, apply to every single case. By March 2002 Paul Wolfowitz was telling Jim Lehrer that "some of them may turn out to be completely harmless." Douglas Feith, undersecretary of defense, raised the hypothetical possibility that some of them might not be threats to Americans at all. What had they learned in the meantime that introduced this smidgen of doubt?

We still don't know, but some indications of the basic demographics of the inmate population have begun to appear, like shadows on the wall of silence, making it possible to draw some surmises. Foreign officials have been allowed to visit and, in some cases, to interrogate their own nationals at the camp. The gesture President Bush made to the Geneva Conventions in February turned out to be more than cosmetic: The ICRC has not just visited the camp where the detainees are held; it has maintained a semipermanent presence there with regular access to the prisoners, most of whom avail themselves of the opportunity to exchange mail with their families through the Red Cross office in Geneva, which is also willing to transmit verbal messages. By the start of this year, some 3,300 letters had been delivered to the detainees and their families.

The mail is subject to censorship and the visitors are extremely circumspect—especially the Red Cross, whose representatives are careful not to jeopardize their access—but information gets discreetly swapped around and a picture emerges. By now more than forty names out of the estimated 650 have come into the public domain, despite the obsessive secretiveness that marks the whole operation. It is now understood by those who try to keep abreast of what is happening at Guantánamo that among the thirty-four or forty-three nations from whom the detainees are drawn—the varying estimates may be explained by dual nationalities in some cases—the great majority are of Arab origin and that, among these, Saudi Arabia accounts for by far the largest group in the camp, just as it did for most of the hijackers on the doomed September 11 flights. Nearly one-quarter of the camp's population—150 persons—are Saudi in background, according to a Yemeni lawyer who has been gathering powers of attorney to represent them; another eighty-five are from Yemen. If there had been any Iraqis among the prisoners, that bit of data would probably have been deployed in the debates over the drive to remove Saddam Hussein. But the awkward facts pointing to Saudi Arabia as well as to adjacent Yemen have been closely held.

It is also understood, by those who try to keep close track, that no non-Afghans are classified as Taliban and that there are fewer than a hundred Afghans in the camp; that everyone else is therefore presumed to be Al-Qaeda; that more than half of the detainees were turned over to the Americans by the Pakistanis,[*] which suggests that some of them, at least, might never have made it to Afghanistan; that some are younger than twenty years old—one, a Canadian by citizenship, was fifteen at the time of his capture; and that most are in their early twenties.

Of these, more than a few appear to have left their homes after September 11 in response to calls at their local mosques to defend an endangered Muslim nation. It was enough that they answered the call; how much training they managed to get and

---

[*]The total was 328, according to Ahmed Rashid; see his article in the *New York Review*, October 10, 2002. An interview with the Yemeni lawyer, Jamil Muhammad Ali Murshid, appeared in *Al-Sharq al-Awsat*, an Arabic newspaper published in London, on September 28, 2002. A translation was published by the BBC Monitoring Service on October 1.

how much action they managed to see before they were captured is open to question. It has also come to be understood, or
at least widely presumed among those who try to stay informed,
that the U.S. officials screening captives in Afghanistan—because of language barriers and an eagerness not to let anyone
significant slip through their hands—had a shaky grip on the
actual identities of prisoners who, in some cases, were being
turned over to them for money with assurances that they were
really and truly dangerous or "interesting" from an intelligence
standpoint, just as any rug that might catch your eye on Afghanistan's storied frontier would turn out to be really and truly
rare.

If these surmises correspond in some measure to reality, the
intelligence officials by now, after months of interrogation,
must have a more realistic idea of how many minnows and how
many big fish, if any, they caught in their net.* But any conclusions they may have drawn about individual detainees—how
dangerous they are, how liable to be brought up on charges before the much debated, yet still unnamed, military commissions
or tribunals—have yet to produce any consequences. Preparations for the legal circus that has been anticipated for nearly a
year now, ever since the White House issued President Bush's

---

*A *Los Angeles Times* report on August 18, 2002, said that American intelligence
officials were deeply disappointed by the gleanings from Guantánamo, which
they attributed to the relative insignificance within the terrorist network of the
detainees who were described as "low- and middle-level." By contrast, in an interview in *Le Monde* timed to appear on the first anniversary of the September 11 attacks, the head of the French counterespionage agency, the DST, Pierre de
Bousquet de Florian, indicated that French officials had gained valuable new information from their interrogations of the six French nationals at Guantánamo.

order reinventing the system of military justice for the war on terrorism, are simply not in evidence in Guantánamo.

At the time the order was issued, the White House was preparing for the imminent capture of Osama bin Laden and other Al-Qaeda leaders. With the fate of the top leaders still unknown, it may seem less urgent to get the commissions rolling. No lawyers or judges have been appointed, no renovations are going on at the old military courthouse where the trials would presumably be held, and no one has been charged. What legal preparations are under way can presumably be found in a Pentagon petri dish, awaiting implantation here. For now, military justice does not seem to be a Guantánamo priority. The administration of justice, after all, is reflexively backward-looking, more concerned with what has already happened than what might happen, and, therefore, not the most pressing issue in the view of security planners.

It's even possible, perhaps even likely, that the first persons to be charged are still somewhere else. The United States has three significant Al-Qaeda leaders in custody, Khalid Sheikh Mohammed, Abu Zubaydah, and Ramzi Binalshibh, each captured in Pakistan. The fact that they are being interrogated in other, as yet undisclosed, locations is another indication that Guantánamo Bay's main function may be that of a holding camp, one where the great majority of inmates will simply be detained without trial for the foreseeable future.* And if this is correct, it

---

*A *New York Times* report by Patrick Tyler on December 23, 2002, said that the Central Intelligence Agency had set up an "interrogation site" in Jordan "to keep Qaeda operatives for questioning in a jurisdiction removed from the United States." Dana Priest and Barton Gellman of the *Washington Post* reported on December 26 that the CIA was also conducting interrogations at Bagram, an air base

follows that the debate about the gestating military commissions has no bearing whatsoever on the fate of most of the detainees.

THAT HOLDING CAMP HAS A NAME. It's called Camp Delta and sits at the southeastern corner of the Guantánamo base, on a low bluff above the Caribbean and a beach known in happier days as Kittery Beach. On the way to the shore, you pass one of the Guantánamo base's few charming features, a yellow diamond-shaped crossing sign with a picture of an iguana. The shore is now laced with electronic sensors and is regularly patrolled by the Army and Coast Guard, on alert for a seaborne rescue attempt by suicidal Al-Qaeda marines. On the inland side of the compound, the small trailer used by the nine representatives of the ICRC—among whom eight languages are spoken—sits just outside the camp's perimeter. Visiting journalists are ferried to the side of the camp facing the sea where they are asked to confine themselves to a "media observation point" marked off by strands of barbed wire and located roughly 200 yards from the nearest cell block.

By day, you get an eyeful of glare off the metal roofs of the cell blocks and a view of guard posts and parallel lines of the high chain-link fences that surround the whole compound, topped and separated by razor-wire coils and covered with green plastic curtains to frustrate intelligence-gathering by the terrorist network. By night, the compound is bathed inside and out by eerie white light cast by halogen lamps on high poles,

---

used by the United States in Afghanistan, and on the tiny Indian Ocean island of Diego Garcia, which the United States leases from Britain.

and sometimes it's possible to make out flickering shadows behind the cell windows. These are covered by steel mesh, not glass, allowing, so you're assured, the breeze off the sea to penetrate the cells, which can also be cooled by fans in the roof when military police guards are moved by their own discomfort, if not that of the detainees, to turn them on.

The flickering shadows, you're told, may be actual Al-Qaeda terrorists. It's as close as reporters ever get these days to seeing them here. (Among the provisions of the Third Geneva Convention that the United States interprets rigorously is one discouraging public display of prisoners. This is out of respect for their "privacy," military escorts explain.) Still, the crepuscular scene at Delta makes vivid the cramped detention regime in which the detainees have lived since the end of April 2002, when they were moved from a warren of cages called Camp X-Ray several miles away. There they had initially been confined in plain, if distant, view of journalists who on one, and only one, occasion in March 2002 were allowed to get close enough to evoke shouted protestations of innocence.

Delta was thrown together for $9.7 million by a private contractor, Brown and Root Services—a division of Vice President Dick Cheney's old company, Halliburton—which flew in low-wage contract labor from the Philippines and India to get the job done, in much the same way that Asians were once brought to the Caribbean to harvest sugarcane. The cell blocks are assembled from the standard forty-foot steel boxes called connex containers that are used in international shipping: five cells to a container, eight containers to a cell block, with four lined up on each side of a central corridor where the lights and fans are installed. Welders cut away three sides of each container, replacing them with sidings of steel mesh, leaving the roof, floor, and one steel wall into which a window was cut. Floor-level toilets were installed—the kind requiring squatting, traditionally described as *à la turque*—and now these are sometimes mentioned as an example of American sensitivity to the cultural needs of the detainees. (Military police guards are the first to tell you that they are much to be preferred over the night soil buckets that they had to empty at Camp X-Ray.)

The detainees are alone in their cells, sleeping on metal shelves fitted with thin mattresses of a sort used in U.S. prisons. But through the chain-link walls they are able to maintain eye contact and conversation, assuming they have a common language, with five others—two on either side and three across the corridor. At 6.8 feet by 8 feet, each cell is only slightly smaller than the cells on death row in Brown and Root's home state of Texas. There, however, the inmates are taken out one by one for an hour's exercise and showers each day. At Camp Delta—where the detainees are never allowed to congregate under any circumstances and where they are periodically shuffled from cell to cell to keep cliques from forming—they are also taken out one by one to exercise and shower, but only twice a week, fifteen minutes each time. In other words, they are in their cells all but thirty minutes a week, unless they are summoned for interrogation. The detainees may be called to interrogation at night as well as during the day. Whenever they are removed from their cells, they are shackled. This regime is uniform for all detainees, except those who have shown defiance that caused them to be moved to "isolation," a standard form of solitary confinement, where they are held in cells with four solid walls blocking any communication with other detainees. The isolation cells, being closed, are the only ones that are air-conditioned. The interrogation rooms are air-conditioned as well.

The ICRC simply does not speak about what it has learned about the treatment of the prisoners. But there has never been a hint that it has had to deal with complaints of physical abuse. I asked an army officer here whether the interrogators used the method of sleep deprivation to get the detainees to open up. He said he was not permitted to talk about interrogation methods. Then citing international rules that do not seem to exist, he volunteered that it was forbidden to keep someone under interrogation awake for more than twenty-four hours. It's possible that the officer had an extremely dry sense of humor. It's possible that he was telling me something. Confusing as his response was, I took it as an answer to my initial question.

According to the officers I spoke to, the rationale behind the tough detention regime is that there may be potential suicide killers among the detainees. Threats to the lives of the guards have been made, defenders of the administration's procedures regularly assert, harking back to Attorney General Ashcroft's contention that these detainees are "uniquely dangerous"—and thus more dangerous, one would presume, than those to be found in a maximum security prison on the mainland. This view was probably colored by the fact that the first American killed in Afghanistan last November, CIA agent Johnny Spann, was beaten to death in the prison uprising at Mazar-e-Sharif.

Actually, it appears, only one threat to the life of a guard has been reported, and that was early on, during the stressful transfer of the first batch of detainees from Afghanistan to Cuba under U.S. Marine guard.* A reservist I met in New York fol-

*According to the Australian press, the man charged with making the threat was a soldier of fortune from Adelaide named David Hicks who converted to Islam after fighting with the Kosovo Liberation Army and later joined Lashkar-e-

lowing the completion of his Guantánamo tour was on the scene when the first detainees arrived. The Marine guards, he said, would not allow them to talk or even raise their heads to look around. They had to kneel with their heads bowed. "They were so scared they couldn't walk, so afraid they couldn't stand," the man said. Navy Seabees working near the compound were equally on edge and stayed that way. "We were just waiting for one of them to take someone's eyes out, just waiting for it to happen," he said. Once the detainees were in the X-Ray cages, or when they were summoned for interrogation, he said, some shouted defiance until they were restrained. A high official of the Taliban ministry of defense, he recalled, was especially obstreperous in those early days at X-Ray.

Since then, resistance has been limited to a bite on a guard's arm, spitting, throwing water, and a hunger strike that gathered momentum early in March 2002 after a Marine guard went into a cage while a detainee was praying in order to remove an improvised turban from his head, not understanding that Muslims cover their heads during prayer. The authorities eventually put two hunger strikers on intravenous drips in the hospital; one of the two didn't finally relent until May 18, following his second round of forced feeding.

The reservist MPs who have been called up to take over guard duty at Camp Delta from the Marines are now regularly told in their cultural awareness classes that they must never interfere with prayer and never touch the Korans that have been

---

Taiba, a Muslim group seeking to infiltrate Kashmir. The *Herald Sun*, an Australian paper, reported on July 8, 2002, that Hicks's family had received a letter from him dismissing the allegation as "a load of crap." The letter went on: "My interrogators admitted that the story was a lie."

placed in every cell like Gideon Bibles in hotel rooms. Prayer caps are also now standard issue, as are prayer mats made of foam rubber. Among the reservists are experienced corrections officers from U.S. prisons who have been less easily flustered, the officer I met in New York said, than the Marines who were more given to shouting and displays of fury.

The fact is that Camp Delta then became largely an Army Reserve and National Guard operation—only one of the six military police companies that guarded at the time of my visit was regular Army—with the call-up personnel changing every six months. When his tour was cut short, Brigadier General Rick Baccus, the commanding officer of the detention operation then, was sent back to his civilian job as director of veterans' cemeteries in Rhode Island. The major assigned to escort journalists was an actor from Queens, one of whose roles was at Shea Stadium as Mr. Met, the prancing team mascot with a large baseball for a head and a goofy smile. The spokesman for the task force handling the interrogations, a retired New York City fire marshal who lost many friends at the World Trade Center, was about to return to the martial arts academy he runs in Forest Hills. If there is any continuity of experience when it came to learning about individual detainees, it had to reside with the interrogators. Finally, for the sake of consistency and more productive interrogations, the previously separate detention and interrogation task forces were merged in October 2002 and placed under a regular Army commander, a post assumed the following month by Major General Geoffrey D. Miller, who had been deputy commander of the Eighth Army in Korea.

AMERICAN SUPPORT FOR the practice of Islam at Camp Delta is not in the least grudging. Eager is the better description, for it's the most convenient way to demonstrate to the world (and, perhaps more to the point, ourselves) that the detainees are being treated humanely. A recorded call to prayer plays over the public address system in the cell blocks five times a day. All meals meet the standards of a Halal diet. An imam—a uniformed U.S. Navy chaplain, among fourteen Muslim chaplains in the armed forces—regularly visits the cell blocks to talk to the detainees; three imams have been rotated out, and Camp Delta is now on its fourth. A selection of religious readings in various languages has also been made available, in addition to the Koran.* Colonel Joseph J. Perrone, Jr., a retired Rochester police officer who was in command at the detention center when I visited, was enthusiastic about his plans for Ramadan, when Muslims fast between sunrise and sunset. He was already in negotiation with the contractors who have taken over kitchen duty in the all-volunteer Army to ensure that the detainees get hot breakfasts at 4 A.M. for the month, two hours earlier than usual, and special meals after sunset.

Americans may be pious about piety, but few people on duty here seem to question the basic proposition that they are deal-

---

*Only lately has the command, prodded by the ICRC, agreed to let in secular material such as manuals and novels in the full range of languages, which, in addition to Arabic and Pashto, includes English, French, Persian, Russian, Urdu, Uighur, Turkish, and the Turkik languages of Central Asia. The ICRC provided some of the material. The Pentagon planned to put up $20,000 to buy books, according to Colonel Joseph J. Perrone, Jr. These would not include any material touching on politics, world affairs, or current events, about which the detainees have been systematically kept in the dark. In the days running up to September 11, 2002, the guards were careful not to let slip that the anniversary was approaching.

ing with a pack of homicidal fanatics. Conversation between the guards and the detainees is discouraged even when it's possible—that is, when a detainee speaks English. By now, guards say, most of the detainees understand the limited repertoire of commands. Outside of the interrogation rooms, where they speak through military and contract interpreters, that's all they get, except for occasional encounters with the chaplain or the Red Cross.

I was told that about one-third of the MPs on duty at Camp Delta worked in their civilian incarnations as police and corrections officers. I asked to speak to some who worked in prisons in civilian life in the hope of getting their more seasoned reactions to what they were experiencing here. Two women, one white and one black, from the same National Guard unit in central Georgia were selected. Sergeant Diane Sanford, the white woman, works at the Frank C. Scott Jr. State Prison in Hardwick; Specialist Tamara Poole, at the Hancock State Prison in Sparta. The regimen at Delta, they said, was tough, but then it was also tough in central Georgia. The time the detainees were doing here was a little harder than conditions in segregation in the prisons where the women normally worked—where prisoners considered threatening were housed—but easier, they said, than Georgia-style isolation. They would call it "high security," the two soldiers said. Whatever it was called, it didn't seem especially new to them.

A similar thought was voiced by Captain Albert J. Shimkus, Jr., who is in charge of the health services for the detainees as well as the uniformed men on the base. Yes, it was true, Captain Shimkus said, that some of the detainees—about 5 percent—were on antidepressant medication. But this would probably be true in any large American prison, he said. Detention is seldom uplifting, I found myself privately conceding, for anyone, any-where. Captain Shimkus said he thought his unit might have to put more detainees on antidepressants as time wore on.

Pharmacology proved to be inadequate to stem a small epidemic of suicide attempts as the months passed under the extremely restrictive detention regime. By February 2003, sixteen prisoners had attempted to take their own lives, three of them twice. Some of these attempts were written off as "gestures," but one detainee may have suffered brain damage as a result of his attempt to hang himself in his cell on January 16, 2003. Five weeks later he was still hospitalized in what was described as stable but serious condition. "The United States and the detaining authorities need to come clean about how the prisoners are being interrogated and how they're being treated before a prisoner dies," Amnesty International commented.

Of course, the two guards I spoke to on my visit had heard inmates threaten the lives of guards in Georgia—that was one way to get into isolation, and, of course, they had seen Muslims praying there too. "Here or at home were they able to tell who's really dangerous?" I asked. "In my mind, I consider all of them are," Sergeant Sanford said flatly. "That's just the way I know I have to think if I'm going to get my people out without any problems."

There were two obvious and fundamental issues that the guards were not asked to consider, by the Army or me. One was that the Georgia system has five grades of detention from the lowest level of security to the highest. At that point, Guantánamo was basically satisfied with a one-size-fits-all approach. Another was that the inmates in Georgia prisons have all been convicted of felony crimes. They have some idea, unlike the detainees here, of when or whether they are getting out. The

Lawyers Committee for Human Rights, in a careful analysis of the consequences for civil liberties of the war on terror, domestically and internationally, notes that the military order signed by President Bush on November 13, 2001, nowhere requires that persons detained under the order be tried by the military commissions it was establishing. "And so," the Lawyers Committee found, the order "authorizes indefinite detention without trial."

But then so do the Geneva Conventions, at least until the end of a conflict. The standard version of the Geneva regime is nothing other than a fairly benign form of preventive detention. Humanitarian organizations, notably Human Rights Watch, take the view that the war in Afghanistan is all but over and therefore that the United States under settled international law faces, or is about to face, a choice between charging or releasing the Camp Delta detainees. Since the Guantánamo detainees have not been granted prisoner-of-war status, the advocacy groups also argue, they should be charged in criminal courts rather than before the promised military commissions, which they view as legally flawed by U.S. as well as international standards. In that case, if they were dropped into the jurisdiction of the federal judiciary, lawyers for the detainees might be able to seek their release on grounds that they had not been read their Miranda rights in Arabic or Pashto, let alone their rights under the Geneva Conventions, before being subject to interrogation here. Amnesty International says the current conditions at Camp Delta "may amount to cruel, inhuman, or degrading treatment in violation of international law." Amnesty said the Guantánamo interrogations should be halted until the detainees had an opportunity to consult lawyers.

These groups, along with many authorities on military justice, have also maintained that the United States had no choice, under the Third Geneva Convention of 1949, but to grant all the captives prisoner-of-war status until "competent tribunals" settled the fate of those whose status as members of an organized fighting force of a nation-state might be open to doubt.

Until now, these requirements have not been an issue for the United States. Without hesitation or controversy, the armed forces efficiently ran more than 1,000 such tribunals after the 1991 Gulf War. In its broadest interpretation, prisoner-of-war status guarantees captives a panoply of protections and rights not to be found at Camp Delta: the right to congregate, to elect a leadership to represent the group to the detaining authority, to prepare their own food, to have musical instruments and even knives, to labor for pay, and—best known of all the convention's provisions—to withhold information beyond name, rank, and serial number. Not least of all, the convention provides for the posting of these rights in languages understood by the prisoners. Instead, the United States classified the Delta detainees as "unlawful enemy combatants"—a term not found in international law, according to the Lawyers Committee.*

---

*Administration lawyers apparently found the term "enemy combatant" in a 1942 Supreme Court ruling (*Ex parte Quirin*, 317 U.S. 1 [1942]), which concerned the case of eight Nazi saboteurs who landed on Long Island and were tried before a military commission set up on the order of President Franklin Roosevelt. The commission condemned the eight to death after the Supreme Court declined to stop the proceedings. Six of the eight were promptly electrocuted—two had their sentences commuted—and then nearly three months passed before the Court reached agreement on a unanimous decision drafted by Chief Justice Harlan Stone. The Lawyers Committee for Human Rights, finding the Bush administration's use of this precedent "particularly awkward," notes that the Nazi prisoners received three rights denied today to the detainees at Camp Delta: the rights to counsel, to a speedy trial, and to civilian review, in this case by the highest court.

Thus, it seems plain that if the administration—with a view to preventing future terrorist attacks—was bent on interrogating and detaining its captives, it was not going to have an easy time with the Geneva Conventions. Its first instinct was not even to try to square what it conceived to be its operational requirements with treaties the United States has long accepted. The administration argued instead that the shadowy terrorist networks it was fighting—with their global reach, tiny sleeper cells, and potential access to weapons of mass destruction—were simply not protected by the established rules of war. Some close observers believe that this view was especially strong at the Justice Department and less strong among military lawyers at the Pentagon, where there is a constant worry about what's termed "reciprocity": the danger that other states might also be tempted to step outside the established conventions when dealing with a downed pilot—in Iraq, for instance—or other American prisoners.

If the administration had been interested in showing what was once called "a decent respect for the opinion of mankind"—if only to sustain the coalition it summoned for its "war on terror"—it might have paid more attention to its experts on military law. The conventions and legal precedents, U.S. leaders might then have heard, are not as hard and fast, as unresponsive to pressing security concerns, as its own civilian lawyers—along with the advocacy groups—appear to have concluded. In other words, there was room for the United States to make a legal case that it had a right under the Geneva Conventions, given the unusual threat it was facing, to establish a system that denied most of the privileges that the Geneva Conventions spell out for prisoners of war.

The monitors of the Geneva regime are repeatedly warned in the actual treaties not to second-guess the detaining authority on issues of security. For instance, article 8 of the convention on prisoners of war warns delegates of the ICRC that they must "take account of the imperative necessities of security of the State wherein they carry out their duties." Article 126 acknowledges "reasons of imperative military necessity" that might interfere with the Geneva regime. A Red Cross commentary on these provisions goes on to say, "Humanitarian principles must take into account actual facts if they are to be applicable." The commentaries also say that the question of what is actually a military necessity "is a matter for the detaining power alone to decide."

What these deliberately elastic treaty formulations suggest, in the view of persons familiar with ICRC procedures and guidelines, is that Red Cross representatives would have had to take seriously any administration argument that Delta's presumed terrorists represented a singular new threat and that therefore it could not be expected to give them the kind of privileges that the Geneva regime envisions for a conventional war and that films from *Grand Illusion* on have portrayed.

Sir Adam Roberts, an Oxford professor of international relations and an authority on the law of war, sees "rank amateurism in both the White House and the humanitarian organizations." At issue here is their reading of articles 4 and 5 of the Third Geneva Convention, which define the legal attributes of prisoners of war and provide for the "competent tribunals" that the detaining authority is supposed to set up in order to resolve cases of doubt. The humanitarian organizations, along with various academic commentators, read these provisions as requiring that each captured belligerent must be classified as a prisoner of war until a tribunal decides otherwise. For its part, the White House appears to have been looking for a way *not* to grant prisoner-of-war status, even temporarily, to anyone connected to Al-Qaeda, so it got itself into the position of denying the need for any tribunals at all.

Roberts argues that the law of war does not divide captive belligerents into just two classes: prisoners of war, and those whom tribunals have found not to deserve that status. He believes there can be another class: captive belligerents who clearly do not qualify as prisoners of war and who therefore don't have to be brought before tribunals because no doubt arises about their status. He would place anyone connected to Al-Qaeda in that category. The notion of an "unlawful combatant" has more standing in international law, in his view, than either the White House or the Lawyers Committee appears to have appreciated. An "unlawful combatant" is much the same as an "unprivileged belligerent," a classification accepted in international law, so he maintains, since it was first used a half-century ago. Article 75 of the First Geneva Protocol of 1977, Roberts notes, covers the treatment of such prisoners and therefore could have been applied to the treatment of most of the Delta detainees.* In this view, it would seem, the law of war is not about civil liberties but about restraining human beastliness.

International law experts and lawyers will continue to debate such issues. The point here is really a political one: The Bush administration appears not to have understood, or cared to un-

---

*Although the 1977 protocols have never been accepted by the United States, article 75 has been recognized in U.S. military law. The article provides for humane treatment and a legal framework for the detention of "persons in the power of a party to the conflict and who do not benefit from more favorable treatment under the Conventions." It also lists the legal rights of a detainee in the event that he is charged with a crime, including his "right to be informed without delay of the particulars of the offense alleged against him."

derstand, that it had more legal arguments—and thus, at least arguably, more legal options—than it brought to bear when it decided that Geneva, by and large, didn't apply or was too much trouble to apply. Here, as in its confrontation with the new International Criminal Court, which the administration is sworn to resist and to recognize, it has shown zero interest in influencing the development of what is termed "international humanitarian law," as the law of war is euphemistically known nowadays.

There is a crying need, a layman might think, for that law to address terrorist acts of mass murder launched across international boundaries. But still unresolved are the questions of whether the war on terror is really a war in some sense that the Geneva Conventions might be stretched to cover and, if so, who gets to decide when it's over. Kenneth Roth, the director of Human Rights Watch, argues that it's no more a war than the war on drugs and therefore that the criminal law must prevail as it does in drug cases. (A former prosecutor, Roth believes it would be possible to use the federal statutes on conspiracy, which heretofore have been used to prosecute organized crime figures, against Al-Qaeda.) This is a principled stand but brings to mind reports that U.S. authorities failed to take custody of Osama bin Laden in 1996 when Sudan hinted he might be made available because the Justice Department didn't think it had enough evidence at that stage—before the 1998 embassy bombings in East Africa—to make a case. Federal prosecutors have shown that they can successfully convict plotters responsible for attacks like the 1993 bombing of the World Trade Center. They cannot reasonably be asked to prevent future atrocities.

Whether the detention regime and interrogations at Guantánamo are preventing future atrocities will probably always be an unanswerable question, but it seems safe to predict that the Delta detainees are not going to be released anytime soon. (It would be "the mother of Willie Hortons," a lawyer remarked, if a released detainee were subsequently connected to an attack.) Yet for all the evasions and ambiguities in the Bush administration's stand on these issues, it still pays lip service to Geneva and therefore can be said to have left the door ajar for the possibility that it might one day engage in a serious effort to reconcile its procedures at Camp Delta with international law. That is what the humanitarian organizations say they have been seeking. It's the administration's failure to respect international law as expressed in the various Geneva agreements, these groups argue, that brings the legality of the detention regime at Camp Delta into question. For its part, Congress has shown zero interest in the Guantánamo detainees, who, after all, are not merely aliens, like the persons detained for immigration infractions in the Justice Department's big roundup following September 11, but foreigners picked up in suspicious proximity to Afghan battlegrounds.

That leaves the current stressful situation at Camp Delta and the question of how long it can be sustained, that is, how long it makes sense to treat all detainees here as potential suicide killers, confined to their small cells for six days and twenty-three and a half hours a week. This is especially so—as a matter of fairness and justice to individuals—if we now believe that some of them are "harmless," as Paul Wolfowitz suggested in 2002. Even Secretary of Defense Rumsfeld, in a rare acknowledgment of human complexity on the other side, once conceded that his collection of "well-trained, hard-core terrorists" might include someone who had been picked up "unintentionally," someone "who just happened to be in there that didn't belong in there."

As of February 2003, there had been confirmation of the releases of only a half-dozen of the original detainees, five Afghans (including one schizophrenic and two geriatric cases) and one Pakistani.* In addition, there have been unconfirmed reports of others being transferred to detention in Muslim countries other than their own where they might be subject to harsher interrogation. For instance, a report in a Mauritanian newspaper, picked up by the Associated Press, told of the transfer of a Mauritanian detainee from Guantánamo to Morocco. Although the capacity of Camp Delta was expanded to 812 in October 2002 and there was once talk of increasing it even further to about 2,000, the detainee population has stayed relatively stable: only about 90 new arrivals have been reported since June 2002.

The ins and outs are normally not announced, making it difficult to get a grip on the actual function of Guantánamo in the continuum of interrogation sites the United States has established, franchised, or rented since September 11. But plans were finally afoot at the start of 2003 to open a medium-security prison at Guantánamo apart from Camp Delta to which Delta detainees who had been deemed to have cooperated with their interrogators and guards could soon graduate. This can be seen as a logical extension of a system of rewards and penalties for de-

---

*U.S. officials had spoken of turning over detainees to countries that undertook to prosecute them for terrorist activities. Britain and Australia, among others, have sent officials to Guantánamo Bay with a view to starting cases. For its troubles the British government was sued for violating the rights of its nationals by interviewing them without a lawyer present. So far no government has been able to give the United States the assurances it apparently seeks that prosecutions might not lead to acquittals and the release of the detainees.

tainees that General Miller has put in place as well as a siphon to relieve the steadily rising pressure inside Delta. Rewards may be minor amenities such as extra blankets or rice. In one reported instance, presumably related to this scheme, a Saudi prisoner was allowed to phone home. With the opening of the new medium-security center, which will have a capacity of 200, the rewards could also include the possibility of congregating in groups of up to twenty for purposes of meals, exercise, or prayer. The ultimate reward for a cooperating detainee—one that has yet to be dangled, let alone offered—might be release from indefinite detention. And the ultimate penalty? Military spokesmen say coolly that it is the absence of rewards; in other words, the unmitigated continuation of the existing regime. But it's hard not to wonder whether it might rather be the threat of transfer to a state—Morocco, Jordan, or possibly Egypt—where interrogators are less bound by restrictions than they still are at Guantánamo; a state, that is, where torture can be threatened and applied.

Under General Miller, the detention scheme appears to be evolving into something more layered and subtle than the one-size-fits-all regime that existed through the first year. But Guantánamo is still what a panel of senior British judges called a "legal black hole" beyond the reach of any court in the world. Only on that distant day when the United States has declared victory in its war on terror, it seems, will we discover how few or how many cases of stark injustice existed beyond Camp Delta's fences. For now, the administration's basic position seems to be to make adjustments but show no sign of relenting in any basic way, perhaps so that the name "Guantánamo" can register in the imaginations of young Arabs as something to be avoided, becoming in itself a kind of deterrent. "It's our Devil's Island, it's our Robben Island," suggested Eugene Fidell, a Washington lawyer who is president of the National Institute of Military Justice.

On the evening I went down after sunset to the media observation point to view Camp Delta with two Turkish journalists and the major who was escorting us, the former Mr. Met, the spectacle got to be more striking for its *son* than for the *lumière* of the halogen lamps: Once my ears managed to sort out the sounds of crickets, a nearby white owl, distant air conditioners, and the lapping surf, I realized I was also listening to a chorus of human voices. Perhaps because of the interventions of guards, the volume tended to fall soon after it rose, but there were still distinct tonal differences among the snatches that came our way on the soft evening air. Sometimes they seemed to be singing, sometimes there were shouts. Variously, I imagined that I heard lamentations, calls to friends further down the cell block, protests, exhortations, and prayers. Even if the words had been distinct, of course, I wouldn't have known.

Then, after a half-hour, as we were giving up on our hopes of actually seeing detainees or their shadows and starting to board our van, the call to prayer sounded over the loudspeakers and we clambered down. It was a recording, but live voices rose to greet it. The Turkish journalists pulled out their video cameras. This was going to be gripping television in Istanbul, the sound of the evening prayers over the ghostly spectacle of Camp Delta. I shut my eyes for a moment, and it was easy to imagine that I was standing on the outskirts of Cairo or Lahore. Finally we drove off, and then the Turkish journalists started to play back their tape. It was a crushing disappointment. They had the images they wanted, but their microphone had not been strong enough to pick up the prayers. The sound of the detainees could not be caught.

CHAPTER 5

Under a Watchful Eye:
Incursions on Personal Privacy

KATHLEEN M. SULLIVAN

P RIVACY IS THE BEDROCK of other freedoms—to think, to differ, to worship, to create households, to pursue intimate relationships. It depends on a tacit assumption that the government will not be watching or listening to what we seek to shield from public view. As Justice John Harlan wrote in dissenting from a 1971 U.S. Supreme Court decision in *United States v. White,* which allowed the government to tape informers' conversations, such electronic surveillance "might well smother that spontaneity—reflected in frivolous, impetuous, sacrilegious, and defiant discourse—that liberates daily life."

After 9/11, the administration proposed an array of new interventions into the privacy of daily life. Two of the more dramatic initiatives—the Total Information Awareness (TIA) project and the operation known as Terrorism Information and Prevention Systems (TIPS)—received enough unfavorable publicity that they have been reined in for the time being. The more technical and insidious, such as the increased latitude for government surveillance granted by the USA Patriot Act, are cause for greater concern. Liberty can be eroded in many small steps as well as a few big ones. And the administration's zeal for privacy erosion continues in new proposals for ever greater surveillance measures that call out for restraint by Congress, the courts, and internal executive rules. To borrow the administration's vocabulary of alert levels about terrorism, the threat to privacy has risen at least to yellow if not yet to red.

Three kinds of recent government actions give rise to concern. The first involves proposed uses of technology that tend in the direction of general searches—that tactic of the British crown that so infuriated the Constitution's drafters. The second involves measures that make it easier for government to spy on us by lowering the threshold of justification for surveillance of individuals and groups. And the third involves measures that require us to make private data more readily accessible to government, increasing the risk of abuse should that data be misused.

Background privacy protection is established by the Fourth Amendment to the United States Constitution, which affirms "the right of the people to be secure in their persons, houses, papers, and effects, against unreasonable searches and seizures"; it also provides that "no Warrants shall issue, but upon probable cause" and "particularly describing" the objects of search and seizure. The reasonableness and warrant requirements do not protect our privacy absolutely, but they place strong procedural constraints on government. By permitting searches and seizures only if reasonable, and interposing the courts between the privacy of citizens and the potential excesses of executive zeal, these constitutional protections help to ensure that law enforcement officials will not engage in dragnets, or general searches, which were anathema to the colonists who rebelled against the British crown. Instead, we enjoy privacy unless and until we do something affirmative to attract particularized suspicion. And modern cases establish that government may no more troll through our personal lives at random electronically than redcoats were permitted to rummage as they pleased through the Founders' drawers.

"Knowledge Is Power"

The extreme case in the general searches category is the Pentagon's Total Information Awareness initiative, disclosed in November 2002. Under the logo of an eye-within-a-pyramid symbol (since removed from the TIA website) and the motto "knowledge is power," John M. Poindexter leads the effort. He is the former national security adviser and Navy admiral, who was previously convicted for lying to Congress about the Iran-Contra affair (the conviction was later overturned on procedural grounds). The project's goal is to aggregate vast amounts of data on citizens and noncitizens alike, from sources including federal, state, and local records, credit card transactions, airline reservations, telephone and Internet service provider (ISP) records, consumer information from health, financial, and retail companies, and live surveillance-camera feeds, such as from those at airports. This unprecedented centralization of private data is meant to enable the government to engage in data "mining" that will allow it to identify suspicious terrorist activity in its early stages.

To be sure, we have already revealed such information to our credit card companies, airlines, banks, and ISPs. Similarly, in our lives as consumers, our purchases enter us into databases whose other users later flood us with additional solicitations.

And the digital "cookies" we silently acquire in our web browsing enable marketers to send customized "pop-up" ads onto our computer screens. What's the loss to privacy if the government simply piggybacks on such disclosures to commercial actors? The Supreme Court has indeed held that, in some cases, when we expose personal information to others, we assume the risk that government snoops might see it too. So it has upheld warrantless government searches of canceled checks that our banks can see, of "pen registers" of telephone numbers we have dialed that a telephone operator could check, of marijuana patches in open fields that small aircraft might fly over, and of garbage bags placed on curbsides that scavengers might access.

But even if, in the digital world, we have relinquished some expectations of privacy by embracing ATM machines, online airline ticketing, and e-mail, a national central data bank of the size and scope of TIA is wholly unprecedented. TIA's proposed *combination* of both comprehensive data aggregation and powerful automated discovery and extraction techniques—by *government* rather than commercial companies with market-enforced privacy policies—resurrects in digital form the Founders' concerns about the danger of general searches. TIA aims through its Evidence Extraction and Link Discovery program to mine large quantities of personal information about individuals and groups in order to detect terrorist potential. Yet as Justice William O. Douglas once wrote in a 1974 dissent in *California Bankers Association v. Shultz*, "In a sense a person is defined by the checks he writes. By examining them, the agents know his doctors, lawyers, creditors, political allies, social connections, religious affiliation, educational interests, the papers and magazines he reads, and so on ad infinitum." Today, our biographies are etched in the ones and zeros we leave behind in daily digital transactions.

Without stringent controls and aggressive oversight, therefore, a data-mining operation such as TIA would pose serious risks. At the extreme it could be a vehicle for politically motivated spying and intimidation reminiscent of the worst features of the J. Edgar Hoover era. It might also permit more ordinary risks such as unauthorized snooping, leaking of information, blackmailing by employees, bureaucratic error, and hacking and identity theft by enterprising high school students or criminals. And it could create a broader if more subtle chilling effect from knowledge that government computers may be watching you and that something you read or someplace you go might form a fragment of a partial terrorist profile.

The revelation of the secret TIA effort eventually aroused enough concern that Congress passed, and President George W. Bush signed, legislation with bipartisan support to rein it in. TIA research now may not proceed unless the administration provides a report to Congress detailing the program's costs, goals, prospects for success against terrorism, and impact on civil liberties. Nor may TIA be used against United States citizens in the absence of legislation authorizing its use and appropriating money to pay for it.

But TIA-style data-banking proposals keep arising nonetheless. The Transportation Security Administration, for example, is developing a program that will create terrorist profiles, analyze databases from sources such as credit companies and criminal records to assign each airline traveler a terrorism risk level (green, yellow, or red), and encrypt those levels onto individual boarding passes. Consumer and civil liberties groups have expressed fervent opposition.

TIA was perhaps an easy target for public outcry, with its suspiciously shadowy origins and sudden unveiling, its ominous title, its pyramid-and-eye logo and "knowledge is power" motto, and its infamous figurehead. Popular attachment to notions of privacy, however, also animated opposition to the White House's proposed Operation TIPS, which would have invited postal and utility workers to report suspicious activity from local neighborhoods to the government over a hotline. Public disapproval once again caused the administration to sharply curtail the initiative, and it was officially banned by Congress in the legislation creating the Department of Homeland Security.

Trapping and Tracing, Sneaking and Peeking

More insidious and therefore more successful is the second category of expanded surveillance measures introduced since 9/11, which involve measures that lower the government's burden in establishing individualized suspicion. Here the problem is not only that indiscriminate searches may inhibit liberty generally but also that targeted searches based on less than probable cause may hit the wrong targets. Many such provisions were included in the Patriot Act, passed by Congress in barely debated political lockstep in the aftermath of the 9/11 bombings. Such measures have elicited less popular outcry than TIA or TIPS but are potentially more dangerous because they are more invisible.

The background protection of privacy in this area lies not only in the Fourth Amendment but also in a three-tiered federal statutory scheme. These protections mirror those required by the Fourth Amendment but are arguably more stringent than the amendment requires. The most restrictive tier applies to electronic eavesdropping. In this first tier, under title III of the Crime Control Act as amended by the Electronic Communications Privacy Act, in order to wiretap a telephone or bug a room a federal agent must obtain an order from a federal district court by showing probable cause that one of a specified set of federal crimes has been, is being, or is about to be committed. The agent also must show that communications concerning the offense will be obtained by the wiretap and explain with specificity which telephone lines will be tapped, what type of communications are sought and from whom, and why normal investigative methods are inadequate. A wiretap may be authorized for up to thirty days, and extensions require a renewed showing of probable cause. Agents must also comply with certain procedures to limit the amount of intrusion upon irrelevant communications, and a targeted suspect must be notified at some later point that the surveillance has occurred. Evidence that is obtained in violation of these strictures can be excluded from later court proceedings.

The second tier of federal statutory protection covers some information that is unprotected by the Fourth Amendment, including telephone company and ISP records that indicate a customer's name, address, phone number, billing records, and the types of services utilized. A federal prosecutor can obtain this information through a grand jury subpoena as long as it is relevant to an ongoing criminal investigation—a much lower threshold than probable cause. Violation of these rules is punished by civil damages, and there is no exclusionary remedy.

The third tier includes "pen register" and "trap and trace" orders. The former is an archaic name for the recording of all phone numbers dialed from a particular phone; the latter is essentially caller ID—it records all telephone numbers dialed in. A federal agent faces even less of a barrier here, in that the information sought need only be relevant to an ongoing criminal investigation. Also, a court may not inquire into the truthfulness of the facts contained in the application. Here again, there is no exclusionary remedy.

In addition to this three-tiered structure, federal statutes create a patchwork of other privacy protections covering other types of information. For example, under the Right to Financial Privacy Act, the government may access bank records by administrative subpoena or written request if relevant to a legitimate law enforcement inquiry. Under the Fair Credit Reporting Act, credit reports require a court order or grand jury subpoena. Cable records, such as information on pay-per-view movies, can be obtained only by satisfying the high standard of "clear and convincing evidence that the subject of the information is reasonably suspected of engaging in criminal activity and that the information sought would be material evidence in the case." But this web of statutes leaves significant gaps. Employers, bookstores, and other retailers are generally free to disclose personal information to federal agents, and agents need only obtain a subpoena to compel production.

Alongside this pre–USA Patriot Act regime for "ordinary" federal criminal investigations stood another separate and distinct regime regulating surveillance designed to thwart foreign intelligence efforts. The Foreign Intelligence Surveillance Act (FISA) was enacted in 1978 as a reaction both to increased fears of terrorism and to concern over the Federal Bureau of Investigation's improper surveillance of citizens such as the Reverend Martin Luther King, Jr., and Vietnam protesters based on their political beliefs. FISA, which originally covered electronic surveillance and was later expanded to physical searches, created a partition between surveillance efforts aimed at foreign intelligence and those aimed at ordinary criminal wrongdoing. (In

Chapter 3, Stephen J. Schulhofer analyzes FISA mainly from the standpoint of accountability; in Chapter 13, ACLU lawyer Ann Beeson describes her experiences litigating the Patriot Act's FISA provisions.)

The key feature of FISA is that it permits wiretaps more readily than the law that governs criminal investigations. Before the Patriot Act, a federal agent had to certify that the primary purpose of the surveillance was to obtain "foreign intelligence information"—that is, information that relates to the ability of the United States to protect itself against attacks, sabotage, terrorism, or clandestine intelligence operations by a foreign power or its agent. In addition, the agent must have probable cause to believe that the target is a "foreign power" or the agent of a foreign power and that each facility at which the surveillance will be directed is being or is about to be used by a foreign power. Crucially, FISA warrants do not require a showing of probable cause of criminal activity. Wiretap orders last up to ninety days, and agents must respect certain requirements. Notification of the target is unnecessary unless the information is used in a subsequent criminal proceeding. Applications for a FISA wiretap are made to the secret Foreign Intelligence Surveillance Court made up of certain federal judges who meet in a secure room at the Department of Justice. The FISA court has been described as the attorney general's playground, only rarely denying or modifying surveillance applications.

How did the Patriot Act alter this pre-9/11 structure? Its key surveillance provisions created greater access to e-mail routing information and expanded the use of "sneak and peek" warrants. It also supplemented FISA with greater authority to obtain consumer information, including library and bookstore records, and with authority to conduct "roving wiretaps." Most significantly, the Patriot Act lowered the barrier between the domains of criminal law enforcement and foreign counterintelligence.

The first controversial innovation in the Patriot Act extends the concept of pen registers and trap-and-trace devices from telephones to e-mail communications in both the criminal law enforcement and FISA surveillance regimes. Analogizing to phone numbers, federal agents may now obtain "to" and "from" information, including e-mail addresses, ISP addresses, port numbers, as well as other so-called noncontent information such as dialing, routing, addressing, and signaling information. They need only to satisfy the low standard of "relevant to an on-going criminal investigation," rather than the demanding standard of probable cause. But unlike phone numbers, which in themselves reveal nothing about a conversation, there is no clear separation between the to/from information in an e-mail and its content. E-mail addresses themselves can have more content than mere phone numbers, even if few would be so bold as to label themselves jihad@aol.com. And orders under the Patriot Act may now capture the addresses of websites that one visits, posing further chill to expressive activities. Finally, a court may issue an e-mail pen register or trap-and-trace order that applies nationwide and to any person or entity "whose assistance may facilitate the existence of the order." Previously, such orders were restricted to a specific jurisdiction and a particular service provider. This provision raises concerns that the government will forum-shop for lenient judges and that objections will be difficult to raise as a practical matter across long distances.

The Patriot Act also expands so-called sneak-and-peek warrants. Warrants normally may not be executed in secret. For example, the Supreme Court has required that police normally knock and announce their presence before entering a house to execute a search warrant. And although prior notice would undermine the point of wiretaps, title III requires that the execution of such wiretaps be revealed to the suspect within a reasonable time no later than ninety days after they expire. But the Patriot Act goes much farther by permitting delayed notification to those whose homes or offices have been physically searched if the issuing court has reasonable cause to believe that immediate notification of execution of the warrant will have "an adverse result." This exception is quite broad, including wherever notification would endanger life or safety, provoke flight from prosecution, or "otherwise seriously jeopardiz[e] an investigation or unduly delay a trial." Under the Patriot Act, a warrant need only provide for notice within a reasonable time after execution, but this period can be extended for good cause. So a federal agent armed with a warrant could sneak into someone's house during the day when nobody is home, rummage through bedrooms, search through computers, copy hard disk drives, photocopy documents and pictures, and, if the court finds "reasonable necessity" for the seizure, even take a floppy disk—all without notifying the targeted person until possibly months later.

A third innovation in the Patriot Act—adding roving wiretaps authority to FISA—is less surprising and troubling. Roving wiretaps allow a single wiretap order to apply to each new phone and computer that a targeted person uses. Title III already provided for such wiretaps, subject to strict requirements. In a world of mobile telephones, restricting government access to a suspect's landline is impractical. The government has claimed that terrorists are especially accustomed to switching phones and other devices to evade detection and that the time saved by roving orders can be crucial. Some critics have -

protested that roving wiretaps will allow the government to cast its net too broadly, unduly intruding on the privacy of third parties—for example, by monitoring all the public telephones in an airport and then deciding which conversations to listen in on. But if the Fourth Amendment protects "people, not places," as the Supreme Court pithily held in the 1967 decision in *United States v. Katz* (extending the warrant requirement to the electronic bugging of a phone call in a telephone booth), then a showing of probable cause to suspect a particular individual of criminal activity logically *un*protects "people, not places" too.

Most troublesome, is the Patriot Act's breach of the line between the domains of criminal law enforcement and foreign spying. Previously, if federal law enforcement officials found information concerning foreign intelligence in the course of a title III wiretap, they could share this information with the Central Intelligence Agency or the Immigration and Naturalization Service solely for law enforcement—not intelligence—purposes. The Patriot Act now allows this kind of sharing. Moreover, the Patriot Act amended FISA to permit FISA surveillance orders to issue whenever "a *significant* purpose" of the surveillance is obtaining foreign intelligence information, rather than requiring that *the* purpose or the "primary purpose" be such spy activity as had been required before. The Foreign Intelligence Surveillance Court of Review, sitting for the first time ever in November 2002, endorsed this relaxation of the crime-spy distinction, holding that as long as the government "entertains a realistic option of dealing with the agent other than through criminal prosecution, it satisfies the significant purpose test." This change gives rise to the concern Schulhofer raises in Chapter 3 that federal agents concerned with fighting ordinary criminal activity will take advantage of FISA's broad definition of "foreign intelligence information" to invoke the FISA procedures as an end-run around the more demanding title III procedures.

The blurrier the line between FISA and ordinary criminal investigations, however, the greater the doubts about FISA's constitutionality under the Fourth Amendment. Searches without probable cause to suspect criminal activity have been sustained only where they reasonably serve "special needs" apart from criminal law enforcement—such as safety inspections of factories, immigration-enforcing border patrols, or, in this case, foreign counterterrorism and counterespionage needs. But the more FISA's function merges with detection of ordinary criminal wrongdoing, the more its procedures should come under the stricter regime of the Fourth Amendment.

The so-called *tangible-things* amendment that the Patriot Act adds to FISA makes this increased spy power all the more threatening. Previously, FISA allowed federal officials to apply for a court order to gain access to only those records held by certain businesses, such as common carriers, public accommodations providers, and car rental agencies. The Patriot Act eliminates these restrictions. Federal agents may now obtain court orders requiring the production of "any tangible things, including books, records, papers, documents, and other items, for an investigation to protect against international terrorism or clandestine intelligence activities, provided that such investigation of a United States person is not conducted solely upon the basis of activities protected by the first amendment of the Constitution."

This authority contrasts sharply with that allowed government in the ordinary criminal surveillance regime outside of FISA, which always requires relevance to an ongoing criminal investigation and permits grand jury subpoenas to be challenged in court. Court orders authorized by the Patriot Act, by contrast, require on-the-spot compliance, since the reasons for the court order may not be disclosed to its recipient, and the recipient may not reveal to the person under surveillance or to anyone else that he has received a request from the FBI. Under this new power, the FBI might compel access to records from bookstores and libraries revealing the readings habits of their patrons. In response, some libraries are eliminating circulation records and Internet records more frequently and are contemplating posting signs warning patrons of the government's new power.

In sum, the Patriot Act, though it does not unleash general searches raising the same concerns as TIA and TIPS, makes individualized suspicion easier to establish and harder to protest through several key but little-noticed provisions. Many of the surveillance powers authorized by the Patriot Act are set to expire after five years, suggesting that these are temporary emergency exceptions to general privacy norms. Yet the Department of Justice, acting without public or congressional input, has recently considered proposing new legislation extending such changes without time limit. Brought to light only through a leak, the proposed Domestic Security Enhancement Act of 2003 would produce broader change than its predecessor, including:

- further expanding the government's authority to place U.S. citizens under surveillance under the authority of the secret FISA court;
- creating a new category of domestic terrorism that encompasses any violent crime and could be used to predicate surveillance that would ordinarily require authorization by Title III;

- allowing federal agents to obtain credit reports without court approval and without notification if they certify that the report will be used "in connection with their duties to enforce federal law";
- authorizing the construction of a database of genetic data from all current federal and state probationers and any "suspected terrorists," where "domestic terrorism" includes "any action that endangers human life that is a violation of any Federal or State law"; and
- creating immunities from suit against informants who wrongly report someone to the authorities.

Checking the tendency of the executive branch in these directions will require internal self-discipline or external constraint by either the federal courts or by Congress. Internal guidelines designed to restrain executive zeal were embraced by past attorneys general in the wake of FBI abuses; the Constitution may require separation of powers, but within the executive branch it is a voluntary decision to separate knowledge among the FBI, INS, and CIA. When the executive branch abandons such self-restraint, as the current administration seems so prone to do, the role of the courts and of Congress in maintaining constitutional vigilance is intensified.

Laudably, some forces in Congress have asserted a watchdog role against the danger that the war on terrorism will erode civil liberties too far. For example, Senators Charles Grassley (R–Iowa) and Patrick Leahy (D–Vermont), along with others, have proposed a bill titled the Foreign Intelligence Surveillance Reporting Act of 2003, which would require public accounting of the number of U.S. persons subject to surveillance under FISA and the extent to which FISA is used for law enforcement purposes. Challenges to Patriot Act provisions have not yet ripened into actions adjudicable in federal courts, but when they do, the courts' insulation from short-term political pressures will make them all the more important as bulwarks against eroding freedoms.

Living in a Glass House

In the third and last type of post-9/11 measure raising serious privacy concerns, the government is using new technologies to increase the ease of access to information related to a person's identity. Citizens are not normally required to take affirmative steps to facilitate government surveillance. We would surely object if the government required us to live in glass houses, carry all of our personal belongings in clear plastic bags, send our mail in glassine envelopes, and leave our houses and drawers unlocked—even if such measures made law enforcement easier. Would the same objections apply to government efforts to gather personal data in digital form on a national ID card?

National ID cards, though they sometimes draw favorable polling numbers, face considerable political difficulties. Privacy is a popular lobbying cry, and the danger of adverse impacts on minority groups creates a civil rights coalition against the idea. Nonetheless, motor vehicle offices are lobbying for substantial federal funding to facilitate the standardization of driver's license procedures, the adoption of fingerprints and other identifiers, and the linking of the databases of each state, which could create a de facto national ID card.

More politically viable efforts to direct such data collection at outsiders are more troubling. For example, the Enhanced Border Security and Visa Entry Reform Act, signed into law in May 2002, requires the government to study and define a biometric standard for ID documents for foreigners, such as green cards, student visas, and border-crossing cards. Scientists at the National Institute for Standards and Technology recently recommended a combination of facial recognition and fingerprint scanning as the federal standard. Pending further study, the INS would incorporate this technology into all documents and install appropriate document readers at all 300 border entry points within the next few years. This statute also requires the INS to integrate its databases into a single biometric-standard-system that can be shared with other agencies, such as the FBI and the Department of State. It is little known that, already, 15 million people (including 10 million American green-card holders, 5 million Mexican citizens with special border-crossing cards, and hundreds of thousands of Canadians) have been issued cards over the past five years that contain encrypted digital photos, signatures, biographical information, and fingerprints.

This law raises a number of unanswered questions. Are there restrictions on whether and how state and local governments, employers, hospitals, and other private parties may make use of the biometric ID cards? Would this lead to abuses and greater risk to privacy? Despite the federal government's efforts to undo the trend, the social security number quickly became an all-purpose identifier that facilitated private-sector data accumulation and mining. The new border and visa law also requires that certain foreign governments that qualify under the visa waiver program adopt biometric passports at a certain date in the future. Will these governments some day demand the same thing of American travelers? If so, then many citizens would possess a biometric ID document, raising new questions about a spiral of mutual government and private-sector piggybacking.

The issue of national ID cards provokes two standard reactions. On the one hand, why care about national ID cards when we already depend upon driver's licenses, passports, and credit cards? Why not take the next step by making such instantly credible identification even more standard? And might more technologically advanced IDs thwart identity thieves and other similar dangers? This view assumes that the governed have nothing to hide. On the other hand, shouldn't we fear national IDs as a kind of loaded weapon? A national database, however benignly motivated, will lie about waiting to be used or misused given the right conditions. This view conjures its own historical narrative of American history, emphasizing the colonial experience and its anathema of general searches. On the "loaded weapon" view, liberty is best protected when data, like political sovereignty, is sufficiently decentralized.

It is no answer to split the difference between these poles by drawing invidious lines between citizens and foreigners, suggesting that we apply norms of security and efficiency to outsiders but less centralization and more freedom for us. A better middle view would assess pragmatically the possible controls and accountability measures that could be incorporated into a national ID. Security and privacy might not be antagonistic values if we pursue strategies for strengthening protections of our computer databases and implementing rigorous controls backed by monitoring and accountability mechanisms. After all, the privacy of national ID card data might be guarded by an independent agency with some insulation from politics, or by judicial gatekeepers who provide limited access only upon a showing of strong necessity.

In the end, the protection of civil liberties depends not upon weak government but upon smart government. New technologies pose not merely an Orwellian menace but also the potential to enhance the accuracy of the individualized suspicion upon which the residual protection of privacy depends. The Patriot Act, however, contains too many shortcuts to such suspicion, threatening values of both liberty and equality. In the absence of self-restraint within the Department of Justice, it will be up to Congress and the courts to ensure that even during the war on terrorism law-abiding citizens retain the right to be let alone.

CHAPTER 6

Who Are "We" Now?
The Collateral Damage
to Immigration

ROBERTO SURO

O N THE MORNING OF September 5, 2001, President George W. Bush welcomed President Vincente Fox of Mexico to the White House at the beginning of a state visit, saying "the United States has no more important relationship in the world than the one we have with Mexico." In his response at the South Lawn ceremony, Fox called for a new migration accord, to be developed by the end of that year, which would "make sure that there are no Mexicans who have not entered this country legally in the United States, and that those Mexicans who have come into the country do so with proper documents."

Although the timetable struck many in Washington as overly ambitious, Fox's goal was widely embraced. Bush told reporters the next day that U.S. immigration policy should "match a willing employer with a willing employee" and that he would move forward with new proposals "as soon as possible." A joint session of Congress cheered the Mexican president when he proclaimed, "We have before us today the opportunity to dramatically change the future of our relationship." Indeed, Fox was not talking just about migration. Instead, he repeatedly described the flow of people between the United States and Mexico as part of a much larger, mutually beneficial interchange that also included goods, ideas, and capital.

For a just a little while, there seemed a chance the United States might dramatically change the orientation of its immigration policy. The prevailing patchwork of ineffective border controls, family reunification preferences, and temporary employment visas would be reforged in the context of a global economy. The movement of people across borders would be regulated as a form of economic interaction essential to growth and prosperity. What would begin with Mexico would eventually change the way the United States dealt with migrants from around the globe. All of that was a real possibility as Fox headed home at the end of the first week of September 2001.

Just about 100 hours later, these ideas and aspirations became relics of that bygone age swept away in the violence of September 11. The crimes that day were perpetrated by foreign nationals who had entered the United States from abroad, and almost immediately the need to protect the country from others who might do the same became the governing principle of immigration policies and procedures. In dozens of individual actions, the federal government took a tough law enforcement approach toward the foreign-born, viewing them with suspicion based on nationality alone. The new Department of Homeland Security was not only put in charge of the borders and ports of entry but also given control over the bureaucracies that determine who will become a citizen, which immigrants are allowed to become permanent residents, and even who gets to visit the United States as a student or tourist. Needless to say, none of the proposals to liberalize and legalize immigration from Mexico moved forward. Rather than blossoming into a dynamic partnership, the nascent friendship between Presidents Bush and Fox withered as frustration mounted in Mexico over the inaction.

What Might Have Been

The tragedy of September 11 is often depicted as a fall from grace. The analogy is particularly apt in the realm of immigration policy because the attacks came at a moment of such extraordinary and rare promise. Measuring the impact of September 11 requires not only an understanding of what has happened since then but also an appreciation of what might have been:

Bush and Fox were both starting their terms. They had quickly developed a personal affinity. Fox, the first Mexican president in seventy years elected from outside the Revolutionary Institutional Party, had a mandate to put aside old antagonisms in favor of new, more positive relations with the United States. Prior to entering politics, Bush had managed a business—a baseball team—heavily dependent on immigration for its talent. He came to the White House from the experience of governing Texas during a time when much of the state's business leadership embraced the new North American Free Trade Agreement as an investment and growth opportunity. He had aggressively courted Latino voters by promising, among other things, to seek a partnership with Mexico on migration issues.

Circumstances and leaders seemed ideally matched in that rare confluence that can make history. The U.S. economy's growth potential looked boundless, as did its ability to absorb ever-increasing numbers of immigrant workers without displacing natives. America's place in the world seemed generally secure, and for the most part Americans took a positive view of globalization and the nation's growing international interconnectedness. At home, relations among different races and ethnic groups had been relatively benign, at least in their outward manifestations. Nearly ten years had passed since the last major expression of intergroup violence, the Los Angeles riots of 1992. Finally, in Washington a consensus had developed in both political parties and among major interest groups that the time had come for major reform of immigration policies and the dysfunctional Immigration and Naturalization Service.

September 11 crushed the opportunity presented by that promising constellation of factors. The law enforcement regime adopted in the aftermath of the attacks has gradually come to influence more and more aspects of immigration policy. Undoubtedly one paradigm—the reform of immigration policies in the light of new economic realities—is dead or, at best, comatose. A new one—the antiterrorism paradigm—has emerged forcefully. What remains to be seen is whether these two ideas will ever have a chance to coexist.

Protecting the nation from potentially dangerous foreigners has been a function of the immigration system at other times of perceived threat, including the Red Scares of the 1920s and 1950s. But the national security imperative had never gained so much precedence so quickly as it has since September 11. Keeping terrorists out and tracking down those who get in could easily become defining missions for the immigration bureaucracy. That would produce a fundamental change in the purposes and character of immigration policy. However, things have not quite progressed to that point yet, at least not as of mid-2003.

Many of the new measures are ad hoc or of limited scope, and the reorganization of immigration functions into the Department of Homeland Security has only just begun. Indeed, both the system of family reunification visas, which is the largest mechanism for legal immigration, and most of the avenues for illegal entry continue to operate as before. Although the number of foreigners granted entry as immigrants has declined since September 11, many thousands continue to make their way to the United States every day. Moreover, the combination of an economic downturn and foreign terrorist attacks has yet to generate widespread expressions of anti-immigrant sentiments. No significant political leaders have tried to energize support by demonizing the foreign-born.

Indeed, there is no backlash comparable to the anti-immigrant polemics of the mid-1990s. Recall that the first World Trade Center bombing in 1993 and an economic recession combined to fuel powerful moves to restrict immigration. In 1994 California voters enacted Proposition 187, a ballot initiative that would have denied public health, education, and social services to undocumented migrants. The Republicans who took control of Congress that year proposed a variety of measures to reduce or discourage legal immigration.

In the days after September 11, President Bush, New York City Mayor Rudolph Giuliani, and other prominent leaders warned loudly against a generalized anti-immigrant backlash. Most of the voices that called for wholesale cuts in immigration in the mid-1990s limited themselves to demanding tougher screening of immigrants and other such antiterrorism measures in the aftermath of the attacks.

Much has changed in the way the United States perceives and treats immigrants since September 11, but the full character and the permanence of those changes are still to be determined. The stage of emergency actions has passed, and the initial bureaucratic realignment is in place. However, many fundamental issues have yet to be broached. Whether the legacy of September 11 for immigration is a series of measures designed to make the homeland more secure or a wholesale revision of the ways the nation relates to the foreign-born is very much in play.

A Muddled, Paradoxical Backdrop

For about a quarter-century, a remarkable balance persisted between the political and economic forces favoring open immigration policies and those favoring restriction. Both have had enough victories to produce an ever more complex muddle of pathways and barriers. The overall result has been a dramatic increase in the size of the foreign-born population, but that great demographic change has been more a result of happenstance than deliberate policies. Even as the United States experienced the largest wave of immigration since the influx from Southern and Eastern Europe at the beginning of the twentieth century, Washington repeatedly took actions to withhold its welcome from the newcomers.

The Immigration Reform and Control Act of 1986 was the most perfect expression of this paradox in the area of undocumented immigration. On the one hand, it imposed sanctions on employers who hired unauthorized immigrants; on the other, it provided an amnesty that granted legal status to more than 3 million of those unauthorized newcomers.

The Immigration Act of 1990 was a similar legislative bargain in the realm of legal immigration. To satisfy the restrictionists, the statute set new numerical limits on the number of permanent residents to be admitted each year; but to satisfy the pro-immigration forces, those limits came in the novel form of a "pierceable cap." The same kind of schizophrenic policymaking continued through the 1990s. With the building of walls and fences combined with massive increases in border patrol manpower, obstacles to illegal entry grew substantially. Yet hardly any resources went to enforcement of employer sanctions. Both family and employment immigration grew, especially during the economic boom years of the last half of the 1990s. But through welfare reform and other measures, legal immigrants lost access to a variety of safety-net programs.

Not surprisingly, this form of policymaking produced a bounty of unintended consequences. The border crackdown, for example, did indeed make crossing into the country from Mexico much more difficult—even deadly in many cases. In response, undocumented Mexican migrants did not go home as often because getting back into the United States had become more bothersome. This soon produced a dramatic change in migration patterns. For decades the undocumented flow had included both settlers and sojourners. Some came to stay, but many others would come to the United States only for a period of months, make some money, and go home, often to return again eventually. Substantial evidence, especially from the work of Douglas Massey, codirector of the Mexican Migration Project at the University of Pennsylvania, now shows that the new border controls—along with the abundance of employment opportunities—encouraged more illegal migrants to settle and fewer to sojourn. The INS estimates that the number of undocumented migrants living in the United States doubled from 3.5 million to 7 million in the 1990s and that the rate of growth actually accelerated during that decade. The unavoidable lesson is that policymakers invite the unexpected when they attempt to direct the behavior of millions of people around the globe on a matter so primal as migration. September 11 did not change that.

The 1990s produced another development in immigration policy that reflected the strength of the restrictionist forces, as well as a new, growing concern with more effective law enforcement pertaining to immigration. Through a series of a regulatory and statutory measures, the foreign-born lost several forms of judicial and constitutional protections in the name of more effective law enforcement. The long-standing concept that an alien has full constitutional protections as soon as one foot is on U.S. soil was not overturned, but some big loopholes were punched into it. Access to the civil court system was severely restricted for individuals fighting for the right to enter or remain in the country. Long-term detention became an ever more common tool not only for those suspected of some sort of misdeed but also for individuals whose immigration status was merely in doubt yet might abscond. In some cases, such as that of Haitian and Chinese boat people, detention was used to deter others from trying to reach the United States to press an asylum claim.

In addition, immigration authorities more frequently relied on secret evidence or secret proceedings to act against individuals allegedly linked to terrorist activities. These measures had various stated purposes, such as speeding up the adjudication of asylum claims or expedited removal of foreigners who had committed serious crimes here. The overall effect of the measures taken by Congress and the administration of President Bill Clinton in the 1990s was to limit judicial review of the adjudication of immigration status and to create an isolated freestanding system within the Justice Department with the power to accuse, judge, and incarcerate individuals as long as they were not U.S. citizens.

Most of what has happened since September 11 has heightened the distinction in the civil rights accorded to citizens and noncitizens while further relying on a law enforcement approach to the screening of immigrants and visitors. Although the laws that govern the number of individuals granted entry into the country remain unchanged, the rickety balance between restriction and openness has tilted forcefully in the direction of restriction on a range of procedures involving the treatment of those individuals.

Building Much Bigger Haystacks

Ten days after the September 11 attacks, Chief Immigration Judge Michael Creppy issued a memo stating that "the Attorney General has implemented additional security procedures for certain cases in the Immigration Court" that "require" all immigration judges handling such cases to "close the hearing to the public." That notification fit a pattern for what became a series of Justice Department administrative actions that curbed due process for the foreign-born in cases somehow related to what had become the war on terrorism. The notification was issued after the new rules had taken effect. Little or no explanation or rationale was offered, and there was no opportunity to challenge the action.

Around the country, federal agents picked up young men from predominately Muslim nations and detained them without pressing any charges. They were held in secret and incommunicado in prison facilities. According to a record of executive branch actions compiled by the American Immigration Lawyers Association, bond was automatically opposed with a boilerplate memo stating: "The [Federal Bureau of Investigation] is gathering and culling information that may corroborate or diminish our suspicions of the individuals who have been detained. . . . The FBI is unable to rule out the possibility that respondent is somehow linked to, or possesses knowledge of, the terrorist attacks." Despite litigation and congressional inquiries, the Justice Department kept the detainees' identities and location secret. At one point, Attorney General John Ashcroft defended his refusal to release the names of the detainees by saying, "The law properly prevents the department from creating a public blacklist of detainees that would violate their rights." The Justice Department vigorously fought off litigation and congressional inquiries that questioned whether the detentions were a gross and wholesale violation of civil rights. Eventually, the dragnet snared more than 1,000 individuals.

There was nothing new about the tactic of using the nonjudicial nature of immigration proceedings to facilitate law enforcement actions that would have been impossible with citizens, but it had never been applied in such a vast and draconian manner. The post–September 11 roundups did set a precedent of another sort, however. Repeatedly thereafter, the Justice Department aimed suspicion at broad categories of foreigners, generating an enormous workload for itself in trying to process them. The Justice Department has never offered a full accounting of the fate of the detainees. However, it appears that a handful were eventually held as material witnesses, and some more were found to be wanted for crimes unrelated to terrorism. The vast majority were held on alleged violations of their immigration status, such as overstaying a tourist visa. Dozens were held for further questioning even after their immigration cases had been resolved either with a deportation order or a voluntary departure agreement. Most of the detainees were eventually released. There are no indications that anyone caught in the autumn 2001 roundups was ever linked to the September 11 attacks or was found to possess any knowledge of them.

Throughout 2002 and thus far into 2003, the Justice Department has used its leverage over immigrants to cast wide nets in the hopes of catching a few potential terrorists. Initially, 5,000 young men recently arrived from nations where Al-Qaeda has a presence were called in for voluntary interviews. That program gradually expanded and eventually grew into a mandatory registration program for all males over the age of sixteen born in a swath of twenty-five Arab or Muslim countries from Pakistan to Libya. Altogether more than 30,000 individuals have been subject to various levels of scrutiny, including examination of their immigration status and a criminal background check with the National Crime Information Center database. This series of steps involved broadening circles of suspicion that encompassed larger numbers of immigrants. Starting with the detainees who had been individually targeted, the Justice Department quickly moved to a wholesale dragnet aimed at entire categories of people based on minimal criteria of age, gender, and country of origin.

Supporters of these programs argue that the effort is justified because of the extraordinary damage that a single individual can cause. Undoubtedly, eliminating a risk to thousands of lives more than outbalances inconveniencing thousands. In the wake of September II, no one can seriously argue that the government should spare any effort if it has a chance to preempt another such attack. However, one can question whether the interview and registration programs targeted at Arab/Muslim men are an effective means of countering terrorism. Critics contend that mass screenings simply create enormous haystacks that may or may not include the proverbial needle. In this view, mass screenings are a wasteful use of resources. Moreover, critics additionally question whether Al-Qaeda operatives and their accomplices are likely to present themselves to federal authorities for registration and questioning.

The registrations are necessary only because the government did not previously attempt to keep track of the millions of foreign visitors and immigrants who come into the country each year. Although that policy has changed, immigration authorities have not kept useful records of where the foreign-born reside or even whether they are still in the country. As a result, the authorities have no ready means of identifying individuals who failed to turn up for registration. Those who agree to be questioned can be scrutinized, but the authorities have no way of locating the scofflaws or even knowing their phone number. One has to assume, moreover, that if the FBI identified any individuals as potential terrorists, it would try to apprehend them rather than wait to see whether they show up to be registered. Finally, the initial post–September II assessments of the intelligence community's handling of the terrorist threat emphasized the failure to adequately process the available information rather than the scarcity of information. As the scope of the registration and screenings increased, so did the quantity of information that had to be processed.

Off the Beaten Track

Many of the initiatives taken since September 11 attempt to remedy the immigration system's failure to track the comings and goings of visitors and immigrants, a weakness that has been well known for more than a decade. The INS routinely reported in the 1990s that about 40 percent of the illegal alien population entered the country legally in one form or another and had simply overstayed visas. While the Clinton administration and Congress undertook an enormous buildup of border controls to block those trying to enter the country without authorization, no parallel action was aimed at these so-called overstayers. The lack of urgency stemmed at least in part from the fact that although they represent a large share of the unauthorized population, overstayers are a tiny fraction of the massive flow of visitors. The first World Trade Center bombing drew attention to the problem when investigators learned that several of the alleged plotters and accomplices had entered the country legally and overstayed. In response, Congress, in the ostentatiously named Illegal Immigration Reform and Immigrant Responsibility Act of 1996, required the INS to begin developing means to track overstayers—but set long lead times for compliance. Needless to say, no systems were in place on September 11, when the attacks suddenly made the issue an emergency matter. As with so much else, what had been just one other concern in the clunky, often haphazard process of developing immigration policies and procedures now came under the aegis of the war on terrorism.

The Entry-Exit Program mandated by Congress in 1996 is supposed to record data on all temporary foreign visitors as they arrive in the county and maintain the information in an automated system enabling immigration authorities to instantly determine whether an individual has overstayed his visa. Starting with airports, the system is supposed to be put in place at all ports of entry between 2003 and the end of 2005. In the meantime, however, the Justice Department, by administrative decree, is rushing into place the National Security Entry-Exit Registration System, which will gather detailed information on visitors "coming from certain countries or who meet a combination of intelligence-based criteria and are identified as presenting elevated national security concerns," according to a Justice Department news release.

In this case, however, the change in the substance and the tenor of immigration policy goes far beyond what has become the suspect class of Arab or Muslim nationalities. In post–September 11 legislation, Congress sped up and significantly toughened plans for the Student and Exchange Visitor Information System, which had been in place since 1996. Since January 1, 2003, for example, schools are required to notify the authorities if an individual on a student visa fails to register within thirty days of his expected arrival and must provide updated information on any changes in a student's address, course load, or field of study. Failure to meet strict reporting deadlines can jeopardize a school's certification for the enrollment of foreign students. Approximately 1 million people in a constantly changing flux will be covered by the new regulations at any one time, according to the Justice Department.

More broadly still, the Justice Department promulgated a regulation in July 2002 that requires any alien—a legal permanent resident or a visitor—to register a change of address within ten days. Ostensibly, this simply enforced a provision of immigration law that had been on the books for fifty years but that had been ignored by the authorities for so long that the proper forms for filing an address change were unavailable at most INS offices.

In addition, however, the Justice Department added what amounts to a classic Catch-22. That regulation requires every alien to acknowledge receipt of a notice that he or she is obliged to provide a valid address. Such notice can be mailed to the alien's last known address. If the alien does not respond, he or she is automatically considered guilty of a "willful" failure to comply, which can produce criminal prosecution or a deportation order issued in absentia. Of course, if the alien has moved from the last address registered with the Justice Department or is simply traveling for a time, he or she will not receive the notice. Thus, a legal immigrant of long standing could leave the country on vacation and, upon returning, find himself detained at the airport and put in secret deportation proceedings without the right to counsel, appeal, or even a phone call. Presumably, this sort of device could make it very easy to snare someone suspected of some involvement with a terrorist group. But then again, the Justice Department has already demonstrated that it considers itself authorized to detain and hold any alien on the grounds of such suspicions alone.

The United States was long overdue for a program that would identify foreign visitors who overstay or otherwise abuse their visas, and such an effort might even have proved to be an effective device for reducing the undocumented population if it were part of a broader, systemic reform of immigration policies and procedures. Overstaying visas has become an increasingly attractive means of residing in the United States because so much else in the immigration system is broken. Backlogs for many categories of family reunification visas that permit permanent legal residency have grown so long that coming to the United States as a visitor, and remaining illegally with relatives until the green card clears, has become an increasingly popular tactic. Indeed, immigration law tacitly acknowledges this practice by allowing the issuance of green cards to thousands of people every year who are already residing here illegally. Many of the Arab or Muslim men deported for violations of immigration status after getting caught up in the mass screenings were simply playing the game according to rules that the federal government has long acknowledged by way of winks and nods.

Dragnet Versus Reform

Failures in one part of the system have bred failures elsewhere in this jury-rigged contraption. The immigration system has been very successful in providing a labor force to a growing economy not satisfied with the number of foreign workers who arrive by legitimate channels. But that has been accomplished at the cost of implicitly accepting a substantial, constant, widely recognized flow outside those channels. The immigration system itself, with the full knowledge of the policymakers, has bred and even encouraged its own lack of legitimacy. After September 11, however, noncitizens who were on the wrong side of rarely enforced rules suddenly found themselves in danger of being treated like criminals.

An overhaul of the immigration system that both regulated and facilitated a flow of immigrants commensurate with the economy's appetite—connecting legal jobs with legal workers, in President Bush's construction—could resolve a host of problems, including the many forms of unauthorized migration.

Issues such as the abuse of student visas could be fixed *en passant* if the system provided an efficient, just means for a foreigner to move from study to work when an employer legitimately required her services. But as part of the war on terror, these matters are being addressed individually, in isolation, and as compliance issues without regard for the failures elsewhere that caused them.

Worse yet, from the point of view of immigration reform, the underlying intent of the new initiatives is not to improve the functioning of the immigration system but rather to make that system a more effective tool of law enforcement. That imperative is understandable at a time of national peril, yet it does not bode well even for the immediate objective of screening out potential terrorists. In order to ensnare a relatively small number of evildoers, the government is attempting to change the behavior of many hundreds of thousands of people without addressing either the proximate or the long-term causes of that behavior. Moreover, because those who abuse visitor and student visas are a small fraction of the total number who travel here on such visas, the new efforts will necessarily collect vast amounts of information on individuals who are entirely law-abiding, thus further clogging intelligence arteries. It is as if a police department decided to record the license plate numbers of every vehicle that passed through an intersection in order to identify those that run a red light.

Cops in the Consulates

Nowhere is the law enforcement imperative more apparent than in the reorganization of the INS into the Department of

Homeland Security, and nowhere does that imperative have a greater potential to have a lasting impact on the entire immigration system. Prior to September 11, a bipartisan consensus was growing in Washington that the INS was due for fundamental reform. The agency had simply proved unable to handle the rapid increase in immigration flows over the preceding twenty years. Substantial increases in manpower and funding seemed only to compound the chaos without breaking any of the logjams. In every major category of responsibility—from border controls to the naturalization of new citizens—the agency was under fire not only for failures to meet basic goals but also for the bureaucratic snafus that seemed to follow one after another. After the attacks, as details emerged about how easily the terrorists had entered the country and remained here, the INS found itself utterly defenseless, regardless of whether other agencies, such as the Central Intelligence Agency and the FBI, might have been more at fault. The last straw came when the INS mailed out visa confirmation notices to two of the hijackers six months after their suicide mission.

The restrictionists and the pro-immigration forces on Capitol Hill came together on an idea that had been kicked around since the mid-1990s: split the INS into two separate agencies within the Justice Department. One would focus on law enforcement; the other would handle visas and citizenship. Put simply, one agency would target those people who were unlawfully in the country or unlawfully trying to reach it, whereas the other would take care of those who followed the rules. The long-standing argument for this plan was that the U.S. Border Patrol, the inspectors at ports of entry, and the investigators who hunt visa violators have different organizational needs and a different bureaucratic ethos than the officials who administer citizenship tests, judge political asylum petitions, and issue residency visas.

In the post–September 11 atmosphere, the emphasis was on bolstering the law enforcement functions, especially defenses against alien terrorists. Nonetheless, pro-immigration forces saw benefits in creating an agency with a customer-service culture that might reduce visa backlogs and the other perils of processing immigration paperwork. With last-minute backing from the White House, legislation to split the INS passed the House of Representatives by a 405-9 vote on April 25, 2002.

But the reform plan took an unexpected turn when President Bush changed his position on the need for a separate Department of Homeland Security, going from opposition to eager support of a massive reorganization of the executive branch. All of the INS's law enforcement duties logically went to the new cabinet department, but so did all of the service functions as well. The restructuring met the bureaucratic imperative of splitting the two sides of the INS into separate organizations. It is much less certain whether the restructuring, which took effect on March 1, 2003, will accomplish the larger, more important goal of creating two organizations with fundamentally different characters and cultures.

The officials charged with ushering immigrants into the nation are now part of a new department with the well-defined mission of preventing terrorist attacks within the United States and coordinating the government response to attacks and other crises. Given the urgency and gravity of that task, the new department would seem to be more narrowly focused than the Justice Department and an unlikely fit for an agency that assists Americans adopting babies abroad and helps immigrants learn to be citizens. Moreover, the new department gained powers over the immigration process that previously had been the exclusive purview of the State Department's consular offices abroad.

As a structural matter, the Homeland Security Act of 2002 consolidates, deepens, and renders permanent the post–September 11 shift to a law enforcement approach to immigration policies and procedures. The legislation creates the new Bureau of Citizenship and Immigration Service, and its stated intent, echoed in administration statements, is for that agency to improve the delivery of services to immigrants, particularly by reducing the massive backlog in visa applications. What remains to be seen is how structure and intent will balance out.

At the outset, structure seems to have the advantage. Within the new department, most of the law enforcement functions performed by the INS will fall to the Directorate of Border and Transportation Security, which will be headed by an undersecretary, representing the third tier of executives just below the secretary and deputy secretary in a cabinet department. All of the agencies that handle the flow of people and goods across borders and ports of entry, including Customs and other non-INS entities, will be consolidated. That ought to increase coordination and efficiency beyond what would have been accomplished with the organization plan that applied to the INS alone.

However, that same Directorate of Border and Transportation Security, which represents the law enforcement half of the immigration equation, is also granted the role of establishing and administering rules governing the granting of visas and other forms of entry to the United States short of citizenship on permanent resident status. While the Department of State will continue to run consular offices where visas are issued and denied overseas, the Department of Homeland Security will have the authority to issue regulations governing those offices, train and evaluate consular officers, place its own personnel in any consulate, and review any visa applications. The intent is to remedy the dangerous disconnect between consular offices and the intelligence and law enforcement agencies charged with tracking foreign citizens who might pose a danger if granted a visa. But those are the few exceptions in a massive flow of people to the United States. The exclusionary function, although it has very grave consequences when it fails, is proportionately a small part of the consular function. The challenge is to perform that role while continuing to welcome the many millions of lawful visitors.

The same challenge faces the Bureau of Citizenship and Immigration Services, which will be a bureaucratic appendage reporting directly to the deputy secretary for homeland security. Its work of adjudicating petitions for permanent resident status, citizenship, political asylum, and refugee status is entirely alien to the primary functions and purposes of the cabinet department. Quite aside from managing the mission paradox, there also will be challenges to ensure that it receives the funding and leadership necessary to ensure its success.

The new Department of Homeland Security is not only creating a new bureaucracy out of bits and pieces pulled from the wreckage of the INS; it will also have to repair all those bits and pieces, which by wide consensus are not functioning properly. In regard to both visitors and immigrants, the challenge to the new department is to balance openness and national security. That is the same mission paradox that bedeviled the old bureaucratic structure, and the change in the organizational charts has done nothing to resolve it. If anything, the inherent contradiction has grown more severe, with the many post–September 11 initiatives to use violations of immigration status as a means of identifying and apprehending potential terrorists.

Ideally, the free and open flow of business travelers, tourists, students, and relatives from around the world should be viewed as an extraordinary resource, indeed a blessing and an advantage. The fact that the United States is by far the globe's most visited nation should be a point of pride. And the free flow of people should be recognized as an essential economic asset at a time when the rapid interchange of information is the key to increased productivity. Moreover, the traffic of visitors should be understood as an exceptionally effective means of recruitment for the immigration system. Immigrants should be viewed as citizens-in-training.

For the past quarter century, the nation's openness to foreign students has allowed U.S. corporations and universities to cherry-pick the world's best scientific, technical, and engineering talent, and this human capital has contributed hugely to the development of a postindustrial information-based economy. Needless to say, substantial sectors of the economy, such as the travel, hospitality, and entertainment industries, depend directly on visitors from abroad.

In a world without terror, the arrival of immigrants would be readily viewed as a positive contribution to the nation's permanent human resources. The economic imperatives so important to President Bush's view of immigration from Mexico before September 11 would take a new precedence in national policy-making. We would move on from decades of stalemate, deal-making, and bureaucratic ineptness. In that ideal world, we would hope for a clearheaded debate about the nature of immigration in our society and the development of a consensus about proper purposes, the size of the flow, and eventually the creation of policies and bureaucracies to carry out that intent.

Those possibilities still exist. As with so much else, we must decide how much we as a society need to change as a result of September 11 and the new world it presents. Changes needed to be made to the immigration system to improve our defenses. But before September 11 there were other, long overdue changes that seemed so ripe when President Fox came to Washington. As with so much else, what remains to be seen in the realm of immigration is whether we can adjust to the new threats and then get back to being the nation we were before that Tuesday morning.

CHAPTER 7

The New American Dilemma: Racial Profiling Post-9/11

CHRISTOPHER EDLEY, JR.

THE CURRENT POLITICAL CLICHÉ is that America's diversity is a source of strength. It has also been the basis upon which we turn on one another. Ask Fred Korematsu, who was the lead victim in the Supreme Court case upholding wartime internment of Japanese Americans. Ask Jim Zogby, president of the Arab American Institute. Or ask members of the nonprofit community groups in the Council on American-Islamic Relations (CAIR). In July 2002, I sat as a member of the U.S. Commission on Civil Rights, listening to presentations in Detroit by CAIR and leaders from the Muslim, Arab, and South Asian communities in the Midwest. I heard a wrenching blend of patriotism and mistrust. They spoke painfully about widespread interrogations and interviews, surveillance at mosques, innumerable immigration difficulties, lack of information on friends and relatives who had been detained, and trusted community charities that were under inves-

I thank Jocelyn Benson and Joy Freeman for their research assistance.

tigation. Most of all, they spoke of government actions that, to their minds, applied the stamp "Possible Terrorist" to whole nations and to entire American communities.

On September 10, 2001, the consensus against racial profiling in law enforcement stretched across lines of party, ideology, and ethnicity. The 2000 presidential candidates had condemned it, and many thought the debate had moved to questions of measurement and practical reform. Two days later this had all changed, along with so much else.

While it is vitally important to wrestle over the proper balance between liberty and security in efforts to manage our risks and fears, racial profiling in this time of terror is but one example of a public policy that imposes an additional risk to us: social trust fractured by dissonance and even conflict, along fault lines of racial and ethnic difference. To complicate matters, we can also see in recent developments how those racial and ethnic differences are *socially constructed* out of, or in the midst of, conflict. I am African American, and I thought Arab Americans were just another shade of white. It turns out they are minorities, too. (It's what poets and rappers have been saying: "You don't have to be black to be a nigger.")

In this sense, racial profiling is only the tip of a wedge of race-freighted issues that threaten to drive Americans apart on homeland security questions today and on who knows what tomorrow. What does it take to generate a cloud of suspicion over an individual, a community, a foreign nation? When, if ever, are color and religion proper elements in generating that suspicion? And if our diversity does indeed divide us in our perceptions of security risks and responses, what are the implications for creating the healthy civic engagement and discourse that must provide the ultimate check on the power of the state?

In this new world, many believe profiling of Arabs and Muslims is indispensable to homeland security. In the immediate aftermath of 9/11, opinion polls suggested widespread support for antiterrorism safeguards directed at Arab and Muslim Americans. Even African Americans were part of this general consensus. By a year later, divisions had emerged. For example, only 36 percent of African Americans supported racial profiling to combat terrorism, compared with 78 percent of whites. Opinion researchers have long noted that civil liberties sensibilities seem comparatively muted when the respondents do not see themselves as the likely object of the imposition.

Of course, because of the pre-9/11 consensus, every official still tries to avoid the term "racial profiling." They argue that actions taken at the border, or against nationals of and travelers from targeted countries, are distinguishable from the pre-9/11 misdeeds of rogue troopers and cops. The distinctions, however, are far from evident to those on the receiving end of heightened state scrutiny.

Yet as far as we know, all of the 9/11 conspirators were Muslim males of Middle Eastern heritage, as were all those convicted for the 1993 World Trade Center bombing. Virtually all of the known trainees at Al-Qaeda camps have been Muslim males. Thus far, everyone arrested after 9/11 on terrorism-related charges is a Muslim male, including two native-born Americans, Jose Padilla and Yaser Esam Hamdi. In contrast, individuals from all walks of life commit conventional crimes, including overstaying visas. And conventional crimes are by definition simply in a different category from acts of mass terror. Only absolutists of the purest sort, whether left or right, can fail to feel some ambivalence in all this. Shouldn't the rules be different and, if so, in what ways?

There have been several developments that illustrate the role of racial and ethnic targeting, including:

- In the fall of 2002, the Immigration and Naturalization Service adopted the Special Call-In Registration Program, whereby adult male nationals of some twenty-five countries are required to submit to being photographed, fingerprinted, and interviewed under oath. Failure to comply is a criminal and deportable offense. Annual re-registration is required, as well as notification to the Immigration and Naturalization Service of any change of address within ten days of moving. Again, any violation is a criminal and deportable offense. Every designated country is Arab or Muslim, with the single exception of North Korea.*

- Visa and border control practices have changed, so that visa applicants from suspect countries now face interviews, fingerprinting, and greatly increased delays.

- In the months immediately following 9/11, there was a program of sweeps in which thousands of Arab and Muslim Americans were interviewed or interrogated—a nuanced difference that depends largely on perspective— for no apparent reason other than nationality or religion.

---

*The Department of Justice and the INS had inadequate resources to explain the program, alert affected aliens, and handle the volume of registrations that were attempted. All of this created massive compliance problems. The political back-lash was such that on January 22, 2003, the U.S. Senate adopted by unanimous consent a bipartisan amendment to the omnibus appropriations bill to halt the program by suspending funding for its implementation. The amendment was dropped in the final legislation.

- At the Treasury Department, investigations of charities in the Muslim community seem to be a necessary element of the global program to combat the financing of terrorism. But from the perspective of many in the affected communities, these moves are assaults on cherished institutions, based on evidence and reasoning that are undisclosed or slight. Muslim-American leaders believe the sociocultural significance of these agencies is not understood by other Americans. The reports of plea agreements seem to have done little to alleviate community concerns.

- The Department of Justice, *Newsweek* reported in February 2003, directed the fifty-six field offices of the Federal Bureau of Investigation to do an inventory of local mosques to help quantify areas of vulnerability and to establish goals for counterterrorism investigations and national security wiretaps. As reported by Michael Isikoff, officials "said the move is justified given continuing concerns about undetected 'sleeper cells' and troublesome evidence that some mosques may be serving as cover for terrorist activity. 'This is not politically correct, no question about it,' said one top FBI official. 'But it would be stupid not to look at this given the number of criminal mosques that may be out there.'"

What Is Racial Profiling?

There is no settled definition of racial profiling. At one extreme, some definitions are clear but uselessly narrow:

"Racial profiling is the use of race, ethnicity, etc., as the *sole* factor." On the other extreme, some definitions simply beg the question:

> Racially-biased policing occurs when law enforcement *inappropriately* considers race or ethnicity in deciding with whom and how to intervene in an enforcement capacity.

Who could favor *that* practice? A typically incomplete definition is reflected in the following statutory language from Massachusetts:

> [Racial profiling is] the practice of *detaining* a suspect based on a broad set of criteria which casts suspicion on an entire class of people without any individualized suspicion of the particular person being stopped.

The flaw here is that profiling can impose many hardships short of detention, and we might agree with the victims that those hardships are not trivial. The General Accounting Office definition is a step better, using a phrase that seems suggestive of the Supreme Court's jurisprudence against so-called racial gerrymandering of election districts:

> [Racial profiling is] using race as a *key factor* in deciding whether to make a traffic stop.

A clunky but sound definition is incorporated in long-proposed legislation, authored principally by Representative John Conyers, Jr., of Michigan:

The practice of a law enforcement agent relying, *to any degree,* on race, ethnicity, or national origin in selecting which individuals to subject to routine investigatory activities, or in deciding upon the scope and substance of law enforcement activity following the initial routine investigatory activity, *except that* racial profiling does not include reliance on such criteria in combination with other identifying factors when the law enforcement agent is seeking to apprehend a specific suspect whose race, ethnicity, or national origin is part of the description of the suspect.

But the syntax of this—a blanket prohibition with a relaxing qualification—has been highly problematic to some in the law enforcement community.

Professor Deborah Ramirez of Northeastern University School of Law champions a virtually identical definition, embraced by the many federal, state, and local agencies with whom she has worked successfully to institute reforms:

Any police-initiated action that relies on the race, ethnicity, or national origin rather than the *behavior* of an individual *or* information that leads the police to a particular individual who has been identified as being, or having been, engaged in criminal activity.

Why Profiling Is Wrong

There are at least six reasons to be concerned. First, and this is often overlooked, is that the factual premise may be incorrect. Law enforcement officials may believe that crooks are more

likely to be black (or terrorists more likely to be Middle East-
erners), but that may simply be a misunderstanding of the realities. If, for example, there is a history of disproportionate
enforcement against blacks, then impressions and even data will
be misleading. Jails seem full of low-level drug dealers who are
primarily African American in part because police do not seem
to bother searching out or arresting comparable offenders in
white and suburban communities. Perhaps the misimpression is
fueled by prejudice or animus, not just ignorance or mistake. In
the case of terrorism, the factual issue about which we could be
mistaken is the ethnicity and nationality of those who would be
terrorists in our midst; Timothy McVeigh, Ted Kaczynski, and
a long line of white male serial killers come to mind.

Second, several researchers and analysts have criticized conventional racial profiling because it is *ineffective* relative to alternative strategies: Too many false positives mean wasted
resources and too few hits on those who actually are, for example, transporting contraband or who are active members of ur-
ban gangs. Studies in New York and New Jersey demonstrated
conclusively that racial profiling by the state police was both
widespread and ineffective: hit rates for interdiction of drugs
improved when the practice was curbed.

Third, there is what one might call "instrumental fairness."
Racial profiling is *unfair* to its victims and the victim community because the practical benefits are outweighed by the costs.
Because the practice is not as effective as less burdensome alternatives, the injuries it causes are gratuitous. Of course, this instrumental unfairness will only be apparent to those who first
come to recognize that, perhaps contrary to intuition, racial
profiling is ineffective.

These first three conceptual concerns are in fact supported by the research evidence. While that evidence relates to conventional profiling, there is good reason to believe the findings and logic are instructive when we think about combating terrorism.

And there are still three other bundles of concerns. The fourth problem is that there are serious systemic consequences for relations with the affected groups. Profiling members of a community can generate a backlash that will undermine needed cooperation, support, and legitimacy from that community and, perhaps, from sympathetic members of the broader public. This potential for community alienation appears to be a very important concern in the many police departments that have adopted active reform programs of monitoring, training, and discipline.

A fifth and related systemic problem is that the practice of profiling may lead individual officers to adopt the stereotypes so deeply that it influences judgment in other aspects of their work. A state police officer trained to be unjustifiably suspicious of black motorists may on his or her next assignment be similarly irrational in selecting investigatory targets after an armed robbery.

Finally, there is the ultimate question of justice, by which I mean something more than instrumental fairness—more than a calculation that profiling is not cost-effective or has systemic costs. That is, even in the unusual circumstance in which the arithmetic strongly points toward profiling, and even if the systemic effects are deemed negligible, we might conclude that the imposition on members of the profiled group is unacceptable. But how *should* we think about such things? How does one, for example, decide whether a progressive income tax, the military draft, or an error-prone capital punishment regime is unjust?

Evidence of Racial Profiling's Ineffectiveness

MARYLAND: A 1996 study found that, although they made up only 18 percent of motorists observed violating traffic laws, African Americans were:

- Twice as likely to have their vehicles stopped (29 percent of all stops);
- More than four times as likely to have their vehicles searched than white and Hispanic drivers (71 percent of all searches).

NEW JERSEY: A 1999 attorney general's report found that the state police of New Jersey used race as a factor in determining whether to stop a vehicle. The study also found:

- Black motorists comprised 27 percent of all motorists who were stopped;
- 53 percent of motorists subjected to vehicle searches were black;
- Of the 3,000 vehicles stopped that led to arrests, 62 percent of the motorists stopped were black.

FLORIDA: Although African Americans comprised less than 12 percent of the drivers and 15 percent of traffic offenders in the state, the 1997 study found:

- 70 percent of motorists stopped were African American or Hispanic;
- 80 percent of all cars pulled over and searched had an African-American or Hispanic motorist;
- the duration of stops for minority motorists was double the time for white motorists.

PENNSYLVANIA: In 1997, the Philadelphia Monitoring Report of the American Civil Liberties Union found:

- Minorities were disproportionately overrepresented in the number of vehicle stops;
- Minority motorists were more likely to be subject to baseless stops than white motorists.

As for the issue of racial profiling, I suggest that debate should focus on the nature of the community we create through the rules we adopt to govern our interactions. Those rules say something about whom we will regard as full members of the community rather than as denizens of some lesser caste. For example, when the U.S. Border Patrol and other law enforcement officers use Latino appearance as a reason to stop cars fifty miles inside the border in the Southwest, or to demand identification from young men in a New Orleans interstate bus terminal, one might well ask whether we want a society in which people with brown skin are required to simply accept that frequent intrusions and relentless suspicion are a "pigment tax" they must pay for the privilege of living near the border or traveling by low-cost public transportation.

The Issue Gets Harder

Let us now turn to post-9/11 profiling. Critics of classic racial profiling argue that *intelligence-driven* targeting is far more effective and fairer. We can apply this insight to the antiterrorism context. Specifically, the blunt and offensive intrusions based on ethnic profiling are instrumentally unfair because they are likely to be ineffective relative to alternatives and, perhaps, ineffective because they divert attention from more serious risks and more threatening individuals. Profiling has enormous systemic costs because it will alienate the very communities and nations from whom we may most need support and cooperation in combating terrorism at home and abroad.

Consider surveillance of mosques. Osama bin Laden, his followers, and those connected with the 1993 bombing of the

World Trade Center espouse Wahhabism, a form of Islam that is preached in a small minority of mosques and other locations. There is really no counterpart or precedent to the strength of that connection between religious teachings and virulent hostility toward modernity and, specifically, the United States. When the public or our officials cast a net of suspicion over all Muslims, it smacks of prejudice, not intelligence—and the mix of the two in our terror-fighting strategies and our private actions seems highly variable. This is the distinction that J. Edgar Hoover blurred between keeping tabs on the Black Panther Party versus the NAACP. It is one thing to seek out and monitor Wahhabis, quite another to be suspicious of almost any Muslim-American leader or social institution or to be nervous when five Arab-looking males travel together.

As for justice, there are surely some greater-good arguments that justify paying attention to race, ethnicity, and religion. Equal protection under the U.S. Constitution, for example, demands a "compelling interest," with a policy "narrowly tailored" to serve that interest. Of course, these phrases, like the crudest definitions of racial profiling, merely beg the question. They invite the deeper investigation of factual accuracy, effectiveness, instrumental fairness, and so forth, as well as deeper debate about the kind of community we are building and who will have full membership in it. That debate must take account of America's growing diversity, and those dramatic changes underscore what is at stake. With our exploding demographic diversity, including the enormous rate of growth of the Islamic population in the United States, it is not too dramatic to claim that our nation's stability in the next generation will depend on finding far better ways to deal with ethnic and religious differences. That, in turn, will require better strategies for constructing communities in which differences are celebrated rather than hardening each group's identity into an impenetrable wall of mistrust.

That mistrust is already at work in powerful ways, with political consequences. There is an argument that racial profiling is reassuring to a fearful and suspicious public because it demonstrates that those who fight terrorism are acting on the suspicions that the untutored public feels; if many travelers are afraid of the Arab-looking passenger, then they are reassured when government targets screening and other measures on that fearsome class. But if the fear is a product of ignorance, bias, or even racism, then the proper response is not to profile based on that fear but to attack the ignorance and bias from which it springs. The circumstance begs the question of whether government will cater to the worst of our popular impulses or whether leaders will assume the burdens of educating and leading citizens.

One thing should be clear in this muddle: *All* of us are put at risk if authorities cater to popular prejudice by adopting ineffective feel-good measures. And the resulting alienation in Muslim and Arab communities here and abroad is counterproductive, unfair, and unjust.

So much of the fear is, indeed, irrational. Estimates of the Muslim population in the United States range from under 1 million up to 9 million, with estimates of Arabs and Arab Americans at 1.2 million (U.S. Census Bureau) to 3 million (the Arab American Institute). There appear to be no estimates of the number of individuals with ties to the twenty-five nations targeted for special immigration procedures. By comparison, there are roughly 5–6 million Jews, about 2.5 million Chinese Americans, 2.8 million members of the Christian Coalition, 6 million PTA members, and 4.3 million members of the National Rifle Association. We have had our homegrown, corn-fed, all-American terrorists. We have not, however, labeled all members National Rifle Association as possible terrorists or potential sources of needed intelligence.

Maybe the Border Is Different

There is a principled argument that border control over goods and people is an indisputable element of sovereignty. The real question, therefore, is whether that sovereign power means that, as government makes those choices of policy, it must adhere to the same principles of rationality, fairness, and nondiscrimination that the U.S. Constitution and political ethos apply to governmental actions unrelated to border sovereignty. The Supreme Court has ruled, loosely speaking, that the constitutional guarantees of liberty are somewhat weaker in matters related to the border and immigration,* and courts have accordingly been very deferential.†

---

*See, e.g., *Landon v. Plasencia,* 459 U.S. 21, 32 (1982) (noting "this Court has long held that an alien seeking initial admission to the United States requests a privilege and has no constitutional rights regarding his application"); and *Saughnessy v. U.S. ex rel. Mezei,* 345 U.S. 206, 213, 215 (1953) (upholding the attorney general's decision to detain an immigrant attempting to enter the country indefinitely and without explanation). But see *Zadvydas v. Davis,* 533 U.S. 678 (2001) (indicating that indefinitely detaining a deportable immigrant who has already entered the country is unconstitutional).

†Most notable (and infamous) is the "Chinese exclusion" case, in which the U.S. Supreme Court upheld an act of Congress that suspended the immigration of Chinese laborers over ten years. The act also barred the return of many legal residents who had previously immigrated from China and who, upon making

However, just because the current Supreme Court's interpretation of the Constitution *permits* some depreciation of liberties in the border zone, that doesn't make erosions of liberty good policy, much less ethically admirable. Ultimately, we must make a political judgment about how government uses that constitutional flexibility.

A second argument is that immigration, customs, and antiterrorism agents at the borders pay attention to nationality, or apparent nationality, not to race per se. In ordinary circumstances, government classifications based on national origin are, like distinctions based on race or religion, subject to strict scrutiny under the Equal Protection Clause. But again, the border is a completely different matter, especially when administering immigration laws, which are by definition focused on nationality. So, the argument goes, while national origin is a suspect classification for most domestic law and policy contexts, it is perfectly appropriate at the border. Therefore, profiling based on apparent nationality is not racial profiling. No matter that nationality, for many nations, is strongly correlated with what Americans would consider to be race. And no matter that the very definition of "race" is socially determined and therefore in flux.

---

temporary visits to their homeland, were denied the right to return to the United States. *Chae Chan Ping v. U.S.*, 130 U.S. 581 (1889). More recent cases have also deferred to the executive or legislative decisions, despite potential equal protection violations. See, e.g., *Sale v. Haitian Centers Council*, 509 U.S. 155 (1993) (upholding an executive order directing the Coast Guard to intercept undocumented vessels transporting passengers from Haiti to the United States and return the passengers to Haiti without first determining if they qualify as refugees; the order did not apply to potential refugees from other countries, most notably those carrying Cuban refugees in the same water passageway).

This line of reasoning bears close examination. Would we conclude that the Chinese Exclusion Act and other waypoints in our history of hostility and discrimination toward Asian immigrants, residents, and citizens was "only" about the sovereign exercise of appropriate attention to national status rather than attention to what Americans thought of as racial difference? There are countless examples in past and current immigration policies that demonstrate the power of color and race, with all its changing meaning. Many things are different after 9/11, but not this.

Maybe Terrorism Is Different

That being said, perhaps *terrorism* is different, for two reasons: the widespread harm caused by its risks and fears, and the scale of the horror when it happens. Surely the balance of liberty and security must be different?

Of course it should. But different in what way? For example, while it is true that the potential horror exceeds that of conventional crime, that makes it all the more important that the investigation and enforcement strategies be *effective*, not merely *political and symbolic*. The small and vanishing probability that any individual Muslim, Arab, or South Asian is actually a threat or possesses useful information means it will be dangerously wasteful to blanket suspicion and resources indiscriminately over all such individuals. True, it would not be as wasteful as going after the population as a whole, but surely our policies should meet a higher standard than not being the stupidest imaginable.

If the intrusion is substantial, then the focus should be narrow. The challenge is how to prevent irrational prejudice or political posturing from infecting our judgments about whether intrusions are substantial and which group definitions are narrow. The challenge is greater because this is terrorism and because those to be burdened are, in the view of most Americans, "others" in the pejorative sense.

Another conundrum is that this otherness is reflected in the poor connections that our security and intelligence agencies seem to have had to the very communities they now seek to study and search. The corrosive use of profiling will, as with conventional policing, create a backlash that undermines the intelligence effort. In the private sphere, what is the natural human reaction a Muslim or Arab American might have to the stares and anxious whispers, day after day, year after year? Does this seem a promising strategy for knitting together our national community in the face of unprecedented expansions of diversity?

Moreover, as our foreign policy fuels mistrust and hostility in the Muslim world, what added propaganda value will America's enemies find in new immigration policies or in the official use of ethnicity and religion as grounds for suspicion? What are the consequences for the struggle against terrorism?

In the final analysis, one lesson from the Japanese internment is that wartime exigencies make "necessary evil" a ready excuse for doing what we shouldn't. We can just apologize later. But if, less cynically, we want to avoid the racist errors of the past, then we have to beware the excuses. It would be absolutely wrong to equate the bitter burden of large-scale internment with the intrusions adopted lately by the INS, the FBI, and other agencies. It is not too soon, however, to warn that the risks of terror, like the risks of war, do not excuse every security measure that might be convenient or popular.

Trust and Community

Not all post-9/11 race-related developments are bleak. Regarding hate crimes, Arab-American leaders and other observers credited the administration of George W. Bush (following Mayor Rudolph Giuliani's lead) with aggressive and effective public leadership to condemn hate crimes and related intolerance, surely reducing the potential number of incidents. Yet there is a disconnect between the rhetoric of tolerance, which condemns private bigotry and stereotypes, and the official practice of targeting these same ethnic and religious communities for antiterrorism efforts. Where is the consistency? If the FBI and INS are free to entertain blanket suspicions based on ethnicity, then why aren't private individuals and companies? Why not encourage private companies to do security checks before hiring Arab Americans or Muslims or before doing business with the nationals of those twenty-five countries included in the INS registration initiative? Why should a landlord feel obliged to be more tolerant than the INS?

The formal, legal answer is that, while the immigration and security context seems to provide some uncertain amount of constitutional latitude—too much, I fear—for unwelcome government attention to race and religion, we have civil rights statutes that include prohibitions on private discrimination based on race, ethnicity, national origin, and religion. So, for example, a hiring practice in which no Arabs or Muslims need apply would be employment discrimination in violation of title VII of the Civil Rights Act of 1964 and hundreds of comparable state and local laws. While the law is less clear, if the private security guards in a New York City office building had a comparable policy of excluding or subjecting to special scrutiny the very same groups that the INS and FBI seem eager to label, the victims would likely have plausible discrimination claims.

This highlights the comparison between public and private morality in the use of stereotypes for risk management. Evidently, there are two standards, as though we trust government to discriminate on our behalf but view it as unacceptably ugly in private practice. But *trust* in the government is an organic product of *community,* and our diverse divisions make the level of trust contingent on who you are and whether you see the government as servant or inquisitor. That, in turn, depends on your past and predicted experiences. For many minorities, the answer has always been fairly clear—and hence the long-standing concern with racial profiling. After 9/11, the answer is clear as well for those with roots in the Arab and Muslim worlds.

To be precise, it is not diversity itself that makes trust more difficult. The difficulty arises when there are hierarchical qualities to the pattern of social and political relationships constructed atop that diversity. The hierarchy means that not all groups feel equally confident of beneficence from the majoritarian government.

A great difficulty is that we in the general public have incomplete information, often necessarily so, about what the government is doing and why. We may know at the most general level (e.g., that some mosques are being watched carefully). But we don't know what factual predicate has been established by policy as the trigger for such surveillance (e.g., how much suspicion, based on what kind of evidence, and how reliable?), and we obviously don't and can't know which specific mosques are being watched. Similarly, we may have suspicions about the basis upon which travelers are subject to special attention at airports and ports of entry, but disclosure of the profiling algorithm would be a tutorial in evasion. An important consequence of this secrecy is that data to inform reasoned judgment about the effectiveness and fairness of racial profiling will not be available to independent analysts. This, in turn, undermines the prospects for restraint and reform.

For some of us, this brings to mind the Hoover-FBI's scrutiny of civil rights leaders, with its tawdry, bigoted paranoia. There were informants among church congregants and at local meetings of the NAACP and the Southern Christian Leadership Conference. That was shameful, almost all concede now. How can John Ashcroft, Robert Mueller, and Tom Ridge explain to the Muslim cleric or Pakistani American awaiting family visitors from abroad (or the rest of us, for that matter) that today's war on domestic threats is vastly different? Is it just that Attorney General Ashcroft is not like his infamous predecessor, A. Mitchell Palmer, who as Woodrow Wilson's attorney general commanded the Palmer Raids against socialist dissidents during and following World War I? Is it enough to say that Robert Mueller is no J. Edgar Hoover? To those innocents who feel themselves potential targets of the state, asserting these differences is far from persuasive. It seems, rather, that we have begun to slide down a slippery slope.

But what awaits us at the bottom of that slope? Politically attuned Asian Americans, and many others, recall that from 1942 to 1946 the United States interned more than 110,000 individuals of Japanese ancestry, including some 70,000 American citizens. Perhaps that is now unthinkable because the number of affected individuals would be overwhelming. Perhaps, more optimistically, we are enough decades past the virulent and even deadly forms of racism that infected America's decisions just two generations ago, when lynching remained a tool of white social order and Asians in many jurisdictions could neither vote nor own property. Again, this presumes much about America's character, and immigrants and minorities, aware of the history and now feeling the sting of labels, have good reason for doubts. The rest of us should not be dismissive.

The Trust Gap

So our history and our diversity contain the wellsprings of doubt and distrust that flow into many aspects of the war on terrorism. In a seminar discussion four months after the 9/11 tragedy, I asked students attending my civil rights seminar at Harvard Law School whether they thought that any of the Afghani detainees at Guantánamo Bay were being tortured by their American captors. To my surprise, all but one or two of the fifteen students thought that, yes, there was probably some torture going on. I asked why they felt that way in the face of strenuous denials by the Pentagon and White House. One woman replied, "If it can happen to a Haitian immigrant, Abner Louima, in a Brooklyn police precinct, why couldn't it happen out of public sight, at a naval base abroad, in time of war?" Subsequent access to the detainees by the media and congressional investigators proved the students wrong. Most of these students were minority, and almost all were politically left of center. They are indisputably on their way to secure positions among the elite class, yet their faith in our government was rather minimal.

The trust gap we see for the domestic war on terrorism extends to our foreign policy and military actions. For example, what should we make of the popular view in many corners of the world that the military edge of U.S. policy in Iraq and elsewhere is shaped by white Christian America's disdain for darker nonbelievers? Much of this is unmistakably noxious anti-Americanism. But can the allegation be so easily dismissed when it resonates with the concerns of patriotic ethnic and religious minorities here at home?

To some foreign audiences, the muscular Christian fundamentalism of so many U.S. political leaders speaks louder than our First Amendment. From our homeland perspective, however, anti-Islam animus seems less plausible than a more diffuse insensibility based on a combination of religious and ethnic differences. We just don't seem to *care* what those people think, or at least not very much (and we care even less about them than we do the French).

Both critiques, foreign and domestic, are informed by the same concern: Whose injuries and sensibilities count in the calculus of our leaders and our majoritarian politics? *And that is the same concern with racial profiling.* So there are complementary dangers. One is that our internal differences will lead us to antiterrorism strategies and risk management that impose differential burdens in a prejudiced, irrational manner. The other is that our aroused self-confidence will lead us to dangerous folly because we miscalculate our national security interest by discounting the injuries and concerns of those whose ethnic and cultural differences we deem beyond the pale. Terrorist behavior is by definition beyond the pale. Stereotypes then sweep in whole nations, regions, and even a great religion.

There is little cause for hope in all of this. War is always hard on liberty, even when waged under that banner. Courts are more likely to be lackeys. No more generous term is deserved when one considers the *Korematsu* case on the internment of

Japanese Americans or today's judicial complicity in the unaccountable use of military tribunals, the suspension of access to counsel upon the thinnest of allegations of security risk, and the indefinite detentions of American citizens deemed by the administration, without judicial recourse, enemy combatants.

The only hope is that, through informed civic discourse, democracy will soon retrieve the inconvenient liberties scatted in the gutter. But whose liberties are they? Democracy does not do well in safeguarding the liberties of "discrete and insular minorities," as Justice Stone famously phrased it. Thus, we have the need for constitutional equal protection and the Bill of Rights. Without the courts to enforce those in antidemocratic fashion, we are in the soup. More precisely, minorities, old and new, are in the soup.

CHAPTER 8

From Saviors to Suspects:
New Threats to
Infectious Disease Research

PATRICIA THOMAS

IN THE LATE 1870S, anthrax bacterium was one of several organisms that Louis Pasteur and Robert Koch used to demonstrate that infectious diseases—far from occurring spontaneously—spread when microbes pass from one living creature to the next. This insight—the germ theory of disease—gave rise to two of the most important developments in the history of science.

Koch turned it into his famous postulates, which biologists still use to puzzle out connections between pathogens and disease. Pasteur put the germ theory to work and, in 1881, discovered that a weak strain of *Bacillus anthracis* could immunize livestock against anthrax disease. Vaccination dramatically reduced incidence among animals and made anthrax rare in humans. More than 120 years later, it is clear that *B. anthracis* played a pivotal role in the development of antibiotics and vaccines that have saved more lives than any public health intervention except for clean water and sewage disposal systems.

In the fall of 2001, this historic organism was unleashed on Americans as a lethal terrorist weapon. The outbreak was detected in Palm Beach County, Florida, where on October 5 tabloid photo editor Robert Stevens became the nation's first anthrax fatality in more than twenty-five years. Within seven weeks, there were twenty-two cases and five deaths. Investigators eventually linked most of these to four letters mailed from the Trenton, New Jersey, area, although who sent them remains a mystery.

Several of the September 11 hijackers had lived briefly in South Florida, and in the beginning local police and agents from the Federal Bureau of Investigation thought they might be behind the attack. After no anthrax spores could be found in their apartment, there was speculation that the organism might have come from Iraq's bioweapons program. Within weeks, however, genetic analysis showed that the attack strain was American: a form of *B. anthracis* widely used by U.S. government laboratories and universities.

Although experts disagreed about the resources and skill needed to generate the super-light spores sent through the mail, investigators were convinced that the perpetrator was an American scientist. FBI agents fanned out to interrogate university professors and researchers who typically see themselves as the good guys in humanity's battle against disease. One scientist, Steven J. Hatfill, had his life upended in the fall of 2002 when the U.S. Postal Service and the FBI searched his apartment while reporters milled outside. Hatfill, who had once worked in a military biodefense lab, was never arrested or charged.

All this led some biologists to "have the sense of being a suspect instead of a savior," said Ronald Atlas, president of the American Society for Microbiology (ASM) and dean of the graduate school at the University of Louisville. "It used to be that when you said you were a microbiologist, people would say you were doing great things to find new cures for disease. Now, when you say you're a microbiologist, people look at you and worry whether you could be doing something wrong."

Under a Microscope

In popular culture, images of scientists range from the saintly Dr. Schweitzer to the evil genius of Dr. Frankenstein. Judging by the responses of George W. Bush's administration to recommendations from scientific experts, the White House view tilts toward the mad scientist end of the spectrum. When elite scientific panels endorsed stem-cell research and nonreproductive cloning as keys to biomedical progress, for example, the administration aligned itself with conservative religious opponents of those technologies. Despite ample evidence that condoms reduce the risk of HIV transmission and a dearth of proof that abortion leads to breast cancer, the administration insisted in each case that the opposite was true. Given that religious ideology has repeatedly trumped scientific consensus, the administration's recent excursions into life-science research should come as no surprise.

Suspicions about biologists are woven into the broad legislative agenda that the administration began developing before the ruins of the World Trade Center stopped smoking. Starting with the USA Patriot Act, Congress has passed a series of laws imposing restrictions on academic researchers studying organisms with weapons potential. Although national security is the rationale for these unprecedented incursions into university and medical school laboratories, many experts believe that these new rules will have the paradoxical effect of slowing research needed to fend off or combat future biological attacks.

The stakes for the public are high. When the government imposes tight controls on nuclear weapons research "you may lose some defense capability, but you're not losing lives," Atlas said. In fact, slowing the development of nuclear weapons could clearly save lives. "But if biomedical research slows, and public health is weakened, then people die," he said. Humanity clearly will not benefit from policies that slow development of treatments and vaccines against global killers such as AIDS, malaria, and tuberculosis—yet this is the research community currently under siege.

Post–September 11 laws, regulations, and directives affecting infectious disease research fall into three broad categories:

- Intense government scrutiny of research on an expanded list of "select agents"—organisms, toxins, or delivery systems that can be used for peaceful purposes or as weapons.
- Exclusion of certain international researchers from select-agents research and mandatory background checks for U.S. researchers to ensure that they are not what the Patriot Act defines as "restricted persons."
- Creation of a "sensitive but unclassified" or "sensitive homeland security information" designation as a rationale for blocking publication of certain research findings generated by government-supported research on open campuses.

At the same time, biodefense research is being stimulated by huge spending increases that will lure hundreds, perhaps thousands, of new scientists into the field. Nowhere is the increase more dramatic than at the National Institute of Allergy and Infectious Diseases, where the budget for bioterrorism projects has soared from $52.8 million to $1.7 billion in only two years. Although part of this huge increase will be used to build special biodefense laboratories, there are plenty of new grants and contracts to go around.

Academic researchers don't know whether to be thrilled at the flood of new research money or deeply disturbed because the government views their organisms as potential weapons, their graduate students as possible spies, and their scientific publications as potential recipes for bioterrorism. But one thing is clear: In a situation this dynamic and politically charged, the scientific community cannot afford to sit back and do nothing.

So far, scientists have successfully used their own institutions, such as the National Academy of Sciences (NAS) and the American Society for Microbiology (ASM), to set limits on their professional behavior before Attorney General John Ashcroft does it for them. Universities are scrambling to comply with new demands and restrictions, solve visa problems for international scholars, install expensive security systems for labs, and negotiate contracts with federal funding agencies that won't trample academic freedom. What follows is a portrait of life-science research for now, after September 11 and the 2001 anthrax attacks, and before bioterrorism strikes a second time.

The Microbes

Microbiologist Theresa M. Koehler, an associate professor of microbiology and molecular genetics at the University of Texas

Medical School at Houston, has been studying *B. anthracis* for twenty years. Since 1997, she has been registered with the Centers for Disease Control and Prevention (CDC) as a researcher who sometimes exchanges samples of the anthrax bacterium with colleagues at other institutions. Before September 11, federal law required registration only for scientists who sent or received infectious agents or biological toxins on the CDC's select-agents list; the government wasn't interested in organisms that stayed put. Nor were researchers obliged to explain why they possessed these materials or to report quantities on hand. The law trusted scientists to make judgments about their own lab practices.

The Patriot Act, signed into law on October 26, 2001, expanded the list of select agents and imposed new controls on scientists who use them. Leading the roster are the so-called Category A agents that cause smallpox, anthrax, plague, tularemia, botulism, and viral hemorrhagic fevers (such as Ebola). A total of sixty-four pathogens that infect humans, animals, both humans and animals, or plants are on the list, which the CDC and the U.S. Department of Agriculture can expand at any time.

No one knows better than microbiologists that viruses and bacteria can be dangerous, which is why they take elaborate precautions to prevent infection or accidental release. The government's idea that some organisms or methods for delivering them can be singled out as "bad," however, signals a shallow understanding of biology. At the University of North Carolina–Chapel Hill, researcher Nancy Davis works on experimental vaccines to prevent HIV, influenza, and other medically important diseases. "You could say that vaccines are always a good thing, absolutely always. But if you have a vaccine that no one else has, and you vaccinate all of your troops against the virus, then that virus becomes a bioweapon. So even vaccines can be a tool for biowarfare," observes Davis, a research associate professor of microbiology and immunology. "Everything is double-edged and is guided by the ethics and morality of the people who have it. Things in themselves are not good or evil."

The Patriot Act requires labs that handle select agents to register with the government, even if they never ship or receive organisms. The new law also demands that scientists document peaceful research purposes for the types and quantities of select agents they have on hand. (In the past, it was enough to declare that the lab was not making bioweapons, which were, of course, prohibited.) The legislation also imposed new restrictions on who is allowed access to certain materials. Scientists who don't comply with these new requirements face penalties that include large fines and imprisonment for up to ten years.

This law, drafted hastily by Attorney General Ashcroft in the aftermath of September 11, was poorly thought out in many regards. One thing the law does *not* do is delegate responsibility for enforcing the new select-agent provisions. The Public Health Security and Bioterrorism Preparedness and Response Act of 2002 put the Department of Health and Human Services (the parent agency of CDC) and the U.S. Department of Agriculture in charge of formulating and enforcing regulations. The new rules set a series of milestones for 2003: Researchers and university administrators had until March to inventory select agents and justify their use, until April to complete background checks on everyone with access to these materials, and until September to make labs physically secure so that unauthorized people did not have access. November was set as the deadline for full compliance with all new rules and regulations.

"The new administrative burden is massive," said anthrax expert Philip C. Hanna, an assistant professor of microbiology and immunology at the University of Michigan Medical School in Ann Arbor. "We're citizens, too. And right now it's hard to say that new rules and steps and oversight and inventories and cross-reference materials aren't important. We're doing our best to comply and still stay in business, and we're going to do that. But it's taken away from other duties."

Complaints about increased red tape and paperwork are universal among scientists who work with select agents. At the University of North Carolina, Nancy Davis and lab chief Robert Johnston use weakened forms of Venezuelan equine encephalitis (VEE) as delivery systems for vaccines against infections including HIV, hemorrhagic fevers, and VEE itself. VEE has been on the CDC's list of select agents since 1997, and these two Chapel Hill researchers have long been registered to ship and receive it. Johnston and Davis have also worked extensively with the Department of Defense and with corporations, as well as with the National Institutes of Health (NIH), and are accustomed to accepting money with strings attached.

"We've always had regulations to follow, but the consequence of a bookkeeping error was losing NIH funding, not going to jail," said Johnston, a professor of microbiology and immunology. He says that the select-agent regulations make him "uneasy" but aren't onerous enough "to prevent me from doing the work." Other scientists, however, may decide that it isn't worth the hassle.

Johnston and Davis are bracing themselves for additional restraints on life-sciences research, perhaps as part of the proposed Domestic Security Enhancement Act of 2003 (Patriot

II). "We don't know how much they're going to try and regulate us, and we don't want to spend 80 percent of our time filling out forms and reports and meeting with inspectors," Davis said. As restrictions pile on, scientists may stop asking certain questions or performing certain experiments. Or their universities may pressure them not to work on certain organisms or diseases.

Already the relationship between scientists and their institutions is being tested by new biosecurity requirements. At the University of Michigan, Hanna says that costly modifications needed to make his anthrax lab secure—as well as biologically safe—"have been hard on my institution." Renovations have also been needed at Koehler's anthrax lab in Texas, where upgrades include a motion-sensitive camera in the isolation room where virulent strains of *B. anthracis* are handled.

Some argue that infectious disease researchers should not complain about laws that essentially align their responsibilities with those of other professions. While tighter select agent and biosecurity rules present a "new form of research oversight" for life scientists, there is no significant difference between these demands and "other accepted measures already in place to regulate the use of radioisotopes and human research subjects," presidential science adviser John H. Marburger III told a congressional hearing in October 2002. In an interview several months later, he predicted that biologists would adjust to the new rules: "Pharmacists who handle potentially addictive drugs have this kind of responsibility, and so do people who handle radioactive materials. [The new regulations] add legal weight to a code of ethics that biological scientists have lived with for years."

The People

There is a good reason why the typical life-science laboratory looks like a Model UN meeting. "Infectious disease is a global fight," says ASM president Ronald Atlas, "therefore we have a particularly international community." Today, 25 percent of ASM members are microbiologists in other countries, many of them trained in U.S. laboratories. Koehler's lab in Texas is typical: Her postdoctoral fellows come from the United States, China, Nigeria, Cypress, France, Germany, Belgium, and Canada.

"They're all great scientists," said Koehler, who worries that applications from top international candidates will soon decline. "I want the best for my lab," she said, and "the fact is, we don't have a large enough pool of Americans qualified to enter Ph.D. programs or continue their research as postdoctoral fellows." Scientists and administrators at other institutions also anticipate empty lab benches in their medical schools and biology departments. This is sure to happen if the rest of the world comes to see Bush's America as a realm that foreign-born professionals enter at their own risk.

There is nothing new about the government's desire to control the flow of American know-how to other countries. During the Cold War, for example, key military and weapons-related research was classified, security clearances were needed to work on these projects, and results were not published. As a further precaution, Soviet scientists were banned from scientific conferences where unclassified but "sensitive" topics might be mentioned.

Visa denial is the classic means for shutting out potential spies and terrorists. After the 1993 bombing of the World Trade

Center, investigators found that one of the perpetrators had entered the United States on a student visa and overstayed after he dropped out of school. Congress swiftly passed laws regulating which students should be allowed into the country, what they would be allowed to study, and how they would be monitored while here.

First came a 1994 amendment to the Immigration and Naturalization Act authorizing the Technology Alert List of sixteen topics that are off-limits to students from "state sponsors of terrorism" (Cuba, Libya, Iran, Iraq, North Korea, Sudan, and Syria). Applicants from those countries are automatically refused student visas, while applicants from certain nuclear powers (China, India, Israel, Pakistan, and Russia) who want to study in these fields are evaluated on a case-by-case basis.

Then, in 1996 Congress voted to create the Student Exchange Visa Information System (SEVIS), a national database into which universities would feed current addresses and educational activities of foreign students and which the Immigration and Naturalization Service would use to monitor compliance with visa restrictions. Universities balked at becoming unpaid record keepers for the INS and opposed SEVIS as a costly intrusion into students' lives. Opposition to this sort of monitoring became politically untenable for educational institutions when the press reported that several of the September 11 hijackers had been granted student visas. The Patriot Act authorized $36.8 million to implement SEVIS and directed 74,000 universities, community colleges, and technical schools to input data for nearly 600,000 international students by January 31, 2003.

Days after President Bush signed the Patriot Act, he also ordered a cabinet-level review of the entire student visa system, with the goal of blocking access not only to subjects on the

Technology Alert List but also to an ill-defined array of sensitive areas. The president appeared to be taking an important step by commissioning this overall assessment of the system. No report has been released, however, and every day nervous officials in U.S. consulates around the world must decide how to handle visa applications filed by students, researchers, and professors.

"Consular officers can only get in trouble for saying 'yes.' They will never get in trouble for saying 'no,'" observed Victor Johnson, associate executive director for public policy at the Association of International Educators. To gauge the impact of post–September 11 visa changes, his organization polled 77 colleges and universities in October 2002. Although undergraduate enrollment levels for foreign students had remained steady since fall 2001, the survey showed an 8 percent drop in international graduate students, postdoctoral fellows, and other scholars. Institutions enumerated 200 cases where scholars expected for the 2002–2003 academic year had been held up by visa delays or denials.

Consular officials are funneling more visa requests to the State Department, where they sometimes disappear for long periods after the FBI or Central Intelligence Agency becomes involved, says Wendy White, director of NAS's Board on International Scientific Organizations. Her office intervenes when NAS members ask for help because their international collaborators, usually senior scientists, are stuck in the system. Although there are "tens, not hundreds" of these cases each year, White said, "we have heard of research programs brought to their knees when key researchers went home for the holidays or for a family funeral and could not get back in." This is dramatically different from the post–World War II era, when the U.S. government rolled out the red carpet for German rocket scientists whose expertise was needed for the space race against the Soviets.

Although universities are concerned about professors and senior investigators, visas for young scholars are a more pressing issue for most campuses. Not even elite institutions like the Massachusetts Institute of Technology can fill their graduate and postdoctoral programs with U.S. citizens. "High-quality American students go immediately into business before they become grad students or post-docs, directly after a bachelor's or master's degree," according to Institute Professor Sheila E. Widnall, who is also a professor of aeronautics and astronautics.

"International students play a big role in providing very, very skilled personnel to American industry and universities," Widnall said in an interview. Since September 11, however, some top candidates have been lured to more hospitable countries. "I know that MIT faculty members have lost graduate students to France, Britain, and Germany—other places where the level of scientific technology is very good," said Widnall, who was secretary of the Air Force during Bill Clinton's administration. In the long run, "I think this is bad for American competitiveness," she said. Ironically, many of the European lab chiefs who are now snapping up talent from around the world were themselves trained in U.S. laboratories.

MIT's high regard for its international researchers became obvious in November 2002, when the *Chronicle of Higher Education* reported that the university had turned down a $1 million Department of Defense contract rather than agree to limit participation by foreign researchers. This project involved "sensitive but unclassified" work, and MIT was not willing to shut out qualified grad students or post-docs who had been born in the wrong place.

The story reached mainstream audiences in January 2003 when the Associated Press reported that MIT had also turned down a $404,000 contract from the National Security Agency for similar reasons. Widnall was initially surprised that MIT's decisions made the news, but she says the coverage is good because "now it stands publicly as an example of the kinds of concerns that the university community is expressing."

It is not uncommon for universities to reject grants and contracts with unacceptable provisions, according to Robert Killoren, president of the National Council of University Research Administrators. The principles of academic freedom dictate that when unclassified research is conducted on an open campus, qualified graduate students can't be excluded for reasons such as sex, race, or national origin. When private companies or federal agencies push for contract language that conflicts with these principles, universities often walk away. Pennsylvania State University, where Killoren is assistant vice president for research, recently turned down a major physical science contract that would have forced the university to subdivide a large laboratory so that foreign graduate students working in the same space could not see what was going on.

The Patriot Act also imposed unprecedented controls on U.S.-born researchers who work with select agents. Of the eight classes of "restricted persons" listed in the legislation, only two apply to foreigners: illegal aliens, and people from countries regarded as state sponsors of terrorism. The remaining six restrict access by U.S. citizens, and some make more sense than others. Few would quarrel with the notion that a "fugitive from justice" or someone "adjudicated as a mental defective" should be kept away from organisms that cause plague and anthrax. But the law also excludes people convicted of any crime carrying a sentence of one year or more, unlawful users of controlled substances, and anyone with a dishonorable military discharge. Given that many of today's full professors came of age during the 1960s, universities could be forced to disqualify researchers who were once busted for smoking marijuana, arrested during antiwar demonstrations, or discharged from the military for being gay.

The Public Health Security and Bioterrorism Preparedness and Response Act of 2002 gave universities until April 12, 2003, to submit the names of all select-agent researchers to the Department of Justice for background checks. Preliminary checking began in September 2002, when campuses were told to find out if "restricted persons" had access to select agents. In an era when employers cannot ask job applicants how old they are or whether they are married, universities were forced to interrogate lab workers about matters that most Americans regard as private.

Many senior scientists, driven by patriotic feelings, volunteered for background checks immediately after the anthrax attacks. Some biologists, like their colleagues in physics and engineering, have federal security clearances that enable them to advise the government about classified research. No boss wants to hire a potential terrorist, and lab chiefs are no exception. But they don't want their relationships with employees undermined by nosy questionnaires.

When the University of North Carolina set out to comply with the Patriot Act, "I thought I was going to lose half my lab, not because they are criminals but because they objected to having that done, as an invasion of their privacy," said Robert Johnston, the vaccine researcher. "I had one friend who said, 'Boy, I wouldn't pass that. I got arrested because I bit a cop during a street demonstration.'" Others were concerned about long-past traffic offenses, some of which carry sentences of one year even if the sentence was suspended. Once the university ascertained that traffic offenses did not have to be reported, people were less anxious about filling out the forms.

Although Steven Hatfill became a household name when he was suspected of being the anthrax bioterrorist, and although he lost his job and his reputation and was hounded by reporters when he ventured outside his apartment, he was never charged with any crime or taken to court. The first scientist charged with violating the Patriot Act's select-agent provisions was Tomas Foral, a little-known graduate student at the University of Connecticut.

A Czech-born U.S. citizen working on the West Nile virus, Foral's troubles started when he moved some thirty-year-old anthrax samples from a broken freezer to the one where his own research specimens were stored. An anonymous tipster saw the anthrax samples in Foral's freezer and, instead of talking to him directly, reported the discovery to the FBI in November 2001. This looked highly suspicious, given that an elderly woman had just died of anthrax in a nearby town, and the FBI was in Connecticut to investigate.

"I am convinced that the student had no ill intent and thought he was doing what we teach all grad students to do: keep specimens," Foral's dean told the *Los Angeles Times* when the case was finally resolved in August 2002. The Justice Department agreed not to prosecute Foral in exchange for community service and some restrictions on his activities.

In January 2003, a researcher in Texas was arrested for making false statements to the FBI about plague samples he had destroyed without authorization. As the Patriot Act and other laws that place national security above civil liberties take hold, more scientists will surely be arrested or banned from laboratories. And if there is a second bioterrorist attack, the dossiers that universities have built on their own researchers, now centralized in a Department of Justice database, may well be the first place the FBI looks for suspects.

The Information

U.S. taxpayers are the world's most generous benefactors of science. The fruits of publicly supported research are routinely published, debated at conferences, and turned into commercial products. President Ronald Reagan articulated the nation's commitment to open exchange of scientific ideas in 1985, when he issued National Security Decision Directive 189:

> It is the policy of this Administration that, to the maximum extent possible, the products of fundamental research remain unrestricted. It is also the policy of this Administration that, where the national security requires control, the mechanism for control of information generated during federally-funded fundamental research in science, technology and engineering at colleges, universities and laboratories is classification.

University faculty and staff who conduct classified research must have security clearances. They work in secure, off-campus laboratories, where graduate students are not involved, and their results are not published without the sponsor's approval. These restrictions are agreed upon before the work begins. For the past thirty-some years, since the U.S. abandoned biological and chemical weapons research, nearly all classified projects have involved electronics, radar, physics, and other areas with clear military and security significance.

In late 2001, when the nation entered a new kind of war, policymakers wondered whether the traditional mechanism of classification would suffice. They worried that the results of some unclassified research would be sensitive, for instance, if findings inadvertently provided tips for fashioning weapons of mass destruction or otherwise threatening homeland security. Not only that, but the anthrax attacks demonstrated that terrorists might be as interested in life-science research as in physics or engineering.

"Biology is the wave of the future. What physics was early in the Cold War, the life sciences are poised to become in the twenty-first century," observed Steven Aftergood, a government secrecy expert for the Federation of American Scientists. Regulating life-science research is a formidable challenge for at least two reasons. First, there is the dual-use problem: The same basic discoveries that help drug designers develop new treatments for a disease may also enable wrongdoers to engineer an outbreak. Second, postgenome biology is a sprawling and diverse enterprise that expresses most of its findings in maddening jargon. Researchers communicate among themselves via hundreds of specialized scientific journals, many of them comprehensible only to others mining the same vein of knowledge. This is not an easy world for government regulators to navigate.

When people in Washington began flipping through some of these arcane journals, which were not usually on their bedside tables, what did they see? Some noticed an article about how to build a better mousepox virus—a close relative of smallpox—in the February 2001 issue of the *Journal of Virology*. Others saw the full genome of the plague bacterium, in press at *Nature* magazine when planes smashed into the World Trade Center and the Pentagon and published a month later. When White House officials became aware of articles like these, they summoned leading biologists, including ASM officers, to discuss the dangers of life-science journals as "cookbooks" for terrorists.

Once this specter had been raised, the scientific community had to act or risk being seen as unpatriotic and arrogant. The leaders of the ASM, which publishes eleven peer-reviewed journals, immediately launched a system for flagging manuscripts "perceived to be sensitive," in the words of Samuel Kaplan, head of the organization's publications board and professor and chairman of microbiology and molecular biology at the University of Texas Medical School in Houston.

Standard practice is to send each manuscript to several peer reviewers—experts on the article's topic drawn from the journal's editorial board or from a large pool of volunteers—who decide if it merits publication. Since December 2001, ASM reviewers have been asked to notify the editor who sent them the manuscript if they think it "raises any eyebrows" about national security, Kaplan said. In addition, any paper about select-agent research is vetted carefully by the journal's editor and by Kaplan "to see if that manuscript has any information that might be considered sensitive."

Scientific reviewers get no tips from intelligence agencies about what the enemy needs to know; nor is there an official definition of "sensitive" information. This leaves them in the same position as judges who must decide what a specific community considers pornographic. "Reviewers say 'If I see it, I'll know it,'" Kaplan said.

"The bioscience community is in the best position to make judgments about what things might be important for terrorists," said John Marburger, President Bush's science adviser and director of the Office of Science and Technology Policy. If authors and reviewers are in doubt about a specific article, they should ask themselves if they would like to see it "in a cave in Afghanistan with passages highlighted in yellow."

There is a precedent for the ASM's approach: During the years leading up to World War II, physicists experimenting with nuclear fission voluntarily stopped reporting their results in scientific journals rather than risk helping Germany build a nuclear bomb. After the United States entered the war, the National Academy of Sciences persuaded 237 scientific journals to withhold publication of anything that might relate to national defense. (At the same time, vital information was privately circulated among scientists working on key projects.)

On February 17, 2002, two months after the ASM's editorial guidelines went into effect, the *New York Times* reported that the government had removed from websites and stopped selling to the public more than 6,000 reports and documents, some dealing with biological weapons research. Some of these documents had never been classified, and others had been declassified decades earlier, suggesting that while the barn might look tidier with the door closed, the cows were long gone.

Along the same lines, a March 19, 2002, memorandum from White House Chief of Staff Andrew Card advised heads of federal departments and agencies that in addition to safeguarding information about weapons of mass destruction, they should now seek to control unclassified information that may be sensitive because it is "related to America's homeland security." Bureaucrats who received this memo, so close to the cosmic one-two punch of September 11 and anthrax bioterrorism, no doubt erred on the side of caution when deciding what should be locked away.

Although the Card memo did not attract much attention outside the Beltway, an article in the July 11 issue of *Science* made headlines everywhere. Eckard Wimmer and his colleagues at the State University of New York–Stony Brook used previously published sequence data to synthesize a poliovirus from scratch. The Department of Defense paid for the project, which Wimmer said demonstrated that terrorists with no access to whole organisms could still manufacture bioweapons—a revelation that to him underlined the need for better biodefense strategies. Although some virologists said the paper was unremarkable and revealed nothing new, that response was shouted down by scientists, ethicists, and policymakers who denounced the experiment as "irresponsible" or "a stunt" and said the world would be better off if *Science* had never published the article.

The Wimmer paper got so much media coverage that once again it became imperative for scientists and government officials to act. Ronald Atlas of ASM promptly asked the NAS to sponsor a high-level policy discussion about managing information that terrorists or rogue nations might use to make biological weapons. Atlas was troubled because several authors had asked ASM journals to publish their articles without detailed "methods" sections, presumably because they didn't want the wrong people repeating their experiments. But this was a radical proposal in a world where progress depends on replicating what someone else has done, satisfying yourself that it is true, and taking the work another step forward. The NAS agreed that biology faced intellectual and political dilemmas, and it scheduled an early 2003 conference on national security and the life sciences. Involvement of the prestigious, well-known NAS reassured the public that the scientific community was doing its best to keep America safe.

The 107th Congress responded to the poliovirus article by passing a resolution decrying publication of research findings with weapons potential and urging publishers and editors not to let this happen again. Congress also scheduled hearings on two of the big issues roiling biology: sensitive information, and restrictions on foreign students and researchers. Atlas, Marburger, and MIT's Widnall were among the witnesses who testified before the House Committee on Science on October 10, 2002. The term "sensitive but unclassified" was uttered so often that it had acquired new gravitas by day's end.

Committee members also became quite familiar with another coinage, "sensitive homeland security information (SHSI)," which Marburger characterized as a new name for information that had always been closely guarded, such as law enforcement data. He said the Office of Management and Budget (OMB) was working on guidelines for how SHSI should be handled by government agencies and those who receive it, including local law enforcement and public health authorities.

Shortly after the hearings, the president of the NAS, along with the heads of three associated scientific institutes, affirmed the scientific community's commitment to national security but lambasted "sensitive but unclassified" as a vague term that "generate[s] deep uncertainties among both scientists and officials responsible for enforcing regulations. The inevitable effect is to stifle scientific creativity and to weaken national security." The statement urged the Bush administration to swear fealty to the Reagan-era principle of using classification as the sole means

for imposing secrecy while placing no restrictions on unclassified research.

Before the OMB could issue guidelines for SHSI, Congress
passed the Homeland Security Act in November 2002. Section
892 defines SHSI as information related to the threat, prevention, interdiction, disruption, or response to terrorist activity, or
information that would help identify or investigate terrorists.
The act also created an agency within the Department of
Homeland Security that will fund research projects at universities and companies. OMB has to take all this into account
when writing new regulations and, presumably, will clarify
whether some projects sponsored by the new cabinet-level department will be labeled "sensitive but unclassified." At press
time, an OMB official said the main focus was on crafting restrictions that apply to government information, not extramural
research.

The NAS did not stand idle and, on January 9, 2003, held its
long-awaited workshop on national security and life-sciences
research in Washington. In his speech, Marburger endorsed
classification as the central means for controlling information
and emphasized that this designation is agreed upon before
projects get underway. "Only in rare and exceptional circumstances should it be necessary to invoke additional controls after
the award," he said.

The following day, editors and publishers of leading life-
science journals met with government officials, scientist-
authors, and security experts to devise a policy for handling
information that might be useful to enemies of the United
States. The new policy, endorsed by the editors of thirty-two
U.S. scientific journals, was announced during the annual meet-

ing of the American Association for the Advancement of Science (AAAS) in February.

"We recognize that on occasion an editor may conclude that the potential harm of publication outweighs the potential societal benefits. Under such circumstances, the paper should be modified, or not be published," the editors said. Only time will tell how often this policy will be invoked. At the AAAS meeting, Samuel Kaplan reported that ASM reviewers had flagged only two of 14,000 manuscripts submitted during the past year. Both were modified and then published. "Nothing was censored—it was really a matter of emphasis in the presentation of material," Kaplan said in an interview.

Anthrax researcher Theresa Koehler, who wrote one of the two papers, is satisfied with how the situation was resolved. For years she has made judgments about which results can be published without reservation, which require prepublication review because funding came from military or intelligence sources, and which results she would never submit to a journal. If she were using *B. anthracis* genes to turn a relatively harmless bacterium into a virulent killer, for example, professional ethics would keep her from attempting to publish it.

Ultimately, Marburger believes that "the biggest impact of all this discussion will be an elevation of consciousness about bioterrorism, and an acceptance of responsibility, within the scientific community." Consciousness-raising and self-regulation is fine for now, but if there is another bioterrorism attack researchers can expect the hammer to fall on academic freedom and scientific publishing. Although Marburger is a physicist who is highly regarded by scientists, he is not thought to have much influence on President Bush. In a time of crisis, the fate of scientific openness will be in the hands of Attorney General Ashcroft and other members of Bush's inner circle.

The Money

For the moment, speculation that post–September 11 regulations will drive people away from infectious disease research seems unfounded. Instead of an exodus from the field, new investigators are being drawn to the government's bioterrorism bonanza. The mother lode is at the National Institute of Allergy and Infectious Diseases (NIAID), where a $1.7 billion appropriation for bioterrorism research lifted NIAID's total FY 2003 research budget to $3.7 billion, a huge 47 percent increase over the previous year. If Congress goes along with the president's FY 2004 request, NIAID's war chest will grow by another 17 percent, to $4.3 billion. In contrast, the projected increase is 2 percent to 6 percent for other institutes within NIH.

The biodefense windfall is broadening the horizons of researchers like Eric Rubin, an assistant professor of immunology and infectious diseases at the Harvard School of Public Health. He has joined a team from Harvard, Brandeis University, and a private company that proposes to carry out molecular studies of *Francisella tularensis*. This organism causes tularemia and is considered a Category A select agent because it has great weapons potential. This is the first time that Rubin, an infectious disease physician whose basic science research focuses on tuberculosis, has ventured anywhere near biodefense work. Yet tuberculosis and tularemia share some infection strategies, and a better understanding of these mechanisms could yield benefits for medicine and national defense, said Rubin.

When Congress throws money at a problem, however, not all of it rains down on the most fertile soil. NIAID will allocate much of the new money through contracts for specific projects, which are not as hotly contested as traditional applications initiated by individual investigators. The latter are rated by peer reviewers, and across all of NIH approximately the top 30 percent will be funded for FY 2004. At NIAID, however, an estimated 39 percent of applicants are expected to succeed. "In terms of knowledge per dollar, it's not going to be as efficient as when it is extremely competitive and you can only fund the *crème de la crème*," Koehler said.

Robert Johnston, the North Carolina vaccine researcher, sees a dark side to the government's sudden largesse. "Pumping all this money into biodefense is going to create thousands of trained people who know how to handle these agents and how to manipulate them genetically. The law of averages say there will be some kooks in the group," he said. "Investing all this money to protect ourselves could actually end up making us less secure."

A more optimistic view is that biodefense spending will pay off in unforeseen ways. The war on cancer, for example, was a huge funding initiative that did not cure cancer but gave rise to molecular biology and spawned the biotechnology industry. Major investments in HIV/AIDS revolutionized scientific understanding of the human immune system, benefiting patients with diseases as seemingly different as arthritis and cancer.

Koehler is left pondering the role played by *B. anthracis*—the pivotal model for pioneers like Pasteur and Koch, the focus of her own career, and the organism that made Americans feel vulnerable in an entirely new way. "We're putting all this money in for one reason, and that's fear. In nature, these diseases are non-issues, yet we're going to great lengths to come up with better vaccines and therapeutics and basic knowledge. AIDS is a problem. Anthrax right now is not a problem. But it could be, and that's why there's all this money."

Although money is necessary for the advancement of science, it is not sufficient. In addition to having adequate resources, investigators must be free to ask and answer questions of their own choosing and to disseminate their results so that other scientists can reproduce or repudiate them. This is the process that has given us thousands of medical miracles over the past century, and it remains the best hope for blunting the killing power of diseases such as AIDS, malaria, and tuberculosis. Despite its tremendous momentum, this great engine of discovery could be stilled if life-science researchers are demonized in the wake of a future bioterrorist attack. If politicians turn into villagers with torches, heading off to find Frankenstein's monster, people around the world will pay the price.

CHAPTER 9

Need to Know:
Governing in Secret

JOHN PODESTA

IN LATE JANUARY 2003, U.S. spy satellites photographed North Korean trucks pulling up to the Yong-
byon Nuclear Complex to begin the process of removing
nuclear fuel rods from its storage tanks. The fuel rods, which
had been safely stored pursuant to a 1994 agreement between
the United States and North Korea, contain enough plutonium
to make five to six nuclear weapons. In the hands of terrorists,
the plutonium, once reprocessed, would constitute the makings
for a series of devastating dirty bombs. The photographs sig-
naled a dramatic escalation of the crisis brewing over the North
Korean nuclear weapons program.

The administration of President George W. Bush reacted to
this new evidence of North Korea's dangerous intentions with a
strategy that has come to characterize its approach to governing: Keep it secret; cover up the evidence.

This was not a case of the intelligence community protecting
its sources and methods of intelligence-gathering at all costs.
The administration was certainly not trying to keep the North

Koreans in the dark about our capacity to monitor these activities. The North Koreans were operating completely out in the open, with absolutely no deception, well aware of the U.S. ability to see exactly what was going on. Indeed, the North Koreans were virtually waving at the cameras.

It was not the North Koreans who were being kept in the dark; it was the American people and their representatives in Congress. While top administration officials deny that they were suppressing intelligence for political reasons, it seems clear, as more candid officials have admitted on background, that the administration was slow to confront the North Koreans publicly for fear that an escalating crisis on the Korean Peninsula would interfere with its public relations offensive against Saddam Hussein.

The administration's embrace of secrecy, so vividly demonstrated by its handling of the Korean episode, has been evident since shortly after the inauguration and increased exponentially after September 11. In addition to the new Department of Homeland Security, three other *domestic* agencies—the Department of Health and Human Services, the Environmental Protection Agency, and the U.S. Department of Agriculture—have been given unprecedented power to classify their own documents as "secret, in the interests of national security." The Justice Department, formerly charged with defending the public's right to know, has become a veritable black hole when it comes to the release of government information. Neither the House nor Senate Judiciary Committee has been able to get essential information about how the Justice Department's sweeping new law enforcement authorities under the USA Patriot Act have been implemented—despite the fact that all the members of these two committees have security clearances. The House committee chairman, Representative James Sensenbrenner, a Republican, had to threaten to subpoena Attorney General John Ashcroft before the Justice Department would answer even the most basic questions on the use of Patriot Act authorities.

In October of 2001, Ashcroft also radically changed the Justice Department's interpretation of the Freedom of Information Act (FOIA). He urged all government agencies to withhold documents if there was any possible legal reason to keep them secret. He told those who reject FOIA requests to "rest assured"—the Justice Department would defend their decisions unless they "lacked a sound legal basis." In so doing, the attorney general reversed the fundamental principle behind FOIA: the presumption of disclosure.

Moreover, the Justice Department also steadfastly refuses to release the names of the hundreds of Muslim men that it detained after September 11. In a recent ruling, Judge Gladys Kessler of the U.S. District Court for the District of Columbia called the secret detentions "odious to a democratic society" and "profoundly antithetical to the bedrock values that characterize a free and open one such as ours." She found that withholding the names of those imprisoned was not permitted under the Freedom of Information Act and ordered their release. The order has been stayed pending appeal.

The focus on secrecy clearly has the blessing of the White House. On March 20, 2002, Andrew Card, my successor as chief of staff to the president, issued a memo that ordered an immediate reexamination of all public documents posted on the Internet. The memo encouraged agencies to consider removing "sensitive but unclassified information." Six thousand public documents have already been removed from government websites. The number of decisions to make a document, video, or audio recording classified, already up 18 percent under the Bush Administration before September 11, continues to grow rapidly.

The breadth and the scope of the redaction of government information is astounding:

- The National Imagery and Mapping Agency has stopped selling large-scale digital maps;
- The Federal Aviation Administration has removed data from its website on enforcement actions against air carriers;
- The Bureau of Transportation Statistics has removed transportation spatial mapping data from its website;
- The Department of Transportation has removed pipeline-mapping information from its website;
- The Agency for Toxic Substances and Disease Registry has dropped its report on chemical site security;
- The Nuclear Regulatory Commission's website was completely down for six months and now has extremely limited information;
- Public access to the envirofacts database posted by the Environmental Protection Agency has been severely limited;
- The EPA Risk Management Plans, which provide important information about the dangers of chemical accidents, including emergency response plans, were removed even after the Federal Bureau of Investigation admitted there was no unique terrorist threat;
- The Department of Energy website for national transportation of radioactive materials was taken down;
- Federal Depository Libraries have been asked to destroy CD-ROMs of U.S. geological water supplies;

- Even access to the Internal Revenue Service reading room has been restricted in the name of national security.

While the administration has been grappling with how to apply the new and slippery concept of "sensitive but unclassified" to their own records, it has pressured the scientific community into applying it to peer-reviewed scientific research. At a January 2003 meeting, convened by the National Academy of Sciences (NAS), administration officials warned that if the scientific journals did not voluntarily censor articles that could compromise national security, the government would likely step in to mandate censorship. Subsequently, the NAS made a pact, drafted with the help of administration officials, to censor articles that could compromise national security. Censorship decisions will not take into consideration the scientific merit of the article. While most scientists recognize the need to have better controls on feedstocks that can be converted to bioweapons, many believe that the new policy may deter research and prevent the dissemination of information that could lead to new defenses against a biological attack such as immunization and quarantine strategies. The administration, however, has more faith in silence than knowledge to protect Americans against a terrorist attack.

The extent of the current administration's preoccupation with secrecy has even bled into the unprecedented effort, directed by President Bill Clinton, to declassify historically valuable records from World War II, the early days of the Cold War, and Vietnam. That initiative, which led to nearly 1 billion pages of formerly classified records being made available to scholars and historians—has nearly ground to a halt despite no conceivable connection to the terrorist threat.

"The Ultimate Regulation"

George W. Bush is certainly not the first president to use secrecy and the control of government information as a weapon to mold public attitudes in support of administration policy. Modern history is replete with examples—from the Cold War to Vietnam to Iran-Contra—of presidents of both parties who sought to avoid public oversight of controversial policies by keeping accurate information from the public. But President Bush's efforts have been unprecedented in promoting policies that expand government secrecy at almost every level, restricting public access to vital health and safety information, and removing publicly generated information from the public domain. Indeed, this president's policies reverse important trends of the last four decades toward more openness in government. Often couched in terms of a necessary national security reaction to September 11, the administration's advocacy of more secrecy in government well predates those tragic events.

It is entirely appropriate and necessary for our country to reexamine the balance among the rights of individuals, the values we cherish as an American community, and the need to secure our nation from the threat of transnational terrorism. But President Bush's embrace of this new culture of secrecy will not only leave our democratic institutions weaker; it may leave the country less secure in the long run.

Of course, there are secrets worth protecting. It is beyond dispute that some information must be closely held to protect national security and to engage in effective diplomacy. Often our interest in protecting the method by which information was obtained is even greater than our interest in protecting its content. For example, when disclosures of classified information mention telephone intercepts, other nations often take heed and find more secure ways to communicate. It is also beyond dispute that unauthorized disclosures can be extraordinarily harmful to U.S. national security interests and that far too many such disclosures occur. They damage our intelligence relationships abroad, compromise intelligence-gathering, jeopardize lives, and increase the threat of terrorism.

Today, we are confronted with an enemy that operates in the shadows—an enemy that will not only tolerate but also actively seek out civilian casualties. These are people hell-bent on acquiring weapons of mass destruction and putting them to use. The operational requirements of a global war against terrorism only enhance the government's legitimate needs to mount actions with complete secrecy. Whether it is arresting suspected terrorists in Naples, Italy, or firing a Hellfire missile from an unmanned Predator at Al-Qaeda leader Abu Ali in Yemen, the ability to mount clandestine operations is essential.

But what's troubling about this administration's approach to secrecy is its conversion of the legitimate desire for operational security into an excuse for sweeping policies that deny public access to information and public understanding of policymaking. President Bush was right when he said in his 2002 State of the Union address that "America is no longer protected by vast oceans. We are protected from attack only by vigorous action abroad and increased vigilance at home." But openness does not destroy security; it is often the key to it. The American people cannot remain vigilant if they remain ignorant. To be sure, some critical defense and security information must be kept from public view, but strengthening homeland security requires public knowledge of potential threats and the public will to take corrective action to deal with unacceptable risks.

Let's recognize secrecy for what it is: Secrecy is government regulation. It is the way the government regulates the flow of information to its citizenry. The tighter one controls information, the more stringent and complex the regulations must be. The late Daniel Patrick Moynihan, a former Democratic U.S. senator from New York, once said that secrecy is the ultimate form of regulation because the people don't even know they are being regulated.

The Risks of Secrecy

One has to ask whether it was genuine security concerns or the pleas of the business lobbyists that led the administration to insist upon a new secrecy provision buried in the recently enacted legislation creating the Department of Homeland Security. That change effectively guts the Freedom of Information Act with respect to vital public health, safety, and environmental information submitted by businesses to the federal government. FOIA *already* prohibited the disclosure of information that could threaten national security. But this new provision prohibits the disclosure of any information that in any way relates to the protection of "critical infrastructure" that private industry labels "sensitive" and chooses to disclose to the government. Not only does the public lose its right to know anything about hazards that could affect their community; now the government is under an affirmative obligation to keep this information secret. The exemption provides a convenient way for businesses to conceal even routine safety hazards and environmental releases that violate permit limits from public disclosure. Shielded from public scrutiny, these hazards are much less likely to be addressed.

Senate negotiators had worked out a compromise, one that was more narrowly tailored to encourage businesses to enhance security protection for critical infrastructure without upending community right-to-know laws. But that compromise was rejected by the administration. The enacted new provision will expose Americans unknowingly to more dangers than they might otherwise have faced.

Similar concerns arise from the administration's approach to dealing with the serious homeland security threat posed by the storage of dangerous toxic chemicals. Industrial manufacturing facilities storing acutely toxic chemicals such as chlorine gas, ammonia, and cyanide present a potentially enormous and devastating opportunity for terrorists. The EPA has estimated that at least 123 plants store toxic chemicals that, if released through explosion, mishap, or terrorist attack, could result in deadly toxic vapor plumes that would put more than 1 million people at risk. The U.S. Army Medical Department's worst-case estimate for a terrorist attack on a chemical plant is that it would lead to about 2.5 million deaths.

While there are more than 75,000 chemicals in commerce and some 20,000 industrial manufacturing facilities storing industrial chemicals across the country, only a small number of chemicals—probably less than two dozen—would be of keen interest to terrorists because they explode into large lethal plumes that kill or maim on contact. It is thus possible to sharply reduce threats in the chemical industry by focusing on a small number of the worst chemicals and a small number of the most dangerous plants. Furthermore, very practical steps are available at these priority facilities to minimize or eliminate them as terrorist targets. The facilities can substitute less toxic alternatives for their most acutely hazardous ingredients; they can convert to "just-in-time" manufacturing, whereby the most highly toxic molecules are synthesized immediately before use rather than synthesized separately and stored in bulk reserve; and they can reduce storage volumes of the most acutely toxic chemicals.

When originally assessing the threat terrorism posed to the chemical manufacturing industry, the administration, led by the EPA and Tom Ridge, who was then the assistant to the president for homeland security at the White House, embraced a strategy of risk reduction. They planned to inspect the worst facilities to ensure that practical and necessary steps to reduce unnecessary risk and to ensure public safety had been undertaken. But after receiving intense pressure from the chemical industry, the administration backed down, settling for voluntary efforts by the industry to strengthen site security by building stronger fences and adding guard dogs—measures that do nothing to eliminate the target or reduce the risk of catastrophic accident. Because EPA is not even requiring that companies report to the government the steps they have voluntarily taken at their facilities, the government lacks needed information about the extent to which this very dangerous class of terrorist targets has been minimized. And thanks to the new secrecy provisions, people living immediately adjacent to these potential targets know less than ever about what is going on behind the chain-link fences. Therefore, local citizens who might be affected the most are less able or likely to demand corrective action.

Now the Department of Justice has floated a new draft of terrorism legislation, dubbed the Patriot Act II. One might have hoped the new proposals would contain the kind of clear regulatory authority sought by the EPA administrator, Christine Whitman, and Secretary of Homeland Security Tom Ridge to reduce the threat posed by these industrial facilities.

Instead, the bill contains a provision that would further restrict public access to existing chemical company reports, which have been mandated by the Clean Air Act, describing the worst-case scenarios that would result from chemical spills, industrial accidents, or explosions.

Showing Stripes, Pre-9/11

Although the administration justifies this broad expansion of government secrecy as a response to new security threats, the administration's preference for secrecy predates September 11 and runs toward areas that have never before been viewed as matters of critical national security. For example, it has removed information from government websites regarding the use of condoms to prevent HIV/AIDS, the fact that abortions do not increase the risk of breast cancer, Labor Department statistics on mass layoffs, and budget information showing state-by-state cuts in federal programs. Withdrawing access to such materials seems to have more to do with satisfying the Republican base or avoiding embarrassment than denying national security secrets to Osama bin Laden.

In the same vein, shortly after his inauguration, President Bush ordered a review of current policy regarding the disclosure of presidential records. He later signed an executive order allowing any current or future president to block the release of *any* presidential record, an order he then used to block the release of documents from Ronald Reagan's administration that were potentially embarrassing to members of the current administration. That executive order violated the spirit, if not the letter, of a 1978 law that affirms that presidential records belong to the public and requires that they be released within twelve years after a president leaves office—subject to narrow exceptions, including national security. The law was passed in response to Richard Nixon's claim that he *personally* owned all his presidential records.

For his part, Vice President Dick Cheney spent nearly a year and a half blocking the efforts of Congress and the Government Accounting Office to acquire information about his energy task force, including the names of energy company lobbyists who attended task force meetings and how much these sessions cost the government. A U.S. district court judge, appointed by President George W. Bush, rejected a lawsuit filed by Comptroller General David Walker against Vice President Cheney seeking the names of the lobbyists. There has been little doubt since the early days of this administration: It does not highly value the principle of an informed public.

Drawing Lines

Before September 11, the administration's predilections toward secrecy had aroused a reasonable degree of scrutiny in the media, best exemplified by the front-page reporting about the vice president's efforts to conceal details about his energy task force. But the post-9/11 environment has given the administration cover to act far more aggressively upon those predilections with virtual impunity. Seizing on that opportunity, the government is concealing important actions with only the most convoluted connections to the war against terrorism. The nation is sure to pay a steep price—as it has so often in the past when its citizens have been unjustifiably kept in the dark.

Taken together, the secrecy initiatives of the Bush administration take us back to an era we had all but forgotten: the advent of the Cold War. Duct tape and plastic sheeting may have replaced fallout shelters, but re-creating a massive bureaucracy to control government information is all too familiar. It can lead to an invidious, paranoid culture of secrecy today, just as it did in the 1950s. By deeming everything under the sun a secret, President George W. Bush has affected our ability to distinguish what's *really* a secret from what's not. This infects the entire system of security classification with ambiguity and weakens the argument for nondisclosure. Perhaps more important, a default to secrecy denies the public the vital information we need to strengthen security here at home. And that is the paradox: The penchant for secrecy undermines our security.

Are we more secure trying to conceal the fact that any one of 123 chemical plants around the country could endanger a million or more people if attacked? Or are we better off informing the public so that they can demand that the risk of terrorist incidents or catastrophic accidents be reduced at those plants?

Similarly, are we more secure by trying to conceal that U.S. customs inspectors are only able to examine 1–2 percent of the shipping containers entering the United States? Or are we better off informing the public so that they can demand that the inspection process be improved by identifying vulnerable loading docks and tracking the movement and condition of each container from the point of origin to its arriving destination?

Are we more secure trying to conceal the Department of Energy's plan to ship high-level nuclear waste within a mile of the congressional office buildings? Or are we better off letting the public know so that they can demand new routes or storage solutions that don't put the Capitol at risk?

We need to find a different approach to these issues that better reflects our fundamental values and our commitment to informed public discourse and debate.

In formulating that approach it would be wise to start with three questions:

Does the information fall within a class that should presumptively be kept secret? Operational plans, troop movements, human source identities, technological methods of surveillance, and advanced weapons designs must continue to command the highest level of protection. But even in those categories there can be circumstances where public disclosure is appropriate and warranted—a classic example being Secretary of State Colin Powell's UN Security Council briefing of declassified intelligence on Iraq's weapons of mass destruction program.

Does the information's important public value outweigh any risk of harm from public disclosure? For example, in the Clinton administration, the White House worked with EPA and the FBI on a disclosure regime of information in EPA's toxic release inventory, including emergency evacuation plans. The public was able to receive important public safety information that the FBI had concluded was of no unique value to terrorists. Likewise, under the leadership of Vice President Al Gore, the overhead imageries dating back to the 1960s from the CORONA, ARGON, and LANYARD intelligence satellite missions were declassified. Disclosing the capabilities of our oldest spy-satellite systems caused no harm to our security while the information proved to be of great value to scholars as well as to the natural resources and environmental communities.

Does release of the information educate the public about security vulnerabilities that, if known, can be corrected by individuals or public action? Justice Louis Brandeis said that sunlight is the best of disinfectants. By that he meant that without openness people would lose trust in their government and government would lose its ability to do its work. But you can take another meaning out of Brandeis's statement: Security flaws in our nation, just like security flaws in our computer software, are best put in the sunlight—exposed, patched, and corrected.

Openness not only enhances important democratic values; it is also an engine of technological and economic growth. America has been a world leader in technology for more than a century for one main reason: Information flows more freely within this country than anywhere else in the world. Scientists and researchers share their results freely and benefit from a highly developed peer-review system.

The need for technological advancement has never been greater. The problems of terrorism are so complex that many of the solutions lie in technologies not yet developed or even imagined. Public knowledge, public scrutiny, and the free exchange of scientific information may not only provide the breakthroughs necessary to stay ahead of our adversaries but also offer a better long-term national security paradigm. As the NAS president, Bruce Alberts, noted, "Some of the planning being proposed [on restrictions of scientific publications] could severely hamper the U.S. research enterprise and decrease national security." And while we certainly need better controls on the distribution of materials and technologies that can be used to create weapons of mass destruction, we need to resist reestablishing the Cold War culture of secrecy across many sciences and disciplines. A new culture of secrecy is bound to influence the direction of discovery, the efficient advancement of scientific knowledge, and our ability to fully understand the costs that come from a science program unchecked by public scrutiny.

September 11 seared into our consciousness the realization that there are strong forces in the world that reject the trends bringing our world together: modernity, openness, and the values we cherish as Americans. But in addressing the problems of international terrorism and homeland security, it is paramount that we remember what we're fighting for. We're fighting for the survival of an open society—a country where people are free to criticize their government, where government is truly an extension of the people. We cannot protect this society by abandoning the principles upon which it was founded.

When we relinquish our role as a beacon of government transparency, we derail our own mission to create a more secure, democratic world. Ultimately, stability can be achieved only through open institutions, where citizens are involved, not excluded from the governing process. This is particularly true in developing nations where terrorists are most likely to find safe harbor. The only way for any government to earn the trust of its people is by conducting its work in the light of day; by exposing itself to scrutiny and criticism; and eventually by finding a system that citizens will accept and respect.

Finding the right balance between confidentiality and an informed public opinion is certainly more difficult than a policy of absolute secrecy or one of unconditional disclosure. But that's the challenge our nation has struggled with for generations, and it's one we will all face in the future. At this critical moment in our history, we owe it to ourselves and our posterity to strike this balance and protect our tradition of liberty.

President Dwight D. Eisenhower, a great military leader,

made the argument succinctly: "Only an alert and knowledgeable citizenry can compel the proper meshing of the huge industrial and military machinery of defense with our peaceful methods and goals, so that security and liberty may prosper together."

CHAPTER 10

Watchdogs on a Leash:
Closing Doors on the Media

JOHN F. STACKS

This administration is more closed-mouthed,
more closed-doored than any in memory.
—Michael Duffy,
Washington bureau chief, *Time* magazine

IN THE AFTERMATH of the terrorist attacks on the United States, the national government has been cloaking more and more of its actions in official secrecy: secret immigration hearings, secret court proceedings, secret detentions, secret wars. Government officials have been prosecuted for sharing "sensitive" but not classified information with the press. Guidelines for abiding by the Freedom of Information Act (FOIA) have been tightened so as to virtually gut the intent of the law. Even presidential papers from prior administrations, which of course belong to the nation, are now sealed unless the sitting and former president agree to their use by historians. The list goes on. The spectacular acts of terrorism on September 11,

2001, have succeeded in keeping the American public from knowing very much about what its government is doing or planning to do, or why.

While there is no doubt some tactical necessity for protecting more of the government's information in a time of terrorist threat, there is also an undeniable need for the public to fully trust and understand its government in such a sensitive time.

The growing uses of official secrecy are well documented and discussed in other chapters of this book. But there is another pernicious and damaging kind of secrecy being practiced by the administration of George W. Bush. Officials in Washington have largely stopped talking to the press except in set-piece briefings. Interviews are refused. Phone inquiries are left unanswered. The public is thus being denied access to the workings of the government it elected. While there are televised briefings, and plenty of photo opportunities, real discussion and real access are denied. The Bush administration has perfected the technique of flooding the cable news operations with enough sound bites and pictures to fill the air with its own message. But it is refusing access to the more thoughtful, long-form journalists who might penetrate beneath the polished message the administration wants delivered. "The sources who really talk with anything resembling honesty are few and far between," says one Washington bureau chief.

A standard tool in drying up the flow of information to the public has always been the practice of stamping government paperwork "secret." After years of attempting to reduce the amount of government material that is classified, and to declassify the mountains of historical documents in the hands of the government, both trends have reversed, according to a paper by former *Los Angeles Times* Washington bureau chief Jack Nelson.

In a paper prepared for the Joan Shorenstein Center on the Press, Politics, and Public Policy at the Kennedy School of Government at Harvard, Nelson reports that in the fiscal year 2001 the total number of classification actions in the government amounted to more than 33,000, an increase of 44 percent over the previous year.

Meanwhile, cabinet officers like Defense Secretary Donald Rumsfeld are calling for jail terms for leakers, and the Federal Bureau of Investigation is investigating members of Congress for allegedly leaking. And as usual, the government is using leaks for its own purposes. As the campaign to gather support for the war in Iraq progressed, the Pentagon repeatedly leaked rough outlines of its war plans as a way of demonstrating its determination to oust Saddam Hussein. The double standard was also in evidence over the handling of periodic taped messages from Osama bin Laden. Shortly after the attacks of September 11, 2001, National Security Advisor Condoleezza Rice convinced the heads of the network news divisions and the cable news channels to sharply censor a videotape of the Al-Qaeda leader. But in another context, as the effort to sell the world on an invasion of Iraq intensified in 2003, the administration made no effort to restrict the broadcast of an audiotape thought to be from bin Laden, urging his followers to avenge an attack on Iraq. The idea was to show the link between bin Laden and Saddam. Fox News, helpfully, broadcast the tape in its entirety.

At the same time, the Bush administration, leveraging national fears about terrorism, reversed existing policy on surrendering documents under the Freedom of Information Act. In a memorandum from White House chief of staff Andrew Card, agencies and departments were instructed to include "sensitive information" in the same category as information affecting national security in rejecting FOIA requests.

Averted Eyes

There was a time, not so long ago, when Washington officials believed it was their duty to talk to the press and thereby to talk to the country. A hardworking reporter in the capital could get an interview, if not this minute, then soon enough to make deadline, if not today, then maybe tomorrow. Officials were selective, of course, calling back first the reporters for the wire services and the big dailies or the three networks, later the newsmagazines with longer deadlines, and then, if time allowed, answering the questions of reporters for smaller news organizations. Reporters for the large news organizations would routinely have background discussions, often in the offices of the top policymakers and from time to time over informal lunches and dinners.

This discourse with the press was regarded not only as part of the job of governing; it was also seen to be in the self-interest of the official and of the government itself. Stories and scripts were being written, and the officials wanted to have their own input, to guide the story toward their point of view, or to steer it against an opponent's position. And if advancing an argument was not sufficient reason to talk with the press, personal ambition was. Press secretaries to the powerful figures in the government saw their primary job as getting their principals' names and faces into the news.

Today the doors of the government in Washington are being slammed in the reporters' faces. The job of the press secretary is now to shut out the press and to keep the bosses' names out of the news. The Bush administration is not interested in communicating with the press except through official spokespersons well versed in the message of the day. Survival in the Bush administration requires, in the words of one veteran Washington correspondent, "keeping your head down and your mouth shut." Press-accessible and unprogrammable officials are quickly sacked. As one Washington bureau chief put it: "This administration's belief in news management is absolutely evangelical." Seymour Hersh, who produced for *The New Yorker* the one piece of unconventional reporting about the special operations missions inside Afghanistan, is one of the most persistent reporters now working in Washington. He has been there for decades and has a vast number of sources. During a panel discussion sponsored by the Libel Defense Resource Center, Hersh said that he felt cut off from the real workings of the administration. "This is scary," he said, "I have never had less of a pulse [of what's going on in government]."

Of course, every administration in history has tried to manage the news by preventing leaks and by trying to orchestrate its message. Some have succeeded more than others. But it is obvious from reading and watching the press, and from the accounts of Washington reporters, that the current administration has become the grand champion of closed government. And what is perhaps even more troubling, the public—full of distrust of the press and the fear of terrorism—is not complaining. More ominously still, journalists themselves have said almost nothing about their inability to cover the Bush administration. So why is this government so closed to the press? Because this government has found it can get away with it.

Every bureau chief has his or her own stories about access

denied. In one case, one large news organization was preparing a major piece on Defense Secretary Rumsfeld. A request to interview the secretary was made to the public affairs office at the Pentagon. The answer was "No." What if we ran the text of the interview, rather than just selected quotes in the story, the bureau chief countered? "Well," said the Pentagon, "only if you run the entire interview verbatim, no cuts, no editing, no trimming for space." How about we run the unedited text on our website and an edited version in print? "No" again. "Thanks anyway," said the bureau chief. Even routine Pentagon coverage has become more difficult. Only regularly accredited Pentagon reporters are permitted to move about the building without an escort; other correspondents who do not cover the Defense Department regularly can enter only with an escort.

Not that it makes much difference to be able to roam freely. One top defense correspondent reports that officers he has known and talked to for years will avert their eyes when they are encountered in the hall, to avoid even the suspicion of being close to someone from the press. One bureau chief recounted the story of a reporter having to interview a department source in the men's room, hoping there would be sufficient privacy so that the source's cooperation would go unnoticed.

Rumsfeld and the top military spokesmen totally controlled the information about the conduct of U.S. forces in Afghanistan and in so doing left out major pieces of information, none of which was in any way damaging to the image of our fighting forces. Thomas E. Ricks, the defense correspondent for the *Washington Post*, noted to Ted Gup, writing for the *Columbia Journalism Review* in the fall of 2002, that Rumsfeld and the other briefers failed to mention the first stationing of U.S. troops in a part of the former Soviet Union, the first firing of a missile from an unmanned aircraft, and the first significant fielding of Central Intelligence Agency paramilitary forces since Vietnam.

In the Department of Justice, all press interviews are conducted with a minder from the press office in attendance, a practice that was once regarded as completely out of bounds and unacceptable by the press. In the twenty years I covered Washington, including the White House, I don't recall more than one or two instances in which press-office people sat in on an interview, including those with the president himself. There is no practice that is more chilling to a free flow of information. The last time I conducted an interview with a minder present was in 1998—in Baghdad.

In another case, *Time* magazine was preparing its annual *Person of the Year* cover. Typically, the magazine prepares two or three pieces and continues to debate the virtues of each choice and to weigh the reporting coming in. Although villains like Joseph Stalin and Ayatollah Khomeini were chosen in the days before the magazine became hypersensitive to its advertisers, *Person of the Year* has in later years become a happy choice, an honorific. In 2002, Vice President Dick Cheney was one possible choice. "Would the vice president sit for a *Person of the Year* interview," the magazine asked? Cheney is so press-shy and determined to not upstage his boss that he passed up the honor.

The Old Rules of Engagement

Recalling the good old days is often not much use in analyzing current events. Memories are gauzy, and nostalgia is a powerful impulse. But it was not so long ago that the closed-door policy of this administration was simply unthinkable.

It is ironic that the greatest days of press access to government occurred in the years between the end of World War II and the war in Vietnam. If danger to the nation is the rationale for secrecy now, surely the Cold War posed an even graver threat to the existence of the republic. Yet in those years the government was a relatively open enterprise.

Reporters, especially the best reporters from the best news organizations, had regular access to the top leaders of government. Presidents had informal discussions with reporters alone and in groups. Cabinet secretaries were easily available to top reporters and columnists. Presidential candidates, rather than moving around the country in a cocoon of handlers and spokespersons, rode the trains and planes of the campaign trail in close proximity to the working press. It was commonplace for even young reporters to get direct and prolonged access to the candidates.

By today's standards, access by the press to public officials was truly astounding. Although he was far from alone in his ability to talk with the powerful, James B. Reston, columnist and Washington bureau chief for the *New York Times,* best exemplified the way the press and the government worked in those days. When he was covering the Department of State during Dwight Eisenhower's administration, Reston would have frequent private meetings with Secretary John Foster Dulles. The two would share a drink, and Dulles, stirring his whiskey with his finger, would share his opinions about world problems, about other members of the Eisenhower administration, and even about the president himself, once complaining to Reston that he thought Ike was a bit too detached from the regular business of government. On another occasion, Dulles outlined to Reston a debate that was raging inside the administration over whether it might be a good idea to launch a nuclear attack on the Soviet Union as a way of ending the Cold War quickly. It was perhaps a precursor to the new Bush doctrine of preemptive war. Reston wrote about the debate and eventually, at a White House press conference, asked Eisenhower his views. Ike denounced the idea and ended the argument in his administration.

Reston, along with others in Washington in his time, had frequent access to the president himself. After a harsh, three-day summit meeting with Soviet leader Nikita Khrushchev, the first person John Kennedy spoke with was none other than Reston, who proceeded to write brilliantly nuanced news reports reflecting Kennedy's pessimistic views of the summit meeting. Reston never mentioned that his source was the president himself.

These days ended in the bitter struggles between the press and the government over Vietnam and Watergate. And the Reston paradigm itself was destroyed when Henry Kissinger, when he was national security adviser under Richard Nixon, seduced Reston into reporting inaccurately Kissinger's role in the infamous Christmas bombing of North Vietnam at the end of 1972. Part of the reason Reston fell prey to Kissinger's manipulations was that the Nixon administration had pretty well bottled up other potential sources for Reston and other reporters inside the administration, not by prohibiting them from talking to reporters—although they tried that tactic—but by excluding even Secretary of State William Rogers from key deliberations about foreign policy.

Gerald Ford restored much of the old amity between press and government, and that cessation of hostilities was at least in part responsible for the healing effect of his administration after the Nixon era. Jimmy Carter, although greeted with suspicion and even condescension by much of the establishment press corps in Washington, was likewise open to reporters.

Ronald Reagan, however, probably ran the most open administration in recent history. Reagan himself avoided much direct contact with the press because his command of detailed information was limited. Still, he would permit the occasional private interview, using his considerable charm and avuncular sweetness to disarm reporters. The White House staff, however, was incredibly accessible to the press corps. The major newsmagazines, for example, had regularly scheduled weekly background sessions with White House Chief of Staff James A. Baker—"feedings," they were called playfully. These sessions were tremendously useful in understanding how the administration worked, what it intended to do, and even provided candid insights into how the president operated in the Oval Office. Others on the Reagan White House staff differed, one from another, in their press-friendliness, but most were as available as Baker. This willingness to talk with reporters played no small part in the success of the Reagan presidency and its generally positive press coverage, despite the fact that most reporters who covered Reagan on a daily basis disagreed deeply with many of his policies and found him to be intellectually limited.

The first President Bush was a good deal more press shy as president than he had been as a candidate for the presidency in 1980. As Reagan's vice president he, too, would see the press fairly regularly but was always cautious about what he said. He feared that he would drift away from the Reagan program which he was working hard to support, despite what must have been deep personal misgivings. It was First Lady Barbara Bush who loathed the press deeply, especially as criticism of her husband mounted. "This George Bush is more like his mother, than like his father, in his feeling for the press," said one Washington bureau chief, "and this feeling extends way down into the administration culture."

Certainly the press has in part earned the contempt now shown it by many politicians and government officials. The unmerciful battering the press administered to Bill Clinton over Whitewater, what was an essentially inconsequential land deal, delivered the message to politicians that once the press frenzy has started it is almost impossible to stop. It does seem in retrospect, and actually appeared to be true at the time, that had the president and first lady made a clean breast of the matter they could have stopped the fuss. But the longer they stonewalled, the more the press growled and chewed. The right-wing scandal machines fed the press's eagerness for dirt, and thus the cycle worsened.

Moreover, some media outlets, with a few notable exceptions, have been gradually taking themselves out of the news-gathering business. Cable television news, for example, seems most happy to substitute noisy provocateurs like Chris Matthews and Bill O'Reilly for serious news shows. CNN, which according to polls by the Pew Research Center is still seen as the most credible source of television news, is bleeding audience to Fox News. Roger Ailes, who runs Fox News, achieved his greatest public relations triumph since he sold America on "the new Nixon" in 1968 with his successful campaign to market his programming as "fair and balanced." Third place MSNBC, taking its cue from Fox, added Joe Scarborough, a conservative former member of Congress, to its evening lineup. His cheerleading support for the war seemed more appropriate for "Sports Center" than for a serious news network.

With the exceptions of the *New York Times* and the Associated Press and, to a lesser extent, the *Washington Post* and the *Los Angeles Times*, the major press organizations have been pruning away their international coverage and severely limiting the amount of space and airtime devoted to foreign news. This turn inward is not because editors are no longer interested in foreign news but because the cost of maintaining foreign bureaus and using up limited space with those stories is not justified by the amount of reader interest they attract. To many business executives in the offices of major news organizations, foreign stories amount to, as one executive at Time Inc. put it a few years ago, "homework." Splashier graphics, shorter stories, and more "service" journalism have replaced the news from abroad. European and Asian editions of the newsmagazine are much more cosmopolitan. In early 2003, a *Time* magazine cover story in Europe featured a well-reported examination of the tensions between Europe and the United States over Iraq. That edition is not available in the United States, where *Time*'s domestic cover was about the power of the mind in healing the body. It is easier for politicians to ignore news organizations that are preoccupied with trying to entertain rather than inform their readers. The television networks have nearly abandoned the actual act of covering news abroad, stationing a few correspondents in key capitals who read the news provided them by wire services. As correspondent Bob Simon said of his CBS network during the Libel Defense Resource Center discussion: "We are no longer a news-gathering organization."

This retreat from seriousness extends as well to domestic news. Once fine newspapers like the *Miami Herald* and the *Philadelphia Inquirer*, both part of the constantly-cost-cutting Knight-Ridder chains, have had their news holes and their news staffs trimmed dramatically over the past decade. The goal has been to increase the rate of profitability of the holding company, and the consequence has been a clear deterioration in the quality of the newspapers the company publishes. Knight-Ridder is far from alone in this cost-cutting, and the result has been a clear loss of quality journalism at second-level newspapers across the country.

Pressure for higher rates of return from already profitable news publications is, of course, directly connected to the conglomeration of these businesses into the media giants that increasingly dominate the news industry. Again with the notable exception of the *New York Times* and the *Washington Post*, where the Sulzberger and Graham families have maintained voting control of their stock, the newspapers, networks, and newsmagazines are under severe cost and profit pressures from their business management. This problem has been exacerbated in recent years by a dramatic decline in advertising revenue that resulted from the post-bubble slump in the economy.

Timid or Intimidated?

One of the great frauds that has been committed against the mainstream media has been the persistent and widely believed allegation that the press tilts toward the political left. Books making these charges, like former CBS correspondent Bernard Goldberg's *Bias* and Ann Coulter's *Slander,* appear with stunning regularity and rise to best-seller status quickly. Leaving aside the question of what might these days constitute a truly liberal political complexion, what gives some credibility to the persistent cries of left-wing bias is that the mass media are not conservative in the sense that they agree, either editorially or in their news judgment, with the movement and religious conservatives who now constitute the core of the national Republican constituency. Except for opinion journals, which target specific ideological audiences, most organs of the American press hug the political center, to the extent they understand where that center is. And the reason is simple: That's where most of their readers and viewers are politically. In the more fractured markets for cable news, Fox has been able to tilt to the right while being more entertaining with its opinionated talk-show hosts. But for most major news outlets, the center is where the money is.

This constant quest for a large audience breeds a real timidity on the part of much of the press, even in the face of a virtual information lockout by the Bush administration. Bush is popular, or has been since September 11, and the press is following the polls. It voiced only mild criticism of the president's policies, even as he prepared a military adventure unlike any in the nation's history. Even the *New York Times* avoided opposing the idea of a preemptive strike on Iraq, contenting itself with pleas for permitting the United Nations inspection process to go on longer. In the wake of the quick military success of the invasion into Iraq, it is reasonable to expect even greater deference to the president—at least for a while longer.

As it tries not to stray too far from the opinion set of its mass market, the press has another problem with its audience. In the period immediately following September 11, the Pew Research Center found widespread support for the idea that the press was professional, patriotic, and compassionate, in the words of the survey. But even before the first anniversary of the terrorist attacks, the measures for all those qualities had declined to under 50 percent of the respondents. The cautionary effects these numbers have on the decisions of the mass media are obvious.

Still, the prevailing attitude, as has always been the case when the nation is at war—however "war" is defined—has been to join what Kathleen Hall Jamieson and Michael Waldman describe as the rally-'round-the-flag effect. They note that this is so not only in the opinion sections of the publications but also in the news sections. They marshal some startling quotes in support of this observation. Dan Rather: "George Bush is president, he makes the decisions, and you know, as just one American, if he wants me to line up, just tell me where." Cokie Roberts: "Look, I am, I'll just confess to you, a total sucker for the guys who stand up with all the ribbons on and stuff, and they say it's true and I'm ready to believe it."

This tendency to be supportive of the government in times of war has been exacerbated, at least in Washington, by a sense of personal danger resulting from the attack on the Pentagon, the planned attack on either the Capitol or the White House, and the sure knowledge that Washington will always be a prime target for another terrorist attack. Speaking to Ted Gup for his piece in the *Columbia Journalism Review*, Evan Thomas of *Newsweek* noted that the press has been muted about the secret detentions of terrorism suspects and immigration law violators. "I think this relates to people being afraid," Thomas said. "They [the journalists] want to keep these potential terrorists—even if they're not—behind bars. Journalists are occasionally people. They share the same fears of terrorism, and they are more willing to look the other way because of that. I am sure that we will decide in retrospect that we went soft on the administration and let them get away with too much. It's inevitable."

The desire to operate on the same emotional wavelength as the audience is part of the economic imperative inherent in the avoidance of offending readers and viewers. This instinct is compounded by another impulse that leads to tiptoe journalism. Most of the conglomerates that own the major media outlets have major business before the government—whether on taxes, or mergers, or communications law. While editors and publishers are being careful not to alienate audiences, their corporate supervisors are cautioning them not to offend the government.

This problem did not arrive the day President Bush moved into the White House; it existed before and will exist under whatever successor follows the current administration. During the Clinton years, for example, *Time* magazine, which had been quite mild, and occasionally even dismissive, of the Whitewater scandal, ran a tough and well-reported cover story on how the White House political staff had been attempting to interfere with the Treasury Department's examination of the failed savings and loan company that had a major part in the Whitewater land deal. Clinton's spokesman never denied the story but instead launched an assault on the cover photo that had been chosen by *Time*. It was a black-and-white, White House stock photo of Clinton and George Stephanopoulos meeting in the Oval Office used to illustrate the fact that Stephanopoulos had been involved in the intercession with Treasury. The White House claimed, preposterously, that *Time* ran this photo intending to show that the president and his aide were actually conspiring on the Whitewater matter.

Soon after the story ran, Clinton himself appeared at the White House Correspondent's Association annual dinner, projected a blowup of the *Time* cover, and then showed a series of obviously fake *Time* covers with Clinton and an assortment of celebrities. The gambit was amusing to many, but not to Time Warner chairman Gerald Levin. Worried about the effect of an angry White House on his company's various pieces of government business, he sent stern word down through the ranks of the magazine's editors, instructing that a more "normal" relationship be established between the magazine and the Clinton White House.

Coverage of Washington is now timid and tentative, careful and controlled. When the U.S. government sent a drone airplane into Yemen, tracked a suspected terrorist, and then destroyed him and the other passengers in his car, most stories raised the obvious questions about the authority for such an assassination inside a country with which the United States is not at war. One person also killed was an American citizen, charged with no crime. Officials made no attempt to justify his killing, other than pointing out that he was in a car with a terrorist. How did we know it was the known terrorist in the car? Was there no way to intercept and apprehend the known terrorist? Who authorized the firing of the missile? In the war on terrorism, questions like that are uncomfortable and unwelcome by the mass audience. Within two days, after Bush administration officials stonewalled the questions, the story died. In his State of the Union address, President Bush even boasted of the assassination and implied there have been others. Only Hendrik Hertzberg of *The New Yorker* took notice of this unprecedented admission by an American president. As White House spokesman Ari Fleischer explained at the time of the bombing, "The president has said very plainly to the American people that this is a war in which . . . sometimes there are going to be things that are done that the American people may never know about."

In one of the rare instances where reporters were able to get administration officials to speak candidly and even against their own interests, the *Washington Post* ran a story in early 2003 describing how the U.S. government was outsourcing some of the more intense interrogations of Al-Qaeda suspects to foreign countries with long records of torture. The piece provoked an editorial in *The Economist*, but there was very little mention of the interrogation policy by other U.S. news organizations. The revelation that John Poindexter, the Reagan aide responsible for much of the Iran-Contra scandal, was employed by the Pentagon to fashion an Orwellian database to gather the most routine information about the activities of ordinary citizens would have caused a media feeding frenzy five years ago. In the current climate, the story got relatively little attention in the general media until the Congress quietly postponed the program.

The press in Washington is not complaining, at least publicly. One bureau chief contacted for this piece was candid in saying that speaking on the record about lack of access to administration officials would only make managing that difficult relationship that much harder. Instead of complaining, Washington reporters are trying to get along with the Bush administration. Some reporters are busy doing puff pieces about various members of the administration—"beat builders," one correspondent calls them—in hopes that they will be let into the tent. In times past, hostility between the press and government often led to tough coverage. Now, the reverse is true. The old danger of getting too close to sources and writing puff pieces about those sources seems to have been reversed. The more the press is kept at bay, the more pliant the coverage has become. Says a veteran Washington bureau chief: "A starving press corps only becomes desperately hungry for small bits. Little anecdotes have become prized commodities because they are so rare. Starvation has been very successful [for the administration]."

The president himself is totally shut away from the mainstream press, having only the most occasional news conferences and, as the selling of the war on Iraq proceeded, a luncheon with conservative columnists. On a long trip to Europe and Russia in his first year in office, Bush never met with the traveling press corps. More astoundingly, neither did his press secretary, Ari Fleischer. "The press secretary was one of the royal attendants," said one bureau chief who made the trip. Bush's televised and carefully scripted press conference just before the attack on Iraq was his first in eighteen months. He has had no on-the-record interview with the big dailies or the newsmagazines since he was sworn in. Only Watergate ace Bob Woodward appears to have achieved great access to administration officials and even got to review presumably classified National Security Council minutes for his recent book *Bush at War*, but his reporting was done retrospectively and not for the daily newspaper. He has traded timeliness for access, and what he is producing is not quite journalism, not quite history.

"I am telling you," Seymour Hersh told the audience during the Libel Defense Resource Center's panel discussion, "this [Bush] crowd has the utmost contempt for us. . . . They really do not care about us. They really do have us figured out." The sad fact of the matter is that the policy of limiting access and limiting discussion is succeeding brilliantly from the administration's point of view. With a political opposition in Congress cowed by many of the same forces that intimidate the press, the usual technique of at least reporting what opponents say is not available to the media. Without lawyers to represent those incarcerated as suspects in the war on terrorism, there are no advocates for the media willing to question, on the record, the misuse of the nation's system of justice. The silence is powerful indeed.

CHAPTER 11

The Fog of War:
Covering the War on Terrorism

STANLEY CLOUD

We don't want the truth told about things here. . . .
We don't want the enemy any better informed than he is.
—General William Tecumseh Sherman,
to a newspaper correspondent in September 1861

G ENERAL SHERMAN WAS NOT BEING merely peevish the day he threw Florus Plympton, a newly arrived reporter for the *Cincinnati Commercial,* out of his Kentucky headquarters. The Civil War had scarcely begun, but Sherman was already in a red-eyed rage about the way it was being covered. "It's impossible to carry on a war with a free press," he roared after the *New York Tribune* revealed his plan to retreat from Kentucky to Indiana. In taking his anger out on poor Plympton, the general raised a question that has been raised in nearly every U.S. war since: How much press coverage of—and access to—U.S. forces in wartime is constitutionally allowed, and how much government and military secrecy is constitutionally justified?

Then, as now, technological advances in the collection and dissemination of news helped drive the debate. The first U.S. war covered by people we would recognize as news reporters was the Mexican War of 1846–1848. In the last year of the war, a group of newspaper publishers, eager for more up-to-date reports, formed a cooperative agency—the Associated Press—so that they could share the high cost of transmitting their correspondents' dispatches by means of a revolutionary new medium, the telegraph. When the Civil War began, telegraph wires capable of moving war news with unprecedented speed were crosshatching much of the nation. For the first time in history, the struggle between the press and the military was joined. It would rage on and escalate through World Wars I and II, Korea, Vietnam, and the Gulf War of 1991. More recently, on the first battlefields of the twenty-first century—from Afghanistan's Hindu Kush to the steamy forests of the Philippines, from Peshawar's back alleys to the deserts in Iraq—the struggle has only intensified.

When the post-9/11 war on terrorism began, large numbers of correspondents—equipped to transmit words, sound, and pictures virtually instantaneously, twenty-four hours a day, seven days a week—were ready to cover the fighting. But U.S. military leaders, waging a new kind of war against a new kind of enemy, kept reporters at bay for several weeks, insisting that U.S. operations on the ground did not lend themselves to coverage. During that period, whatever information was available came, more often than not, from high-level Pentagon briefings, not from firsthand reports by independent correspondents in the field. As the focus shifted to Iraq in 2003, questions about how that war would be covered were far from resolved. The Pentagon promised journalists a new kind of access to U.S. troops—"embedding." But while some saw that as a hopeful sign, others saw it as a trap.

Wading into the Pool

The 1983 war in Grenada was the first full-scale U.S. invasion of a foreign country to occur in complete secrecy since at least the end of World War II. Following the conflict, a consensus arose in Washington that the American people do, after all, have a right to some ill-defined measure of independent reporting about what the Pentagon does in their name, with their money, and with the bodies and lives of their children. Even the Pentagon brass—perhaps sensing that they may have stretched their constitutional authority a bit thin in Grenada and belatedly appreciating how the media can sometimes play a role in the glorification of war and warriors—seemed intent on reform. They appointed a commission, chaired by General Winant Sidle, a retired former Pentagon public affairs officer, to investigate how the press was treated during the Grenada operation and how to avoid a repetition.

On the Sidle Commission's recommendation, the Department of Defense in the mid-1980s created the National Media Pool. The pool consisted of a group of journalists, rotated quarterly, who were to accompany U.S. troops during the *earliest phase* of any major combat and provide text, pictures, and sound for the use of the news media as a whole. Once the pool had done its work, the press would be on its own to cover the rest of the war as best it could, with or without the military's assistance. Despite its apparently benign provenance, the DoD pool became in practice a rather sophisticated attempt by the Pentagon on the one hand to *permit* combat coverage and, on the other, to *control* it. But journalists in the Washington-based national press corps, many of them pleased and flattered to have been consulted both before and after the pool's creation, seemed to welcome its advent as a long stride in the right direction.

That rather naive view soon came into serious question. During the war between Iran and Iraq in 1988, when Kuwaiti oil tankers were reflagged and escorted out of the Persian Gulf by U.S. warships, and again in 1989, when the U.S. invaded Panama in order to depose and arrest its strongman ruler, Manuel Noriega, DoD pool reporters were kept away from most of the action and subjected to stringent controls. The skimpy reports the pools were able to produce were subjected to "security review" and often censored, even when the controversial material was merely embarrassing and had nothing whatever to do with "operational security."

But it was during the Gulf War in 1991—Operation Desert Storm—that journalists discovered just how hideous a monster the DoD pool had become. When the fighting finally began in January, after a long buildup in Saudi Arabia and elsewhere—a buildup that was itself inadequately covered because of what the Pentagon called "host-nation sensitivities"—the pool concept became the basis for reporting the *entire war*. At the press headquarters in Dhahran, Saudi Arabia, the Defense Department established a vast system of local pools, with the promise of easy access to selected military units in return for the press's agreement to play by the military's rules. Among those rules: no interviews with military personnel unless a public affairs officer was present; no photographs or identifications of dead or wounded U.S. troops; and, of course, "security review" of all copy, film, tape, and photos. These restraints and others largely resulted in watered-down, secondhand coverage and such long delays in the transmission of many stories that they were effectively robbed of their news value. The system was so pervasive and effective that only the most daring, skilled, and perhaps foolhardy reporters—dubbed "unilaterals" by the Pentagon—attempted to cover the combat on their own.

The Gulf War thus had the dubious distinction of being the most undercovered all-out American war in modern history. Except for the work of a few "unilaterals" and the CNN correspondents who reported, with obvious limitations, from behind the lines in Baghdad, there were hardly any unofficial pictures, film, or tape of combat. Stories based on actual observation of combat were also scarce. The Pentagon made almost a fetish of showing official film of cruise missiles and so-called smart weapons in action—flying down ventilator shafts, obliterating command posts, taking out surface-to-air missile sites, and so on—but those pictures turned out much later to be misleading, both in terms of the weapons' actual level of usage and their record of accuracy.

The government's pictures also grossly misrepresented the conflict's real nature. One of the great tank battles in the annals of war was fought in the Iraqi desert. Yet no journalist or other independent observer was on hand to write history's first draft. What's more, on those few occasions when something approaching coverage of actual operations was permitted, the results would be deceptive. Journalists who accompanied U.S. Marines as they prepared to land on the beaches of Kuwait, for instance, were deliberately misled into reporting that the Marines were the primary assault force. In leaking this story, the military hoped Saddam Hussein would not shift his coastal defense assets to the north where the main attack would in fact originate.

A Beachhead at the Podium

In any war, there is usually a good deal of on-the-job training for the correspondents, who, not surprisingly, tend to be relatively young and eager. During Desert Storm, for every veteran like CNN's Peter Arnett, there were many more reporters who were covering their first war. The problem was compounded by the fact that, since the establishment of an all-volunteer military during the Nixon administration, fewer and fewer reporters have personal experience with the military. All this came into sharp focus when the U.S. command's televised press briefings in Dhahran became a mainstay of the coverage—especially the briefings presided over by the U.S. commander, General Norman Schwarzkopf. While the general stood more or less patiently at the podium, reporters who were unable to get to the fighting asked questions. For the most part, the questions were sensible and serious, but some were silly, unnecessary, or unanswerable. Schwarzkopf responded to the latter with skillful bemusement or anger. Thus, he became a TV star, and the press sank to new lows in public opinion polls.

Until twenty-five or thirty years ago, briefings by federal officials of all kinds, military and civilian alike, were usually conducted—unlike presidential press conferences, for instance—without live TV cameras present. This permitted a certain rough informality and kept the briefer and his questioners on a relatively equal footing: journalists and their sources, trying, in their messy and unappealing way, to arrive at a semblance of the truth. But at a point in the late 1970s or early 1980s, the TV cameras began to be turned on for briefings, in part because the TV networks were demanding it and in part, I believe, because some officials came to realize that it was very much in their interest to grant the networks' wish. With the cameras on, and various stately, TV-friendly logos ("The White House," "The State Department," "The Pentagon") having materialized in the background, briefings became little more than performances by all concerned—performances to be to be judged by the TV audience and other critics, including the reporters' editors. Were the questioners well-dressed, polite, pertinent, and cool? Did a given briefer handle himself or herself with aplomb and a ready grasp of the facts? But these competitions for the favorable opinion of viewers were unequal. Well-coached and well-prepared briefers usually appear knowledgeable and in command, while questioners all too often seem by turns bumptious, obsequious, ridiculous, or ill-informed (which, of course, they very often are, or they wouldn't be asking questions).

Thus it was in Dhahran.

General Schwarzkopf and his subalterns stood at the podium in their desert-dun battle fatigues and their spit-polished boots, with their maps and pointers, and forbore to answer questions from a raucous, ill-tempered pack of journalists, some of whom didn't know an SOF from a sofa or a Hummer from a Volkswagen. While the real war progressed in the desert, and pool reporters flailed about in an almost pitiful parody of war correspondence, the public back home was treated to hour after hour of briefings that made Schwarzkopf a hero and the press— including, unfairly and unfortunately, the many reporters who *did* know their stuff—laughingstocks.

More than a decade after the war, Pete Williams, who was the Pentagon's chief spokesman before becoming a correspondent for NBC News in 1992, told me: "The trouble with the Gulf War was that General Schwarzkopf simply wouldn't *hear* of allowing reporters to be in place before the fighting began. He was afraid they would give it [the plan of attack] away."

Not long after the war ended, both sides in the press-military debate once again began to express concern about the way reporters had been treated and about the mostly lackluster coverage that resulted. A series of negotiations between the Pentagon and the media led in 1992 to the approval of a set of nine principles, the most important of which were the first ("open and independent reporting will be the principal means of coverage of U.S. military operations") and the second ("pools are not to serve as the standard of covering U.S. military operations").

A New Kind of War

When the World Trade Center and the Pentagon were attacked by Al-Qaeda terrorists on the blue-crystal morning of September 11, 2001, the administration of George W. Bush wasted little time in declaring the current war on terrorism. Although Bush persuaded the Congress to support him, his was anything but a formal declaration of war. Terrorism is a tactic, not a state against which war may be declared. In that sense, the war on terrorism is the same as the war on drugs or the war on poverty—a metaphor rather than a legal process or description of the relationship between nations. Bush nevertheless made clear that this war would also be against Al-Qaeda–friendly *nations*. That presidential declaration and Bush's decision to make Afghanistan the first major battlefield in the war opened yet another chapter in the story of the press versus the military.

It was on October 7, 2001, less than four weeks after the Al-Qaeda attack, that carrier- and land-based U.S. warplanes began striking targets in Afghanistan as part of the newly christened Operation Enduring Freedom. The initial targets were Al-Qaeda training camps, which were obliterated in fairly short order. Almost from the outset, however, it was obvious that the United States also intended to go after the Afghan government, then under the control of pro–Al-Qaeda Islamic fundamentalists known as the Taliban. In a matter of days, the first U.S. combat troops arrived in small, clandestine groups—occasionally, as the current assistant secretary of defense for public affairs, Victoria Clarke, put it—in groups as small as "ones and twos."

They came from surrounding countries (Pakistan, Uzbekistan, Tajikistan) and from the USS *Kitty Hawk,* operating in the Arabian Sea. Some of the Americans were in uniform, some not; some were Army, some from the Central Intelligence Agency. They carried a lot of cash with which to buy off Afghan warlords, and they tended to move fast over extremely difficult and mountainous terrain—in vehicles, on horseback, on foot—and did *not* tend to answer questions. Soon they had linked up with and recruited fighting units of the Northern Alliance, anti-Taliban Afghanis who in the 1970s and 1980s had fought *alongside* the Taliban (as well as Al-Qaeda and the CIA) against invading forces from the Soviet Union.

As Operation Enduring Freedom intensified, journalists in Washington and elsewhere were beginning to wonder if they were seeing another Grenada in the making. True, a number of reporters—thirty-nine of them, representing twenty-six news organizations, according to the Pentagon—were allowed on board the aircraft carriers from which many of the air strikes were launched; and another 100 were at Ramstein Air Force Base, Germany, where flights of C-17 transports with humanitarian aid for the long-suffering Afghan people originated. Aboard ship and in Germany, the reporters were subject to rules imposed by local officers, acting on instructions from the Pentagon. Certain parts of the aircraft carriers containing classified equipment were declared off-limits, for instance, and there were obvious bans on reporting mission targets before they were hit. The rules were not especially onerous, however, and reporters were able to conduct interviews with pilots before and after they had flown missions. Still, the correspondents were far from the fighting, and their reports provided little more than fleeting glimpses of what was happening.

And where was the DoD pool that was specifically designed to cover the early phase of any combat? *Time*'s national security correspondent, Mark Thompson, was one of the designated pool reporters during the last quarter of 2001 when the fighting began. Not long after 9/11, he and the other pool members were given vaccinations and told to be ready to move on short notice. They waited—and waited. Nothing happened. "The war began on the seventh" of October 2001, Thomson recalled,

> and as the time went by, we all had a sense, or a fear, that the Pentagon was going to try to do all of it without activating the pool. But at that point, it was still pretty much just an air war, and we told ourselves, you know, no big deal. Once they go in on the ground, the pool will be activated, and we'll be covered. I

mean, we all know the pool's sort of lousy, because you only get half a loaf with it, if that. But when you've got nothing at all, half a loaf begins to look pretty damn good. And we never even got that.

Assistant Defense Secretary Clarke insists that, apart from reporting by those aboard certain aircraft carriers and at Ramstein AFB, there was nothing to cover in the first weeks of the war—or nothing that the Pentagon *wanted* covered. "If you look at the criteria for when and how and where the pool is supposed to be activated . . . you *find* me a circumstance in Afghanistan where it would have been appropriate to deploy the DoD National Media Pool. You can't." And why weren't pool reporters put aboard the *Kitty Hawk,* at least to interview special operations teams on their return? "What we had aboard the *Kitty Hawk,*" Clarke says, "were forces we don't acknowledge exist, using special tools and tactics and techniques, some of which still haven't yet—amazingly—become public. . . . [The *Kitty Hawk*] was a platform from which very unique members of the U.S. military operated. We [the Pentagon's public information office] actually sent people out there to take a look and research it [as a potential site for the pool], and they came back, and [Defense Secretary Donald] Rumsfeld and I looked at them, and I said, 'I'm with them. We're not going to do it.'"

There was no significant access on the ground until U.S. bases were established inside Afghanistan, and by then the fighting had essentially become a manhunt for Al-Qaeda and Taliban leaders, especially Osama bin Laden and the Taliban's Mullah Mohammad Omar (both of whom, at this writing, appear to be still at large). In any case, it wasn't long after the Pen-

THE FOG OF WAR

tagon finally did allow reporters to enter Afghanistan that serious coverage problems developed. The question of civilian and
so-called friendly fire casualties—"collateral damage," as the
military euphemism has it—caused the most difficulties. Civilian casualties are inevitable in any modern war, but they are
more prevalent when belligerents deliberately operate within
the civilian community, as the Vietcong and North Vietnamese
did in Vietnam, as Al-Qaeda and the Taliban did in
Afghanistan, and as Saddam Hussein's forces did in Iraq.

The most written-about civilian-casualty incident during
Operation Enduring Freedom was probably when a U.S. air attack on a village that was believed to be (correctly, the Pentagon
still insists) a source of antiaircraft fire resulted in the killing of
members of a local wedding party. By early 2002, the Taliban
was making a major issue of civilian deaths, and some American critics were accusing the press in this country of downplay-
ing the story. The full truth may not be known for some time,
but a January 2002 interim report by the Project on Defense
Initiatives in Cambridge, Massachusetts, tentatively concluded:
"If all Taliban government and Afghan refugee accounts of the
numbers of civilians killed or wounded in the bombing campaign are taken at face value, they would suggest a total of more
than 5,000 killed and 10,000 wounded. . . . It is likely that the
actual toll is less than one-quarter as many."

There were also several friendly-fire incidents during the period of heaviest fighting in Afghanistan—from October 2001 to
the battle of Shah-i-Kot in early March of 2002—although a
number of correspondents on the scene concluded that they
were, as William Branigin of the *Washington Post* put it, "pretty
rare." Perhaps the best known, in terms of military-press relations, occurred on December 5 near Kandahar, when a B-52

bombing run resulted in the deaths of three U.S. servicemen and the wounding of nineteen others. A locally organized pool of reporters and photographers tried to cover the story, but they were confined to a warehouse by Marine commanders and were unable to interview either the wounded victims as they were brought in or those tending them. When Washington bureau chiefs complained to Clarke, she sent them a letter in which she said: "We owe you an apology. The last several days have revealed severe shortcomings in our preparedness to support news organizations in their efforts to cover U.S. military operations in Afghanistan."

Although Clarke's apology ignored the fact that this kind of thing had happened repeatedly in the post-Grenada past, it was nonetheless welcome. Better still, she went on to pledge that the Defense Department would set up information centers in Afghanistan and try to avoid any repetition of the incident. By the time this was done, however, the air war and attacks by U.S.-supported troops of the Northern Alliance had significantly reduced the resistance of Al-Qaeda and the Taliban.

Almost a year later, Clarke said:

When the Marines went into Camp Rhino [a U.S. Marines camp near Kandahar], a lot of media went in with them, and from then on, when we had more and more boots on the ground, more military on the ground, it was full and open coverage. The press was anywhere they wanted to be. We did make mistakes. A Marine . . . on December 6 made a bad mistake and prevented reporters from covering the return of friendly fire victims. Went against the training. Went against the policy. Made a mistake. We fixed it. And we instituted better training and better policies.

The question is whether the fixes are permanent and will prevent similar "mistakes" in the future.

Whatever the answer, the relative lack of sanctioned access for journalists in Afghanistan may actually have worked out for the best. With the DoD pool out of action for the most intense part of the fighting, and access limited, the press was pretty much on its own. The results were instructive. Operating on combinations of instinct and experience, many journalists—mainly Moscow-based correspondents at first, followed later by others—made their way to Pakistan, Uzbekistan, and Tajikistan. There they filed stories about the governments surrounding Afghanistan and their supportive but often uneasy relationship to the war on terrorism, about the spread and impact of Muslim fundamentalism, about the Muslim "street" and its attitude toward the United States. They also tried to get to U.S. forces that were by then massing in those countries, but as in the first Gulf War buildup, the Pentagon blamed "host-nation sensitivities" for keeping them at arm's length. From the surrounding countries, journalists entered Afghanistan at different times and by different routes and managed to link up with Northern Alliance forces and sometimes even with U.S. Special Operations Forces. The journalism they produced was often first-rate, far superior to anything likely to be found in any pool report ever written.

This kind of reporting doesn't necessarily work only in so-called proxy wars. For the most part, it was the way reporters covered the U.S. military's operations in Vietnam and the rest of Indochina: By one means or another, they got themselves to where the action was (often by informally hitching rides on U.S. or Vietnamese aircraft) and either covered it or covered its aftermath. To be sure, there are certain kinds of wars or, more likely, battles in which independent coverage is all but impossible and some sort of government assistance is necessary—even with strings attached. But government assistance really should be the *last* resort, not the first.

The cost of independent coverage can be heavy, though. Early in 2002, *Wall Street Journal* correspondent Daniel Pearl was kidnapped by a Muslim fundamentalist organization in a back street of Karachi, held captive, forced to appear in a propaganda video, then gruesomely murdered—all as he attempted to report a story from the point of view of Muslim fundamentalists. Elsewhere, Kathleen Kenna of the *Toronto Star* was seriously wounded inside Afghanistan when a grenade was thrown into a van in which she was riding. At least eight other journalists from the United States and other countries were killed during the fighting—an extremely high toll for so relatively short a war.

Embedded with the Troops

Despite the good work of "unilaterals" in Afghanistan, journalists had many legitimate complaints about the way the Bush administration controlled the flow of information—including complaints about how the DoD pool was used (or not used) as well as how sources inside the Pentagon seemed to dry up as the war on terror progressed. Clarke and her boss, Defense Secretary Donald Rumsfeld, insist that only unauthorized leaks dried up, but some longtime Pentagon reporters dispute that. They insist that it became increasingly difficult to reach people in the Pentagon who were once good sources of accurate information. "I used to run into officers all the time in the hall," said one correspondent about covering the war in Afghanistan. "I'd say,

'What about this or what about that?' And they'd help me out. That's over. Now we're reduced to just covering Rumsfeld's briefings." Those televised briefings made Rumsfeld, like General Schwarzkopf before him, something of a media star, illustrating once again that, with the cameras on, briefings are the briefer's métier.

Afghanistan was, in effect, a proving ground—not only by the military but by the press. There, even print reporters came to the battlefield loaded down with new technology—satellite phones, video phones, and the like—that allows instant reporting from almost any spot on earth. This technology is a military commander's worst nightmare: Just by sending a message to his home office, a reporter can inadvertently reveal his position and the position of the troops he is with. Nevertheless, in Afghanistan the military appeared to develop a new appreciation for the way serious, professional reporters operate. (Clarke says she has had that appreciation all along but that "others further up the food chain" came to it more recently.) Based in part on the way reporters handled stories dealing with civilian casualties and friendly-fire incidents, there was a greater willingness—in principle, at least—to let the press be the press and to minimize attempts to control it. "I don't think it's an accident," Clarke says, "that the preamble to the Constitution calls for the common defense of the country, and the First Amendment deals with freedom of the press. I don't think [the Founders'] priority in that document is an accident. I think both [concepts] are very important. And I think the worst thing in the world, for us and for others, would be if we didn't have a free and aggressive and open and robust press, covering everything we do."

Of course, a "robust" press can cause—sometimes *should* cause—heartburn in people who are trying to fight a war. But what Clarke and some of her superiors say they are beginning to understand is that journalists who are allowed to do their job may in effect counteract an enemy's propaganda by investigating and reporting the facts of situations that others are attempting to exploit. Says Knight-Ridder's Washington editor Clark Hoyt:

> Not too long ago, in the aftermath of the heavy fighting in Afghanistan, I attended another bureau chiefs' meeting at the Pentagon, and Secretary Rumsfeld came in and talked to us about how he was committed to getting a lot of journalists into the field with the military. And someone asked him if he was saying that because it was a principle of his—that he believed that there should be more reporters in the field—and he said, 'Well, yeah, it's a principle of mine.' But the real reason—he was very candid about it—was a completely self-interested one. He said they were already concerned that the Iraqis were going to be putting out false information about what U.S. troops in Iraq might do in the event of a war and that he wanted independent eyewitnesses there to refute claims of atrocities, targeting of civilians, things like that. I think that was a lesson he learned in Afghanistan.

It was this sort of thinking in the Bush Pentagon that led to the idea of "embedding" reporters—the military has already begun to refer to them as "embeds"—with military units during combat. The idea is really a throwback, with certain modifications, to the way it used to be before there were DoD pools and all the other features of the elaborate superstructure of press control that the military has built over the last couple of decades—the way it was, for example, on D-Day 1944. In combat situations, a reporter—or reporters, depending on the size of the unit—would be placed with a military outfit and stay with it in the way reporters used to accompany units in World War II—not as guided, controlled guests but, in effect, as reporters covering a regular beat. During the Pentagon's preparations for war in Iraq, it was already canvassing its commanders at all levels—from company to corps, from squadron to wing, from ship to fleet—to determine which units and which headquarters would be suitable for "embeds" and for how many. Once that was determined, the Pentagon informed interested U.S. and foreign media outlets how many slots were available—about 600 was the ultimate figure—and asked for the names of reporters to fill them.

The media have also been adjusting their thinking. When the Pentagon announced in 2002 that it would be holding occasional "boot camps" for journalists—voluntary, weeklong training sessions at military bases around the country in such things as fitness, weapons familiarization, and first aid—reporters signed up in large numbers, with the understanding that there would be no strings attached and no attempt to prevent combat coverage by reporters who had not attended boot camp. During a conference on the press and the military in wartime, held at the National Press Club in Washington in early 2003, there was a great deal of talk about embedding and boot camps—and favorable reaction from participating journalists. One of them, *Newsweek* assistant managing editor Evan Thomas, was typically upbeat. "It seems to me," he said, "that this administration—the Pentagon certainly—has finally gotten the message."

Based on past experience with these kinds of schemes, skepticism was in order, however. Another participant in the National Press Club conference, Paul McMasters, First Amendment ombudsman for the Gannett Foundation's Freedom Forum, noted that journalists have had their hopes raised before every post-Grenada military engagement, only to see them dashed once the shooting started. "You all remind me of Charlie Brown trying to kick the football," McMasters said to the journalists in the room.

He had a very good point. Embedding and other schemes had to be tested under fire. There were a few primitive attempts at embedding during the fighting in Afghanistan, but the most intense part of the action there lasted only five months, less if we don't count the time devoted to the air war. During the war in Iraq, embedding seemed to work quite well. The coverage provided by embedded print and TV journalists was, on the whole, excellent. This may have been due in part to the relative ease with which U.S. forces advanced and the relatively light casualties they suffered. The true test of all the new goodwill and trust between the Pentagon and the media will likely come on some other battlefield of the war on terrorism, when emotions are running high and things are not going as well as they seemed to in Iraq.

What, for instance, about censorship and "security review"? In Iraq, at least at first, the Defense Department's thinking on that score may be summed up in the phrase "security at the source," meaning it was left to individual unit commanders and individual "embeds" to work out the details for themselves. There were general guidelines from on high for all concerned, but the specifics were for the most part left to the people in the trenches. Says Clarke: "I don't think there are too many journalists . . . out there [embedded with military units] who . . . want to do anything to put themselves at risk, much less the people around them."

As the war on terrorism proceeds, and as additional reporting from the embeds with U.S. and allied forces in Iraq and elsewhere pour in, it will become clearer just how committed the Pentagon is to the latest attempt to strike a balance between what's good for the military and what's good for the press. But in the end, after all the discussion and all the debate, after all the negotiating, after all the pushing and pulling, it will come down to a single and quite simple fact: If a war—any war—goes badly for the United States, and the press has not been allowed to cover it as freely and fully as possible, the American people will be among the last to know.

CHAPTER 12

The Go-for-Broke Presidency:
Can National Unity and
Partisanship Coexist?

E. J. DIONNE, JR.

HERE IS THE CENTRAL CONTRADICTION of George W. Bush's presidency: He can be a commanding and unifying leader who rallies the country behind the war on terrorism and foreign policy endeavors aimed at transforming the world. Or he can be a partisan and ideological leader who tries to radically alter domestic policy and politics.

Bush, however, sees no contradiction. He has decided that his will be a go-for-broke presidency, an administration in which no priority will give way to any other priority.

Politically, he has sought to use the authority he gained after 9/11 to achieve a historic realignment toward the Republican party. If that meant using war and domestic security to batter the Democrats in the midterm congressional elections, so be it. If Democrats were embittered as a result, that was their problem, not his. Domestically, the president has pursued a conservative agenda far more ambitious than Ronald Reagan's. Bush is determined to do two things: First, tilt the tax code toward the interests of the well-off—or, as Bush would see it, toward investors and entrepreneurs; and second, create a long-term hole in the federal budget that will, over time, force deep cuts in domestic programs. If Bush wanted an economic "stimulus" plan that would shower the maximum number of benefits on the smallest number of the most financially comfortable Americans, he could hardly have done better than his proposal to eliminate the taxation of most dividends.

And then Bush would reorder the world. While he's cutting taxes, he's increasing military spending to bolster America's fighting forces. The war with Iraq was aimed not just at ridding Saddam Hussein of dangerous weapons (and at ridding Iraq and the world of Hussein) but also at rearranging the politics of the Middle East. This will mean years of engagement—years of political and economic reconstruction. The president insists the United States can do all that, as well as pacify North Korea and still carry on the war against Al-Qaeda. And we hear nary a word about the potential for unintended consequences, the concept that is one of conservatism's greatest contributions to the public policy debate.

Conservatives have been ecstatic over Bush's boldness. They praise him for betting the farm on the midterm elections and winning. They are pleasantly astonished at the ambition of Bush's tax proposals. They cheer his unapologetic swagger, embodied in down-home declarations such as his scoffing at the idea of giving United Nations weapons inspectors more time in Iraq: "This looks like a rerun of a bad movie and I'm not interested in watching it." And the more the wimpy Europeans complain—especially those irritatingly unreliable French—the more certain Bush's supporters are that he's on the right track.

This essay is being written just after the fall of Baghdad, and it would be an act of exceptional recklessness to predict how the war and its aftermath will affect American politics. Bush's supporters have argued that victory in Iraq will create a surge of popularity for the president that will ease the passage of all his domestic initiatives. His opponents believe that with the end of the war the nation's attention will turn back to domestic issues and economics—areas where Bush's standing in public opinion has been relatively weak and, absent an economic upturn, will remain so. In both cases, the wish is the father to the thought. And both views could underestimate how large a role Iraq will play in domestic politics in the months and years ahead. Victory itself calls forth a new domestic debate over America's obligations to rebuild Iraq, the costs of a long-term occupation, and the obligations to repair international alliances broken during the bitter debate that preceded the war. The debate over just the budgetary costs will affect every other debate over taxes and domestic spending.

What can be said with certainty is that the run-up to the war did not heal political divisions. It's difficult to imagine that even the relatively easy and overwhelming victory will heal the breach between Republicans and Democrats seen in 2002. The months immediately after the GOP's historic triumph in the midterm elections were the most troubled of Bush's post-9/11 presidency. The polls offered one measure: Support for Bush's Iraq strategy headed south between November and March 2003, recovering only when war became an inevitability. On the domestic side, approval of his handling of the economy was halved between his post-9/11 high tide of popularity and early March. At that moment, only four Americans in ten in a *New York Times*/CBS News poll approved of Bush's economic performance—roughly the proportion of the Republican base in the electorate.

The president, of course, would say that he doesn't make decisions based on polls. But the polls reflected a genuine and significant problem: The more Bush has pursued an ideological agenda at home, the more he split the country and alienated potential friends abroad.

To understand what the president decided to throw away, it's worth recalling the depth of bipartisan unity that existed in the months after 9/11. I'll never forget calling a Democratic political consultant in the week after the attack and asking him his thoughts on Bush. This highly partisan Democrat replied: "I actually went into church and knelt down and prayed that he'd be successful. He's ours. He's all we've got. Pray God that he's going to do what's best for our country." Such sentiments lasted well beyond the initial shock of the attacks, translating into genuine political support for Bush's foreign policy goals. There was hardly any dissent from his decision to wage war on the Taliban in Afghanistan—partly, it should be said, because as a response to the aggression of 9/11, it was a war that made sense to most Americans, including most Democrats.

Republicans might counter that Democrats were petrified, for their own political reasons, of saying anything negative about Bush. There's some truth to that assertion, but it understates how authentic the feelings of national unity were at the time. For example, it would not, in principle, have been unpatriotic for Democrats to press the administration hard and immediately for explanations of the intelligence breakdowns that preceded the attacks. Republicans, for their part, were not in the least reluctant to blame the attacks on Bill Clinton, who had been out of office for eight months. Just days after the attacks, Richard Shelby, a Republican senator, explicitly criticized Clinton for restrictions on the Central Intelligence Agency's recruitment of informants overseas, saying that "the Clinton curbs have hindered the work of our human intelligence agents around the world." Shelby was not alone in voicing this view. But Democrats held their tongues for months.

On the issues of domestic security and civil liberties—the central concern of this book—Democrats rallied to the president despite misgivings. They gave overwhelming support to the USA Patriot Act. It was striking during the debate over the bill that such libertarian opposition as there was came from the farther ends of the political left and political right. The unlikely alliance between former Representative Bob Barr, the Georgia Republican, and Maxine Waters, the California Democrat, symbolized both the possibility of unusual coalitions, and the fact that they were, at the time, marginal. Some of the strongest criticisms of the administration on liberty questions came from the political right—*New York Times* columnist William Safire was especially forceful—even as many liberals and Democrats (with important exceptions such as Senator Russ Feingold of Wisconsin) chose, for the moment at least, the side of security.

Democratic bitterness is directly related to the sense of many in the party that they were played for suckers. That feeling was especially pervasive after last year's elections. "The fact that the administration used 9/11 in the last election, that they seemed intent on using the president's role as commander in chief as a way of soliciting votes, has created a hardening of partisan lines that will be felt until the end of this administration," Representative Chaka Fattah, a Democrat from Philadelphia, declared last winter in a comment typical of his party's mood.

Senator Dick Durbin of Illinois said that he and many fellow Democrats remained incensed that Bush and his party went after then–Senator Max Cleland of Georgia for allegedly being soft on homeland security. Cleland's offense against the safety of the nation? He supported civil service and union protections that Bush opposed within the new homeland security department. "This is something that gnaws at us," Durbin said. "A decorated and disabled Vietnam veteran would be discredited because of his stand in the homeland security debate?" Senator Mary Landrieu of Louisiana poured a little extra Tabasco on her comments about Cleland's defeat: "He left three limbs in Vietnam. He's already served his country in more ways than any of us ever will. The president came in with a very personal and very vicious attack, using the homeland security issue to unseat a man who fought on the Armed Services Committee to give the guys in the battlefield everything they need. It didn't mean a thing to this president."

Landrieu had her own issues with Bush. A Democratic hawk, she strongly supported him on Iraq and called for even higher levels of defense spending. She also voted for his tax cut. Nonetheless, Bush threw everything he had into trying to defeat her in the December runoff that ensued after she failed to capture a majority of the vote in November. She won anyway, and it's useful to hear her out. She won't be on the ballot again until 2008, so she can speak more plainly than some of her more politically vulnerable colleagues. "For Democrats who were trying to work with the president on national security issues and support a more hawkish stand than might seem natural for a Democrat, this president discounts it, ignores it, and acts as if it's not relevant," she said. "Any time the country is poised for war and about to engage on behalf of the security of the country, it's very important that the president make that the priority and make everything else come in second. Unfortunately, the president has done exactly the opposite of that." Like many of her colleagues, she sees the country as increasingly polarized. "Unfortunately, the president has earned this polarization," she says. "It hasn't just happened. He pushed it to happen."

I can imagine Republicans and conservatively inclined readers saying: "Of course Landrieu is angry. Of course the Democrats are frustrated. But will any of it matter if everything works out well with Iraq, and if the economy comes back strong?" Well, sure. If things go perfectly in the months ahead, Bush is likely to win reelection in November 2004. The problem is that Saddam's ouster marked the beginning, not the end, of America's commitment to Iraq. If Bush genuinely wants to create a new foreign policy, as Harry Truman did after World War II, does he not need to build the same bipartisan bridges that Harry Truman did? As Landrieu's comments suggest, he has already blown up bridges to the very sort of Democrats on whom he is likely to depend.

Life being what it is, it's also likely that the coming months will not be perfect—for Bush or for the country. Smart presidents engaged in large foreign policy projects understand the need to make sure the opposition stands with them in difficult times. At the beginning of World War II, Franklin Roosevelt was explicit about this: "Dr. New Deal," he declared, had given way to Dr. Win the War." FDR jettisoned many New Deal dreams in order to unify the country against Nazi Germany and imperial Japan.

Bush prepared for war with Iraq with far shallower support than his father had twelve years earlier, despite the closely split congressional vote on the 1991 Gulf War and despite the rallying of Americans to the cause of the most recent Iraq war once it became inevitable. Under the first President Bush, even opponents of the war respected the skill with which the administration rallied international support. Under the second President Bush, even supporters of the war were troubled by the failures of diplomacy and the alienation of potential allies. And having used security issues for partisan purposes, this President Bush has diminished his ability to ask for support on purely patriotic grounds. He left himself with no political net beneath him if something went wrong. And by using his popularity on foreign affairs to push for domestic policies that Democrats genuinely despised, he made those in the opposition who actually support his objectives abroad look like chumps.

Politicizing Homeland Security

Democratic bitterness cannot be understood apart from the debate over the creation of the Department of Homeland Security, which will long stand as one of the sorriest episodes in the history of partisanship. The idea for this vast new bureaucracy was embraced at a moment of maximum political advantage and pursued with a relentless focus on electoral calculation. By turning domestic security into a divisive and partisan issue, President Bush helped win his party an election. But at what cost?

Recall that the president resisted creating this department for months after 9/11. Calls for the new security structure came largely from Democrats, especially Senator Joe Lieberman. Then, on June 6, 2002, Bush abruptly announced on national television that he had switched sides and embraced the new department. What was going on at that moment? For weeks, the news had been dominated by stories reporting the failures of U.S. intelligence and law enforcement in the days and weeks leading up to the terrorist attacks. Suddenly, Congress was asking the obvious question: How could this have happened?

It was not exactly a line of inquiry the administration welcomed, and Bush's speech just happened to come on the first day of testimony from whistle-blower Coleen Rowley, the chief legal counsel of the Federal Bureau of Investigation's Minneapolis field office. Surprise: Bush overshadowed Rowley. Dan Balz noted in the *Washington Post* on June 7 that Bush appeared on television as he was "struggling to regain the initiative" on security. While the president retained the confidence of the country, Balz wrote, "his administration is no longer immune from questions or criticism about what happened before Sept. 11, and whether everything is now being done to make the homeland safer. . . . In recent weeks, Bush has faced the first sustained scrutiny since the terrorist attacks." The result: "signs of declining public confidence in the government's ability to combat future terrorism."

Given this opening, did the Democrats respond to Bush's speech with partisanship? No. As they did so often after September 11, they turned the other cheek. Then Senate Majority Leader Tom Daschle, regularly vilified by the Republicans as a mad partisan, called Bush's remarks "encouraging." Representative Jane Harman of California, one of the Democrats' leading voices on security, called Bush's proposal "bold and courageous."

The natural move from here would have been authentic bipartisanship to get a bill passed. After all, the differences between Bush and the Democrats were so small that then–Senator Phil Gramm, a Republican from Texas, noted that 95 percent of the homeland security bill that was finally approved after the election had been written by Democrats.

But getting a department created before the election was clearly less important to the president than having a campaign issue. He picked a fight over the union and civil service protections, and Republican senators filibustered various efforts to reach a compromise on the issue. In late September 2002, Bush went so far as to charge that the Senate—meaning its Democratic majority—was "not interested in the security of the American people." And just to make sure that the bitterness of the election was sustained, House Republicans larded the final bill with a list of special interest provisions, including one protecting the pharmaceutical giant Eli Lilly from lawsuits relating to a mercury-based vaccine additive that plaintiffs claim caused their children's autism. The shamelessness was breathtaking. The Democrats' worries over employee rights were characterized as a concern for "special interests." But the drug companies that had made such large campaign contributions were presumably immune from the special interest charge.

At least two prominent Democrats, Senator Bob Graham of Florida and Representative David Obey of Wisconsin, were mystified as to why their party had not been able to make more out of the homeland security issue in 2002. Obey, the ranking Democrat on the House Appropriations Committee, argued for months that the administration was providing far less money than is needed for a long list of security priorities. "It's almost like they've made a conscious decision that you can't defend against all contingencies, so let's just cover the basic ones, and save every dollar we can for tax cuts," Obey said at the time. Graham, the chairman of the Senate Select Committee on Intelligence, saw the administration as "lethargic" in dismantling terrorist networks inside the United States and said the country should be debating how much more needs to be done.

But Obey and Graham went largely unheard. Because the real homeland security debate never happened, one might view Bush's maneuverings as brilliant politics. But it was brilliance bought at a high price. The next time the president's defenders try to evade tough questions about his policies by declaring that homeland security should be above partisan politics, his critics will chuckle knowingly.

Bearing Any Burden?

There can be no doubting Bush's boldness in pursuing his objectives and his success in stymieing Democrats. They never quite knew how to respond to Bush's marriage of patriotism and partisanship. Yet history suggests that when democratic nations face foreign policy challenges, their leaders usually pursue domestic policies designed to promote social solidarity and national unity.

During World War II, Prime Minister Winston Churchill was acutely aware of the need to rally Britain's poor and working classes and give them a stake in victory over Hitler. And so it was under the auspices of the twentieth century's greatest conservative that the foundations of Britain's robust system of social insurance were laid. Churchill recognized that a time of war places a special obligation on the governing classes to those who benefit least from a nation's social and economic arrangements.

Bush, by contrast, has done all he can to benefit the economic elites and to undercut the government's commitments to the least fortunate. This is not a liberal fantasy. Conservatives acknowledge that Bush's long-term goal is to reduce the federal government's capacity to act—yes, to spend—without saying so publicly. The large tax cuts the president put on the table, conservative columnist Donald Lambro wrote candidly, "are, in effect, Mr. Bush's stealth initiative to curb future spending—big time." Exactly. And if you look carefully, most of the spending cuts will be in programs for the poor and near-poor.

Stealthy redistribution upward is the central theme of Bush's domestic agenda. Under the cover of promoting growth, Bush is shifting more and more of the tax burden from the wealthy. That's the effect of his proposal to eliminate the dividends tax and the huge new tax loopholes the administration tried to sell as "savings" incentives, and moderate Republicans bridled at the size of his proposed tax reductions. Mercifully, the administration eventually backed off the savings initiative. In the meantime, Bush proposed to create long-term incentives for states to cut their programs to help the poor.

On Medicaid, for example, Bush proposed to give states modest fiscal relief up front—not anything close to what they needed, of course—but only if they accepted the transformation of Medicaid into a block-grant program and cuts in later years. The cuts were disguised by declaring that whatever Medicaid relief the states get now would be a "loan" to be paid back within the next decade. "The federal government is acting like a loan shark," said Ron Pollack, executive director of Families USA, a group that battles for expanding health insurance coverage. "The federal government is dangling a little money before the states now, and then takes it back." In later years, the federal government would get out of the business of giving the states certain automatic protections against increased health care costs or a rise in the number of the uninsured. The result, Pollack said, will be "waiting lists, a reduction in services, and higher premiums, deductibles, and co-payments."

Robert Greenstein, executive director of the Center on Budget and Policy Priorities, a think tank that advocates programs for the needy, said states would be pressured to reduce medical coverage for the working poor—the very people the president praises over and over again for their responsibility. But, somebody's got to pay for this dividends tax cut. Too bad it may have to be the children of low-income working parents. Other long-term cuts affect the poor, too. According to Greenstein's center, the number of children receiving child-care subsidies would drop by 200,000—to 2.3 million—by 2007. If housing programs were run through block grants, that also could lead to real cuts in services to the poorest Americans.

The president's program is neither conservative nor compassionate. It is radical in its stealthy way, and it threatens to undermine the federal government's rather modest commitment to helping states and cities assist their poorest residents. Yet by pushing so many of the fiscal problems so far down the road, Bush hoped to insulate himself from the political costs of his choices.

The great defect in the administration's call to arms in Iraq was the shortage of candor about the sacrifices entailed in its bold venture. This helped explain why so many Americans outside the ranks of the president's most fervent supporters—including Americans who agreed entirely with Bush about the genuinely evil nature of Saddam Hussein's regime—found it difficult to give their wholehearted assent to the endeavor until it happened. At that point, Americans rallied to the troops, and against a dictator whom Bush was right to call evil.

John F. Kennedy is legendary for declaring that the United

States was willing to "pay any price, bear any burden, meet any hardship, support any friend, oppose any foe, in order to assure the survival and the success of liberty." But what price did President Bush ask of us and, in political terms, of himself? Right up to the eve of war, the answer was: precious little.

This was the significance of the president's resolute refusal to put a price tag on the war in advance. It was a price tag that involved not only treasure but also the commitment of tens of thousands of American men and women in the military to a very hard task, likely for years to come. But instead of following Kennedy's example by speaking of the difficulty and expense of his course, the president and his lieutenants played down the potential costs or simply feigned ignorance. Asked by Tim Russert on *Meet the Press* before the war whether it might cost $100 billion, Vice President Dick Cheney wouldn't discuss the potential burden. "I can't say that, Tim," Cheney said. "There are estimates out there." Note the denial of responsibility in that phrase "out there," as if the administration had no estimates of its own. Russert also asked whether "we would have to have several hundred thousand troops there" in Iraq "for several years in order to maintain stability." Cheney replied: "I disagree." The vice president wouldn't say how many troops we would need but said that "to suggest that we need several hundred thousand troops there after military operations cease, after the conflict ends, I don't think is accurate." In other words: Don't worry about it.

The reluctance to challenge Americans extends to domestic policy. In the run-up to the invasion of Iraq, the president told his wealthiest supporters to party on. How else is one to interpret his call for the repeal of taxes on dividends? These tax cuts proved too much even for some in the president's own party. A group of eleven moderate House Republicans led by Mike Castle of Delaware and Amo Houghton of New York wrote their leadership just before the war began declaring their opposition to $1.4 trillion in tax cuts. "The war against terror and the crisis in the Gulf are of key concern to the American people," they said. "However, meeting these challenges should not cause us to abandon our party's commitment to fiscal responsibility. . . . We must pursue a budget policy that fairly limits both spending and tax reductions to those that are absolutely needed at this time." Key Republican moderates in the Senate, as we've seen, effectively challenged the cuts, too.

In a time of war, it should not fall to this honorable handful of House members or Senators to state the obvious. A government proposing revolutionary departures in foreign policy should not pretend that its objectives can be pursued painlessly and with no disturbance to its domestic objectives.

Supporters of the war regularly chastised their opponents for refusing to face the reality of Saddam Hussein's threat and the need for radical measures to eliminate it. In the wake of war, it will be their turn to face reality. From a desire not to unsettle the delicate foundations of their political coalition, supporters of a grand new American role in reordering the world have held their tongues about the cost of their enterprise. They have not said what price or burden or hardship they are asking of their fellow Americans, especially of their own supporters. Perhaps President Bush will lead by breaking the silence and asking more of us—and of himself. Rallying a nation to war demands sacrifices from everyone, including the president of the United States. It calls for a serious debate over the meaning of patriotism, as well as a challenge to assumptions about how patriots are defined.

A Patriotic Response

In *The Right Man*, his book about the Bush presidency, former Bush speechwriter David Frum offers an analysis of "compassionate conservatism" that includes a nice throwaway line about liberals. "Bush described himself as a 'compassionate conservative,'" Frum writes, "which sounded less like a philosophy than a marketing slogan: Love conservatism but hate arguing about abortion? Try our new compassionate conservatism—great ideological taste, now with less controversy." Then came Frum's line on liberals: "Conservatives disliked the 'compassionate conservative' label in the same way that people on the left would dislike it if a Democratic candidate for president called himself a 'patriotic liberal.'"

Frum's point is fair enough: Conservatives hate having to add the adjective "compassionate" to their label because doing so implies that they once lacked compassion. Liberals presumably would dislike adding "patriotic" to their label because doing so would imply that they once lacked love for their country. What can't be ignored is that Bush was smart to embrace the compassionate conservative idea. He knew perfectly well that a large number of Americans were suspicious—for good reason, I'd argue, but never mind—that conservatives really didn't care enough about the poorest in our midst.

"Compassionate conservatism" was a brilliant slogan that did three things at once. It acknowledged that conservatives had a problem. It insisted that conservatives really did care about the poor. And it tried to change the debate about poverty by claiming that advocates of programs outside government, especially church-based programs, had better ideas about how to help the poor.

By the same logic, it is time to proclaim loudly and without apology that there is such a thing as patriotic liberalism—or, in keeping with the locations of the day, patriotic progressivism. Of course, there should be no need to do this. Liberalism, the philosophy of Franklin D. Roosevelt and Harry Truman, waged and won America's war against Nazi Germany and imperial Japan and laid the groundwork for the successful battle against Soviet communism. Jimmy Carter's campaign for human rights created the ideological underpinning of Ronald Reagan's successful Cold War policies.

But contemporary liberals should acknowledge they have a problem. Yes, some of it is a problem of demagoguery by their opponents. Tom DeLay has gone so far as to accuse Democrats of being the "appeasement party" because of Democratic presidential candidate Howard Dean's opposition to a war with Iraq. If opposing a war proposed by a president automatically makes somebody unpatriotic, then Abraham Lincoln was an unpatriotic appeaser for opposing the Mexican War as a young congressman in the 1840s.

In fact, liberals split on the Iraq war. Even among opponents of Bush's policies, most shared a proper revulsion toward Saddam's regime, and few engaged in reflexive anti-Americanism. But for liberals, it is simply a fact that since the Vietnam era their cause and the cause of patriotism have not enjoyed the close link in the public mind that was so powerful in the days of FDR's presidency. In the wake of 9/11, that's a genuine problem for liberals.

The solution is not defensiveness but an aggressive attempt to define patriotic liberalism. It would include a strong emphasis on service to the country. Senators John McCain and Evan Bayh have proposed expanding service opportunities for young

Americans so that 250,000 slots would be available for those who want to give a year to their country. Short-term enlistments in the military could also be encouraged. Patriotic liberals would support the call of a commission convened by CIRCLE (the Center for Information and Research on Civil Learning and Engagement) and the Carnegie Corp. to have our schools place a new emphasis on civic education. This would include a genuine rigor in the teaching of government and history and a new emphasis on extracurricular activities now endangered by budget cuts.

A patriotic liberalism would contrast itself to a radical individualism that rejects any idea of a "common good." It would emphasize both rights and responsibilities. It would tell corporations that move offshore to escape taxes that they have obligations to their country at a time of war and domestic threats. It would urge that we spend what's needed to defend ourselves at home against terrorism. A bipartisan group organized by the Council on Foreign Relations issued a report in October 2000 entitled "America—Still Unprepared, Still in Danger." Led by former Senators Warren Rudman and Gary Hart, the panel concluded that "America remains dangerously unprepared to prevent and respond to a catastrophic attack." Ideological posturing is no substitute for practical measures to strengthen our first responders, especially at the local level. And as Rudman has noted, secrecy is often the enemy rather than the friend of security. "Obviously we've got security concerns about a number of things," Rudman said, "but sometimes secrecy is a haven for covering up mistakes."

Patriotic progressives would argue that the preservation of freedom is a common project requiring a commitment of citizens to one another across the lines of class, race, and gender. It would also celebrate the fact that the friends of liberty can be found all across the philosophical spectrum. It would insist that a free republic will not prosper if too many of its citizens feel deprived of opportunities. Patriotic liberalism would declare that we are all in this together. It's an old-fashioned thought that, at this moment, would be a radical challenge to the status quo.

CHAPTER 13

On the Home Front:
A Lawyer's Struggle
to Defend Rights After 9/11

ANN BEESON

*I pause as we enter the mosque. I've never been in a
mosque before, and the people I am meeting are taking
off their shoes. Is there, as usual, a hole in my stocking?
My worry is trivial. These Americans have much more
to fear. It is December 2002, and I am visiting Muslim
communities in southeastern Michigan to plan a
constitutional challenge to the USA Patriot Act.*

S A LAWYER for the American Civil Liberties Union,
I have fought to protect constitutional rights for eight
years. Nothing has prepared me for the reality of civil
rights litigation after September 11: terrified clients, disrupted
communities, unprecedented executive power, secret courts,
deferential judges, gag orders, and a disinterested public. A new
civil liberties crisis emerges almost daily. ACLU lawyers around
the country post frantic cries for help on our Internet discussion

board. Passengers who appear to be Middle Eastern are kicked off airlines when ladies with poodles report that they are "suspicious." Hundreds of men are detained indefinitely on minor immigration charges, and the government won't even tell us who they are. The Justice Department announces Operation TIPS, a plan to recruit a million volunteers to report "suspicious activities." A Muslim man driving a car in Philadelphia with a bumper sticker in Arabic is arrested and held for months. The Federal Bureau of Investigation conducts countless "voluntary" interviews of Muslims, South Asians, and Arabs. Hundreds of Iraqis are arrested in California when they comply with the FBI's "special registration" program, causing widespread panic among the growing number of other immigrant groups required to register nationwide. The Defense Department announces the Total Information Awareness initiative, a massive database that will profile Americans using their travel, finance, health, and education records. A student in Michigan is suspended for wearing a T-shirt with the words "Bush is a Terrorist." The FBI announces a plan to count mosques in communities across the country to help set quotas for surveillance orders. Nuns on the way to a peace rally are held at the airport because their names appear in error on a terrorist "no-fly" list. The press and public are denied access to secret deportation hearings in the name of "national security." New York City refuses to allow citizens to march in protest of war in Iraq.

The cause of the current civil liberties backlash makes the work that much harder. Like all Americans, I was traumatized by the September 11 terrorist attacks. The ACLU office is just a few blocks away from ground zero. Every day for five years, I had arrived at the World Trade Center each morning on an 8:45 train from my home in New Jersey. I was at Newark airport that morning, on a plane turned back before takeoff when another plane was hijacked from the airport. A Texas native, I considered loading up my family and heading west, never to return to Manhattan. When I rode the ferry to work on my first trip back into the city, I wanted to pull the Statue of Liberty in a little closer. For months after the attack, the foul smell of the smoke from ground zero was an ever-present reminder of what had happened. Outside my window, I heard the constant clang of scraping metal as cranes on barges sorted twisted debris from the destroyed buildings.

In this climate, it was hard to stay focused on my goal as one of many lawyers galvanized to fight the erosion of rights after September 11: challenging the constitutionality of the Patriot Act, which vastly expands the government's authority to spy on Americans.

More Spying, More Secrecy

Congress passed the Patriot Act a mere six weeks after September 11, while we at the ACLU were still recovering from the shock of the attacks and cautiously suggesting that Americans could be both safe and free. The Patriot Act is a law enforcement wish list of new powers rejected by Congress as too broad on several prior occasions. While increasing executive power, the Patriot Act simultaneously reduces checks and balances like judicial oversight, public accountability, and transparency. Though a number of Patriot Act provisions have serious civil liberties implications, after much research and analysis we focused our advocacy efforts on two in particular. The first, which I'll call the personal records provision, lets the government obtain records about anyone—from libraries, Internet service providers, hospitals, and any business—by merely arguing that the records are "relevant" to an ongoing terrorism investigation. The second, which I'll call the wiretap and secret search provision, makes it easy for the government to listen in on phone calls and conduct secret searches of homes and businesses. Both provisions authorize an intrusive federal fishing expedition without first requiring the government to establish that the person whose phone it taps or whose records it wants is any threat. Both violate the Fourth Amendment's prohibition against unreasonable searches and seizures, and both seriously jeopardize First Amendment rights because expansive government spying inevitably discourages people from speaking out.

The Patriot Act provisions are actually amendments to a previously obscure federal law called the Foreign Intelligence Surveillance Act (FISA). (FISA changes are also analyzed from different standpoints by Stephen J. Schulhofer in Chapter 3 and Kathleen M. Sullivan in Chapter 5.) Ironically, FISA was originally enacted in part to curb rampant abuses of executive surveillance powers. During the Cold War and the McCarthy era, the FBI routinely installed electronic surveillance devices on private property in order to monitor the conversations of suspected communists. The FBI's COINTELPRO wiretapped Martin Luther King, Jr., and other dissidents and antiwar protesters solely because of their political beliefs. The Central Intelligence Agency illegally spied on as many as 7,000 Americans in Operation CHAOS, including individuals involved in the peace movement, student activists, and black nationalists. The Church Committee's report, issued in 1976, disclosed that the FBI had compiled more than 500,000 intelligence files on individual Americans and domestic organizations, including 65,000 new files in 1972 alone. The report concluded that "unless new and tighter controls are established by legislation, domestic intelligence activities threaten to undermine our democratic society and fundamentally alter its nature."

During the same era, the U.S. Supreme Court wrote in *Berger v. New York* that "few threats to liberty exist which are greater than that posed by the use of eavesdropping devices." Noting the danger that wiretaps will intercept innocent communications, the Court applied the Fourth Amendment right to privacy to wiretaps:

> The traditional wiretap or electronic eavesdropping device constitutes a dragnet, sweeping in all conversations within its scope—without regard to the participants or the nature of the conversations. It intrudes upon the privacy of those not even suspected of crime and intercepts the most intimate of conversations.

The government nevertheless continued to abuse its domestic spying powers in the name of national security.

FISA was enacted in 1978 to govern surveillance of foreign powers and their agents inside the United States. The statute created the secret Foreign Intelligence Surveillance Court, now composed of eleven federal district court judges specially appointed by the chief justice of the United States. The FISA court can grant or deny government applications for surveillance orders. It sits in secret and does not publish its decisions. The government is the only party in a FISA proceeding, and very little is known about how the court functions. Between 1979 and 2001, reports to Congress show that the FISA court approved without modification 14,031 out of 14,036 surveillance applications.

While FISA was enacted to curb McCarthy-era abuse, the standards that govern FISA surveillance have always been substantially less stringent than the Fourth Amendment requires in criminal investigations. The Fourth Amendment prohibits warrantless and unreasonable searches. A search warrant normally requires "probable cause" to believe that the target has committed, or is about to commit, a particular criminal offense. The Constitution also normally requires notice to the person whose information is searched. FISA orders don't require criminal probable cause or even delayed notice to the person whose privacy has been compromised. Unlike searches conducted in normal criminal investigations, 99 percent of all FISA targets are *never* informed that their homes have been searched or their phones tapped, because the information is never used in a subsequent proceeding. Most targets—including the *innocent*—never receive notice and an opportunity to be heard on a claim that the surveillance violated their constitutional privacy rights. In other words, the government could have a record that you bought this book, and you would never know it.

When FISA was first enacted it applied only to a relatively narrow and strictly delineated class of "foreign intelligence" investigations. That is no longer the case. Since 1978, Congress has amended FISA on numerous occasions, each time adding new surveillance tools to the executive's foreign intelligence toolbox. As a result, FISA as it exists now bears little resemblance to the statute that Congress enacted in 1978. Federal law imposes more rigorous standards for wiretaps in normal criminal investigations, but 66 percent of all federal wiretaps are now conducted through the secret FISA process. The number of

FISA applications per year has risen from about 200 in 1979 to nearly 1,000 in 2001.

Though we knew that expanding FISA's spying powers under the Patriot Act could lead to abuse, it would be difficult or impossible to prove. The only real oversight rested with the highly secretive FISA court. The law also imposed a strict gag order on businesses and individuals who received court orders for personal information. How could we protect privacy rights with no way to learn who the government was watching? How would we find clients when the government *never* had to notify even innocent victims of its spying? We had to find out more about how the government was using these new powers.

Using the Freedom of Information Act

In August 2002, we filed a Freedom of Information Act (FOIA) request for information about how the Justice Department was implementing its new powers under the Patriot Act. Earlier in the summer, representatives in Congress had become concerned about expanded surveillance and sent Attorney General John Ashcroft a series of written questions. Ashcroft stalled but finally responded to Congress. The questions asked for information on how often, and in what contexts, the Justice Department had used its new spying powers. Though none of the questions from Congress asked Ashcroft to reveal information about specific targets of FBI investigations, Ashcroft submitted the bulk of his responses to Congress under seal because he claimed that making them public would jeopardize "national security." Our FOIA request asked the government to provide us with the documents Ashcroft improperly sent to Congress in classified form; it also sought general information about the use of new surveillance powers, including the number of times the government had:

- Directed a library, bookstore, or newspaper to produce records, for example, the titles of books an individual has purchased or borrowed or the identity of individuals who have purchased or borrowed certain books;
- Initiated surveillance of Americans under the expanded Foreign Intelligence Surveillance Act;
- Investigated American citizens or permanent legal residents on the basis of activities protected by the First Amendment (e.g., writing a letter to the editor or attending a rally);
- Conducted secret searches of homes and businesses.

When the Justice Department refused to respond quickly, we filed a lawsuit to force an answer. Even after we filed the lawsuit, the government continued to stall. After a hearing, we were encouraged when a federal judge gave the government only two months to respond. Despite the ruling, the government sought three additional extensions. Its excuse for the third extension was an anticipated winter storm. On the phone, the government lawyers claimed that "the FBI doesn't come to work when it snows." I couldn't decide whether that made me feel more or less safe.

Eight months after our initial request, the government provided just over 300 pages of heavily redacted documents. It continued to withhold numerous other responsive documents on national security grounds. Nonetheless, some documents it provided gave us valuable information on how the government is exercising its new powers—information that may help in our lawsuits to challenge those powers. For example, the government gave us several completely blacked-out pages apparently listing surveillance applications, which confirms the repeated use of the new powers. In another internal FBI memo titled "What do I have to do to get a FISA?" the FBI states outright that it is not required to satisfy the ordinary requirements of the Fourth Amendment to spy on Americans.

We also learned that the government was aggressively using another little-known power broadened by the Patriot Act—National Security Letters—to obtain sensitive records from banks, credit reporting agencies, and Internet service providers. These administrative subpoenas require no judicial approval at all, even from the FISA court. The FBI director or a delegate simply writes a letter asserting that the records are "relevant to an authorized investigation to protect against international terrorism," and a financial institution or Internet service provider—subject to a strict gag order—must turn over the personal records. The information we obtained through the FOIA case made us more determined than ever to challenge these broad new spying powers.

Spies in the Stacks

While our FOIA litigation continued, we began planning to file two related lawsuits to challenge the Patriot Act personal records provision. Of all the Patriot Act spying powers, this provision perhaps most invokes the specter of Big Brother—it is so broad that it authorizes the government to find out what books we've been reading. Using this power, the government can obtain *any* personal records by merely asserting that they are relevant to an ongoing terrorism or intelligence investigation. In direct conflict with the Fourth Amendment's protection against unreasonable and warrantless searches, the government does not need to establish probable cause that the person whose records it seeks has done anything wrong. In fact, the personal records provision authorizes federal officials to go on fishing expeditions even when they are not investigating a particular person at all. The government can merely ask for a list of every person who has checked out a particular book, say, on Islamic fundamentalism. A gag order in the law prevents public libraries, universities, and other businesses served with these orders from telling anyone about them.

In the first case to challenge the provision, we plan to represent Arab and Muslim community groups who believe the government is using the law to obtain their records in violation of the Fourth Amendment. In the second, we intend to file a First Amendment challenge to the gag order on behalf of libraries and other businesses that receive the court orders for information. But first we needed to identify potential clients who were at risk of surveillance and businesses subject to the orders.

In December 2002, we scheduled our first set of meetings to offer legal representation to Arab and Muslim community groups, as well as to libraries. We decided to visit Michigan first, because the ACLU of Michigan was already working closely with local communities in other post-9/11–related cases. Our first meeting with Arab community leaders was in Dearborn at a local Lebanese restaurant. I was lucky to be traveling with Jameel Jaffer, a talented young lawyer who had recently joined the ACLU and would share the task of explaining our planned constitutional challenge to this complex but frightening law. I hoped his presence as a South Asian Muslim would put our potential clients at ease, but that turned out to be a nonissue. Everyone we met was grateful to local ACLU advocates like legal director Mike Steinberg, who also joined us in the meetings. At first, as we devoured huge platters of delicious food, the meeting seemed no different than many others I'd had with clients to plan challenges to unconstitutional laws. Then the stories began to come out, and the fear became palpable. Prominent community members had already been detained for months without charges. Though many of those we met were citizens, nearly all had family members who were not; they faced a much greater threat of retaliation from the government. Nonprofit organizations that provide much-needed social services to new immigrants were afraid they'd lose state funding if they helped with the lawsuit; the group had received threatening phone calls from state legislators warning them not to make public statements that could be seen as opposing the government's antiterrorism efforts.

Each meeting that followed was more depressing. Amid cartoon characters and dangling mobiles, we met with a prominent Muslim pediatrician who described colleagues in other cities whose children had been terrified by midnight FBI raids. At the mosque we visited, a widely respected cleric had been detained for months without charges and subjected to a secret deportation hearing. Though the ACLU and others had challenged the secret hearing on behalf of Congressman John Conyers and the press, that battle was just beginning. The Muslims we met were understandably certain that the mosque was bugged. I began to envision my own FBI file.

Muslim students at the meeting described the silencing of activism and dissent on campuses. Many had already been "voluntarily" interviewed by the FBI and had been asked intrusive questions about their political associations, religious beliefs, and family members. One student was afraid to help his younger brother check out books for a high school report on guns because he thought the FBI would find his borrowing habits suspicious. Many feared that the government would not renew their student visas if they spoke out on political issues at all. Some had stopped giving to any charities based in their home countries for fear they would be arrested for supporting terrorism. All were afraid that participating in a lawsuit opposing the Patriot Act would cause the government to investigate and retaliate against them. Community organizations feared intrusive and harassing government efforts to gain access to their membership lists and financial records.

The only uplifting meetings were with local libraries eager to support the privacy rights of their patrons and to join in a constitutional challenge. Some brave library board members even offered to check out a series of controversial books in hopes of setting up a test case if the FBI subpoenaed the circulation records. But while some libraries had received informal requests from the FBI, none had yet been served with a Patriot Act order.

We returned to New York sobered. After researching the legal rules on discovery, and discussing the potential for retaliation, we concluded that our clients' participation in a lawsuit against the federal government would pose very real risks. We were still determined to file the lawsuit but needed to proceed cautiously.

Litigating in a Secret Court

As if snooping into reading habits and personal records was not enough, the Patriot Act also threatened to vastly expand the government's ability to listen in on phone calls, read e-mail, and conduct secret searches without complying with the Fourth Amendment. The Patriot Act—theoretically, at least—now authorizes the government to use FISA searches and wiretaps as an end-run around the Fourth Amendment even in normal criminal cases.

Here's how. Before the Patriot Act, to get a FISA wiretap the government had to certify that the "primary purpose" of the surveillance was foreign intelligence and show probable cause to believe that the target was a "foreign power" or an "agent of a foreign power." In the classic case, the government met these tests when it wanted to bug the Russian embassy. The Patriot Act amended FISA to allow the government to obtain a wiretap or search order where only a "significant purpose" of the surveillance is foreign intelligence. Civil liberties advocates fought the amendment because we feared the change would allow the government to get a secret FISA wiretap when the government's primary purpose is not foreign intelligence gathering but criminal investigation. But since we had no access to internal FBI guidelines interpreting the new authority under the Patriot Act, and since innocent victims of FISA surveillance will never know the government is spying on them, we had no obvious way to challenge the new powers.

In early September 2002, I returned from a two-week vacation to incredible news. It was revealed that in May the FISA court had issued a historic decision—the first it had ever published—rejecting Ashcroft's bid for the broadest possible interpretation of new powers authorized by the Patriot wiretap and secret search provision. The ruling was the first time since 1978 that the secret court had ruled against the government. The decision was disclosed after Senator Patrick Leahy and other members of Congress concerned about the secretive FISA process had written to the FISA court asking for information. In response, the FISA court published its May ruling, which the government had just appealed. Since the government had never previously lost, this was also the first-ever FISA appeal. Under the terms of the statute, the special Foreign Intelligence Surveillance Court of Review would convene for the first time to hear the case.

We scrambled to absorb the opinion and galvanize quickly for action. The FISA court made a point of documenting over seventy-five instances in which the government had abused its surveillance power *even before* the Patriot Act. The FISA court then rejected Ashcroft's interpretation of the Patriot wiretap and secret search provision, recognizing that Ashcroft wanted to use FISA as a way to evade the Fourth Amendment in criminal investigations.

Because the government was the only party in the case, there would be no one to oppose the government's view on appeal. Working with other civil liberties groups, we decided to try to file a friend-of-the-court brief to argue that FISA would be unconstitutional if used for normal criminal investigations. Filing briefs like this is routine in a regular federal court. But this was unprecedented—how do you file a brief in a secret court? Normally a lawyer would call the clerk's office for advice, but there was no number listed for the secret court. We finally resorted to calling the judges (in their capacity as ordinary federal trial court judges) but were told—unsurprisingly—that we couldn't talk to them personally. We sent a letter to all three judges advising them of our intent to file a brief in late September and asking how to proceed. Days went by with no word, and we grew more anxious that the FISA court of review would decide the case before we could file our brief. Then I picked up the phone in mid-September, and an unfamiliar voice said she was our contact for the secret court. My blood raced—it felt like I was talking to Deep Throat. She said the judges had not yet decided whether they would accept our brief but that we could file it with the FISA clerk—who, it turns out, works for the Justice Department. So much for separation of powers! My contact was decidedly not the secret FISA clerk—perhaps the judges thought it inappropriate for our go-between to be a Justice Department employee.

On a Monday morning in mid-September, as we rushed to finish the brief, an inside-the-Beltway news columnist reported that the FISA court of review was hearing secret arguments in the case that very day—in a highly secure location inside the Justice Department. Solicitor General Ted Olson, the highest-powered Justice Department lawyer, was presenting the argument himself (he normally appears only before the Supreme Court). Along with members of Congress who were turned back at the door, we denounced the secret hearing.

A few days later, we filed our brief, not knowing whether the court would even consider it. A couple of weeks later, I got a call from my secret contact again. She asked whether I had received an order from the court accepting our brief. It turned out that the court had issued the order soon after we filed. Apparently the court in its secrecy had neglected to send us a copy of the simple order. We became the first members of the public to ever receive an order from the secret FISA court of review. The style of the order itself was dramatic. As if for special effect, the FISA court of review had opted for a particularly gothic font. Where the parties are usually listed—*United States v. John Smith*—this order merely said *In re: Sealed Case*. The case number, typically a number representative of the thousands of cases filed in a particular court, said simply #02-001. The court, like us, seemed to be operating by the seat of its pants.

On November 18, 2002, the FISA court of review issued its decision and reversed the ruling of the lower FISA court. The court recognized that the case presented difficult constitutional questions but concluded that if the new FISA powers "do not meet the minimum Fourth Amendment warrant standards, [they] certainly come close." The opinion gave the Justice Department the green light to broadly expand its spying on Americans without first establishing probable cause and without *ever* providing notice to the persons it targets. The U.S. attorney general can now suspend the ordinary requirements of the Fourth Amendment to listen in on phone calls, read e-mail, and conduct secret searches of Americans' homes and offices. Ashcroft held a press conference to laud the ruling, saying the new powers would "revolutionize" the Justice Department's use of FISA. He announced plans to train government agents nationwide to use the new powers.

Because the Justice Department was the only party in the court and won, there was no one to appeal the decision to the U.S. Supreme Court. After engaging in heated internal debate, and consulting with other legal experts and Muslim, Arab, and South Asian groups who feared they were being targeted under the law, we decided to take a radical step: We would move to intervene directly in the Supreme Court and ask them to review the ruling. If the Court granted review, it would be the Court's first case involving post-9/11 threats to civil liberties. Representing the American-Arab Anti-Discrimination Committee, ACCESS (a Michigan-based social services agency for recent immigrants), the ACLU, and the National Association of Criminal Defense Attorneys, we filed our motion and brief in the Supreme Court on February 18, 2003. We argued that the Supreme Court must be the final arbiter of the constitutional limits of government surveillance. Certainly such issues should not be decided by courts that sit in secret, ordinarily do not publish their decisions, and allow only the government to appear before them. But in a one-line order issued in late March, the Supreme Court denied our petition to intervene and refused to hear the case. We will continue to press the courts to play their vital role in preserving constitutional rights and checking executive power. It remains to be seen whether they will rise to the task.

Times of Urgency

When the government sought new powers in the war on drugs, Justice Thurgood Marshall warned of the danger of abandoning constitutional rights in a crisis:

> History teaches that grave threats to liberty often come in times of urgency, when constitutional rights seem too extravagant to endure. The World War II Relocation cases and the Red Scare and McCarthy Era internal subversion case are only the most

extreme reminders that when we allow fundamental freedoms to be sacrificed in the name of real or perceived exigency, we invariably come to regret it.

Like past civil rights advocates who fought for justice in the midst of a national crisis, we are certain to lose some of our battles. Fundamental liberties will be eroded in the name of national security and the war on terrorism. Our only consolation in the long run may be that we didn't give up the struggle. There will be no similar comfort for the countless people whose rights are forever lost.

GREG ANRIG, JR., is vice president of programs at The Century Foundation and the former Washington bureau chief of *Money* magazine.

ANN BEESON is the associate legal director of the American Civil Liberties Union and is currently leading efforts to challenge the government's expanded surveillance powers under the USA Patriot Act. In November 2001, she argued before the United States Supreme Court in *Ashcroft v. ACLU*, a challenge to the Child Online Protection Act, and she was named one of America's Top 50 Women Litigators by the *National Law Journal*.

ALAN BRINKLEY is the provost of Columbia University. His published works include *Voices of Protest: Huey Long, Father Coughlin, and the Great Depression*, which won the 1983 National Book Award; *The End of Reform: New Deal Liberalism in Recession and War*, and *Liberalism and Its Discontents*.

STANLEY CLOUD was *Time* magazine's Washington bureau chief during the Gulf War. He covered the war in Indochina from 1970 to 1973 and was *Time*'s Saigon bureau chief for the last year and a half of that period. With his wife, Lynne Olson, he is coauthor of *The Murrow Boys: Pioneers on the Front Lines of Broadcast Journalism* and the forthcoming *A Question of Honor*.

E. J. DIONNE, JR., is a syndicated columnist and senior fellow at the Brookings Institution. He is the author of *Why Americans Hate Politics* and *They Only Look Dead: Why Progressives Will Dominate the Next Political Era*. His most recent book is *United We Serve: National Service and the Future of Citizenship*, coedited with Kayla Meltzer Drogosz and Robert E. Litan.

CHRISTOPHER EDLEY, JR., has taught at Harvard Law School since 1981. He is a founding codirector of The Civil Rights Project, a policy research think tank based at Harvard, and is the author of *Not All Black and White: Affirmative Action, Race, and American Values*. He served in the administration of President Bill Clinton in several capacities, including special counsel to the president. He is currently serving a six-year term as a member of the U.S. Commission on Civil Rights.

RICHARD C. LEONE, president of The Century Foundation, has held government, business, and academic posts, including stints as chairman of the Port Authority of New York and New Jersey, president of the New York Mercantile Exchange, and faculty member at Princeton University.

JOSEPH LELYVELD was executive editor of the *New York Times* from 1994 to 2001. Previously, he served as the *Times* managing editor, foreign editor, and correspondent in London, New Delhi, Hong Kong, and South Africa. He is the author of the Pulitzer Prize–winning book *Move Your Shadow: South Africa, Black and White*.

ANTHONY LEWIS, formerly a longtime columnist for the *New York Times*, is the author of *Gideon's Trumpet*; *Portrait of a Decade: The Second American Revolution*; and *Make No Law: The Sullivan Case and the First Amendment*. He frequently writes about international affairs but also covers U.S. domestic issues, including politics, law, and a variety of social issues.

JOHN PODESTA, the former chief of staff to President Bill Clinton, is currently a visiting professor of law at Georgetown University Law Center and a senior fellow at the National Resources Defense Council. He served as a member of the United States Commission on Protecting and Reducing Government Secrecy.

STEPHEN J. SCHULHOFER is the Robert B. McKay Professor of Law at New York University Law School. He is the author of *The Enemy Within: Intelligence Gathering, Law Enforcement, and Civil Liberties in the Wake of September 11*. He has written extensively on police practices, criminal law, and criminal procedure.

JOHN STACKS was deputy managing editor and chief of correspondents for *Time* magazine. He was a Washington political correspondent for fifteen years, then served as eastern regional bureau chief and deputy chief of correspondents for *Time*. He is the author of *Scotty: James B. Reston and the Rise and Fall of American Journalism*.

KATHLEEN M. SULLIVAN is the dean of Stanford Law School, where she also holds the Richard E. Lang Professorship of Law as well as the Stanley Morrison Professorship of Law. She is a coauthor of *New Federalist Papers: Essays in Defense of the Constitution* and a coauthor of the casebook *Constitutional Law*.

ROBERTO SURO is director of the Pew Hispanic Center. Previously, Suro spent twenty-seven years working as a print journalist for a variety of publications, most recently the *Washington Post*. He is the author of *Strangers Among Us: Latino Lives in a Changing America*; *Watching America's Door: The Immigration Backlash and the New Policy Debate*; and *Remembering the American Dream: Hispanic Immigration and National Policy*

PATRICIA THOMAS has written extensively about science, medicine, and health policy. She has been a Knight Science Journalism Fellow at the Massachusetts Institute of Technology and a visiting scholar at the Knight Center for Science and Medical Journalism at Boston University. She is the author of *Big Shot: Passion, Politics, and the Struggle for an AIDS Vaccine* and former editor of the *Harvard Health Letter*.

Exploring fundamental questions concerning American liberty and national policy is central to The Century Foundation's project on homeland security. Thus, when Peter Osnos and Paul Golob from PublicAffairs approached us about organizing this volume, we were eager to move forward.

Peter and Paul were insightful and creative partners throughout the process of putting together this publication. We are also grateful to their colleagues at PublicAffairs, including David Patterson, Robert Kimzey, Lisa Kaufman, Gene Taft, and Nina D'Amario. At The Century Foundation, we received abundant input and support from Christy Hicks, Carol Starmack, Tova Wang, Leif W. Haase, Martha Paskoff, Cynthia Maertz, Maureen Farrell, and Alex Baker. The Century Foundation's homeland security project, which directly led to this book, is funded by the John D. and Catherine T. Mac-Arthur Foundation and the John S. and James L. Knight Foundation. We are enormously grateful to Jonathan F. Fanton and Arthur M. Sussman at MacArthur and to Hodding Carter III and Eric Newton at Knight for their foresight and support. In addition, John Seigenthaler, who has guided much of The Century Foundation's work related to the media and homeland security, provided his usual wisdom. While not an overnight job, this book was produced very quickly. That could not have happened without the support and assistance of Meg Cox Leone and Jeanne Reid.

The distinguished authors published in these pages exerted their talents to the fullest on a very tight timeline. We thank them for bringing light to this important topic.

PUBLICAFFAIRS is a publishing house founded in 1997. It is a tribute to the standards, values, and flair of three persons who have served as mentors to countless reporters, writers, editors, and book people of all kinds, including me.

I. F. STONE, proprietor of *I. F. Stone's Weekly,* combined a commitment to the First Amendment with entrepreneurial zeal and reporting skill and became one of the great independent journalists in American history. At the age of eighty, Izzy published *The Trial of Socrates,* which was a national bestseller. He wrote the book after he taught himself ancient Greek.

BENJAMIN C. BRADLEE was for nearly thirty years the charismatic editorial leader of *The Washington Post.* It was Ben who gave the *Post* the range and courage to pursue such historic issues as Watergate. He supported his reporters with a tenacity that made them fearless, and it is no accident that so many became authors of influential, best-selling books.

ROBERT L. BERNSTEIN, the chief executive of Random House for more than a quarter century, guided one of the nation's premier publishing houses. Bob was personally responsible for many books of political dissent and argument that challenged tyranny around the globe. He is also the founder and was the longtime chair of Human Rights Watch, one of the most respected human rights organizations in the world.

. . .

For fifty years, the banner of Public Affairs Press was carried by its owner Morris B. Schnapper, who published Gandhi, Nasser, Toynbee, Truman, and about 1,500 other authors. In 1983 Schnapper was described by *The Washington Post* as "a redoubtable gadfly." His legacy will endure in the books to come.

Peter Osnos, *Publisher*